The
DISCOVERY
of
EGYPT

ALSO BY LESLIE GREENER

High Dam over Nubia

Moon Ahead

No Time to Look Back

The DISCOVERY of EGYPT

LESLIE GREENER

Dorset Press   New York

To the
Director-General and personnel of the
Service des Antiquités de l'Egypte

This edition published by Dorset Press
a division of Marboro Books Corporation,
by arrangement with Viking Penguin,
a division of Penguin Books U.S.A., Inc.
1989 Dorset Press

ISBN 0-88029-396-9

Printed in the United States of America
M 9 8 7 6 5 4 3 2 1

Contents

Illustrations

Acknowledgments

I do not take kindly to collaboration in writing, but when my friend John F. Keane offered to dig with me into the mountain of books piled up for search, the making of this book became at once a genial and often hilarious partnership.

If our book is read with pleasure, as I hope, it will be mostly due to his flair for spotting precisely those events and characters most suited to develop this tale of the revelation of Egypt to the Western world. That John Keane was elected to the Committee of the Egypt Exploration Society during our collaboration seemed to me a most happy augury for what he has made my happiest writing experience.

My thanks go out, too, to my Field Director at Luxor, Dr Charles F. Nims, of the Oriental Institute, University of Chicago, for his constant encouragement and for so kindly checking my script; to Dr Edward Wente, of the Oriental Institute, for his patience in answering many questions insoluble by me; to Mr Peter Clayton, for being ever willing to search London for obscure facts and pictures; to Mr Frank Leek, F.S.A., F.R.N.S., for similar kind help; to my friend of former Cairo days, Professor Bryn Davies, for allowing me to use his account of Henry Salt's marriage; and finally to the Cambridge University Press, for permission to quote the comment on Sir John Mandeville from their *History of English Literature*, and the extract from *Thomas Young* by Alexander Wood and Frank Oldham.

It will be appreciated that, in the interests of clarity, a number of the quoted passages have had to be slightly abridged.

1 The Living Egypt

'YOUR Highness, I can see that it would be scarcely respectable, on returning from Egypt, to present oneself in Europe without a mummy in one hand and a crocodile in the other.'

Father Géramb spoke thus lightly to Mohamed Ali in 1833. This unusual Trappist, who had been a monarchist general—and prisoner of Napoleon Bonaparte—could speak his mind to the Pasha of Egypt. The two old soldiers must have enjoyed one another's company; and Father Géramb's drollery was not far-fetched at the time. A craze for ancient Egypt had spread over Europe since Napoleon's Expedition to Egypt at the turn of the century.

The great Expedition had been a military disaster for France; yet it had been a triumph for French culture through the achievement of the band of men of arts and letters who had accompanied Napoleon's campaign up the Nile.

Never before, and perhaps never since, has a description of a foreign land been made so completely, so accurately and so fast, or under such difficulty, as that which these men made. The huge volumes of their *Description de l'Egypte* were a revelation to Europeans. Especially was their imagination fired by the five volumes depicting the mighty ruins encountered by the artists, writers and engineers as they followed the armies up the river. Scene after scene of temple, tomb and pyramid was presented to awed readers who turned the pages of superb engravings. Many of the sketches from which the plates were made had been drawn while the smoke of battle still drifted over the field. Readers had an enticing first glimpse of the mysterious relics of ancient Egypt, about which almost nothing was known. Until then only solitary travellers had ventured into this almost forbidden land in search of curios for rich patrons. Their journeys had been hazardous, the information they brought back fragmentary, and their drawings mostly unreliable.

Now educated Europe absorbed the new knowledge of Egypt greedily. Napoleon's Expedition had opened the door, and Mohamed Ali Pasha, who made himself master of Egypt soon after, opened the country to European travellers. The vogue for things Egyptian invaded not only the cabinets of learned men but the salons of all elegant folk. It influenced furniture, dress styles and even the coiffure of the period. Father Géramb was right in jesting that the traveller returning from the Nile could scarce keep countenance without an Egyptian object in either hand. Egyptology had begun. It has continued to fascinate ever since.

Nobody knows yet how this civilization, perhaps the most ancient of all, began: whether its elements entered the Nile valley from outside, or whether it evolved on its own. We are presented almost suddenly with those eternal monuments that have been with mankind through the entire period of written history: the pyramids of Egypt, set up by a people who could already write, and build perfectly in stone.

Here by the Nile lies Memphis with its secrets still only half revealed; and farther up Thebes, another capital, with painted tombs of Pharaohs and the acres of Karnak's courts and pillars; and the short-lived City of the Sun where Pharaoh Akhnaton lived with Nefertiti; and thousands more, literally, of temples, tombs, and buried towns remain from the most ancient times of Egypt. The Greeks and the Phoenicians who civilized the Mediterranean drew the first inspiration of their arts and science from the well of Egyptian culture; and later the Greek city of Alexandria on Egypt's coast was long the centre of learning in the ancient world.

But the old Egypt was melting away by then. Christian beliefs came to jostle the old gods out, and presently all knowledge of the ancient civilization of the Egyptians was totally lost, even to the Egyptians themselves, who dwelt in that same Nile valley among the tremendous ruins covered with pictographic writing incomprehensible and mysterious as the monuments themselves.

Yet Egypt's history was so long that it could contain its own archaeologists even while the ancient civilization still flourished. A man of the time when the temple of Abu Simbel was fresh-hewn out of the mountain in Nubia would have regarded the pyramids as very ancient monuments. They were more than two thousand years away from him: more remote in time than Jesus Christ from us.

One such man was Khaemwase. He was a son of Ramses the Great who caused great Abu Simbel to be made, and a High Priest of Ptah. It was written of Khaemwase that he passed his time wandering about the necropolis of Memphis reading the inscriptions in the tombs of the Great Ones and the writings on the walls of temples, as well as the books in the sacerdotal library. Khaemwase's interest in antiquities was so great that he marked his visit to the pyramid of King Unas by an inscription that was found in 1937, more than three thousand years afterwards, by the French archaeologist J.-P. Lauer.

His Majesty has ordered it to be proclaimed that the chief of the masters of artists, the Setem-priest Khaemwase, has inscribed the name of the King of Upper and Lower Egypt, Unas, since it was not found on the face of the pyramid, because the Setem-priest Prince Khaemwase much loved to restore the monuments of the kings of Upper and Lower Egypt.

Although Khaemwase is the first Egyptologist on record, it is not likely that his motivation was altogether similar to that which moves his fellows in the science at the present day. In the year 1250 B.C. he had no need of historical research: he was living in the midst of history that was well known then. And the inscriptions obviously gave him no trouble to decipher.

What he was after was magical texts, a perfectly acceptable

subject of research at the time. If a man had a reputation for learning, it applied especially to his skill in the art of magic; and Khaemwase was a magician of renown who knew how to compose powerful writings, some of which are still with us. Papyrus No. 3248 in the Louvre contains magical formulae attributed to him. We have to make some adjustment to this if we are to give the ancient Egyptians a sympathetic understanding, for magic was as natural as the air to an Egyptian, and quite as necessary. Thus Setem Khaemwase did not seek to reconstruct the past, but to collect the magic wisdom of the past; and the obvious place to look for that would be among the tombs. Learned men who had preceded Khaemwase to the shadow world would include in their tomb decoration some of their favourite magical texts to help them along in their new life, and they might even have some of their more potent books of magic buried with them. Books of those days were, of course, rolls of papyrus sometimes many feet long, tied neatly with string.

A thousand years after Khaemwase died his renown as an antiquarian was still so strong that tales were told in which he was the hero of fantastic and sometimes salacious adventures in his hunts for buried wisdom of the ancients. A scribe named Ziharpto wrote one of these tales down during the reign of Ptolemy II.

Khaemwase, the story goes, longs to possess the most magical text of all: the wonderful book of the god Thoth, whose formulae would enable a man to enchant the earth, the sky, the mountains, and understand the language of birds and beasts. He could even use them after he was dead and emerge from the tomb in his earthly form.

Khaemwase tracks the precious book-roll down to the tomb of a deceased wizard-prince, Nenefer-ka-ptah, and his wife Princess Ahura. With no compunction Khaemwase breaks in. There, sure enough, is the book, lying shining with potence between the mummified Nenefer-ka-ptah and the spirit-double, or *ka*, of Ahura. These two sit up and beg him not to touch the book. Heedless, Khaemwase threatens to take it by force. Nenefer-ka-ptah replies by a challenge to play him at draughts for it. But when the dead prince beats him three games running, Khaemwase snatches up the book and leaves.

The magical revenge of Nenefer-ka-ptah and his wife is not long coming. Khaemwase, strolling in the forecourt of the temple, perceives the most beautiful woman he ever saw and is overcome by desire for her. He sends his page across to offer 900 grammes of gold for an hour of her; to which she replies haughtily that she is a sacred virgin and no mean person. However, she invites him to her house.

The woman's name is Tbubui, and her house luxurious. She hands him a gold cup brimming with wine and invites him to rest, to which his forthright reply is, 'That is not what I came for.' But he is obliged to endure a day of hot desire, and when he eventually suggests that they accomplish what he came for she repeats, 'I am a sacred virgin and no mean person. If you desire your pleasure of me you will make me a contract of maintenance and money.'

A scribe is brought and the contract drawn up. But each time Khaemwase says hopefully, 'Now let us accomplish what we came here for,' she makes a fresh and ever more exorbitant demand which his burning desire will not allow him to refuse —even her final ghastly ultimatum: 'If you desire your pleasure of me then cause your children to be slain so that they may not dispute your possessions with my children.' As she invites him at last to 'come into this chamber', he hears the dogs crunching the dead bones of his children in the courtyard below.

He lies on a bed of ivory and ebony, and Tbubui lies beside him. But he has barely accomplished what he came for when she opens her mouth enormously and lets forth a scream like a gale of wind.

Khaemwase wakes up far off, lying in filth without a stitch of clothing. It is all a magical deed of Nenefer-ka-ptah to render him impure and a criminal so that he will lose his supernatural power. Princess Ahura was impersonating the seductive Tbubui, and the children are safe at home. The moral ending to the story is the remorse of Khaemwase, his penance and restitution of the book.

Mariette found the papyrus containing this story in 1864, in the tomb of a Coptic monk, of all places. This early Christian monk must have been one of the last Egyptians who understood the ancient writings before they were lost in the darkness of the Middle Ages. It is also of interest that Marie

Corelli, one of the most widely-read novelists of our grand-fathers' day, used one of the principal points in this story for her strange book, *Zizka Charmezel*: the return to earth of an Egyptian princess to avenge herself on an enemy.

The story of Khaemwase gives a vivid idea of the picture of life in the Underworld as the Egyptian saw it, with family affairs continuing in the tomb. And it suggests that the notion of violating any religious principle by disturbing a tomb in the interests of knowledge was totally absent from the Egyptian way of thinking.

There was one thing, however, that the Egyptians would not tolerate: the effacing of a dead person's identity. To destroy his mummified body or to obliterate his name was worse than robbery. It was murder—murder to the nth degree: the deceased died a second and much more terrible death, for his spirit was extinguished for eternity.

The Egyptians, being the first to live history, were of course the least able to learn its lessons. They were the first to try to beat eternity, with their pyramids and deep concealed burials. It was death they tried to cheat. Kings, and others who could afford to, left endowments for the maintenance of their tombs and the provision for their needs in the next life, naïvely believing that the endowment would go on through eternity; for this civilization had yet to experience the instability of human institutions as well as the friability of stone.

The passage of time showed up the sad fact that trust funds have a way of being applied to other things after a couple of centuries or less. So there arose the extraordinary situation of a dead man falling on hard times because his investments were failing him. Not only was his tomb in danger of being robbed for lack of guards, but he was starving to death as well. Since life hereafter was an extension of life on earth, the *ka* of the defunct needed food and drink, and he needed remembrance. Certainly the victuals were symbolic and transmuted by magic into phantom nourishment, but it was the real stuff that his trustees were supposed to bring—loaves and wine—and the words of remembrance had to be recited to preserve his identity.

To provide against these horrible possibilities, inscriptions were placed at the entrance to tombs, or on a tombstone-like stela, to warn off trespassers: 'Any man who does harm to this

tomb will be judged with me by the great god,' is the usual
threat. This was in part to deter those who might use the tomb
as a handy quarry for material to build their own. But how to
guard against alienation of a mortuary foundation was the
constant preoccupation of a tomb proprietor—before he
occupied the tomb, naturally. Since money dividends had not
been invented in those innocent times, the prudent man set
aside land, the usufruct of which would pay for the guarding
of his tomb and the nourishment of his soul in perpetuity.
Numerous inscriptions refer to the ugly fate that awaited those
who might appropriate such foundations to other purposes. A
warning posted by a man named Senna is quite moving:

> This piece of land which I have constituted a funerary endowment
> I have given to my loved wife Disenk, and I have done that for
> Disenk because of the great attachment for her that reigns in my
> heart. Such persons as may take this land from Disenk, I will
> appear with them to contest the matter before the great god, lord
> of the sky.

Warnings were often followed by the claim, 'I am an
accomplished soul, knowing all the secrets of magic,' to let
the evil-doer know that his victim could outmatch any magic
aids to his abominable schemes. This is as near as we come to
the celebrated 'Curse of the Pharaohs', whereby calamity is
supposed to fall upon those who disturb the eternal rest of
Egypt's kings. In fact there is no record of an imprecation
written on a Pharaoh's tomb. Those quoted here are all from
private burials, and the 'Curse of the Pharaohs' is a lively
myth concocted by a journalist of the 'twenties after the
discovery of Tutankhamon's tomb. It was a good story, as was
that of Khaemwase.

As time went by it became all too clear that the family would
forget its dead, or become extinct; or that the priests of the
spirit-double would break contract. So tomb-owners turned to
cajolery, and we witness the strange plight of a dead man
become beggar. Antef, on his 12th dynasty stela, beseeches:

> O you who live on earth, every mortal, every priest, every scribe,
> every official, who enters this tomb hollowed in the ground: if
> you love life and would ignore death, and be favoured of the gods

of your town, and not taste the terror of the nether world, but would be laid in your tombs and leave your possessions to your children! Then recite the words written on this stela, thus: Glory to Amon, Lord of Karnak, that he may give a thousand jugs of wine, a thousand loaves, a thousand bulls, a thousand geese, a thousand sachets of perfume to the *ka* of Antef.

He is not begging for real goods: that would be too much to expect of a passer-by. Antef asks only that his name be remembered and a prayer made to the god to provide for the nourishment of his *ka*. This formula recited by a living voice was a true charm that effectively procured for the *ka* the enjoyment of all the good things on the list. 'I have just done that,' said Maspero in 1878, after translating Antef's stela to an audience of Orientalists at Lyon. 'By the simple fact that I repeated to you the formula, the *ka* of Antef has received the repast promised by the prayer. It is a piece of good fortune that he hasn't had for a long time.'

2 Greeks and Romans in Egypt

MAGIC and appeals for sympathy failed to protect the dead of ancient Egypt. Their tombs crumbled and were filled by wind-blown sand. Yet slowly; almost as slowly as the magnificent civilization decayed that had created them.

The occupying Greeks, and after them the Romans, looked upon the temples and the religious customs of the Egyptians with condescending toleration. Portraits of the Ptolemies and of Roman emperors were carved on temple walls, but they were in the interests of politics, and had no sincere spiritual affinity with the native religion. The ruling races knew little more about ancient Egyptian beliefs than the British in India knew about Hinduism, except that the Greeks saw the counterpart of some of their own gods in the more ancient gods of the Egyptians. The temples were something to go and visit as a tourist. The grand religion of the Pharaohs that once had disciplined the whole Nile valley had shrunk to a quaint native custom, to be tolerated and used as a vehicle of administration, but not to be taken seriously.

Nearly a century and a half before Alexander took Egypt for the Greeks, the Greek historian Herodotus went there to collect material for a book. The country was under Persian domination, and already the custodians of the old religion were on the defensive towards outsiders. This may account for some of the tall tales told to the visiting historian, who wrote:

Now the priests told me that Cheops enjoined all the Egyptians to work for him . . . The period of oppression of the people was

ten years for the construction of the causeway . . . But twenty
years were expended on the construction of the Pyramid itself . . .
Now, the sum that was spent on radishes onions and garlick, for
the workmen, is marked in Egyptian characters on the Pyramid;
and, as I well remember what the interpreter, as he read over the
writing, said to me, it made up a sum of sixteen hundred silver
talents . . . Cheops, they continued, descended so low, that for
want of money he placed his own daughter in a chamber, and
charged her to get a certain sum of money . . . She not only obtained
the sum appointed by her father, but on her own account was
minded to leave a memorial behind her, and asked each of her
visitors to give her one stone for the work. Of these stones, they
said, the Pyramid was built which stands in the middle of the
three before the Great Pyramid.

Since Herodotus is one of the few authorities on whom early
travellers from medieval and modern Europe had to rely, it is
natural that we find these tales repeated in their works,
frequently believed. One wonders if the translator of the
radishes and onions was smiling inwardly at his credulous
tourist. It is not at all certain that the pyramid ever was
inscribed in hieroglyphs; and it is very unlikely that Cheops
would have written the records of his commissariat on it.
The great Egyptologist Mariette wrote of Herodotus in a letter
to his friend Desjardins in 1874:

I detest this traveller who came to Egypt at a time when the
Egyptian language was spoken, who with his eyes saw all the
temples still standing; who only had to ask the first comer the
name of the reigning king, the name of the king who preceded him,
who only had to refer to the first temple for the history, religion—
for everything of interest concerning the most fascinating country in
the world. And who, instead of all that, tells us gravely that a
daughter of Cheops built a pyramid with the fruit of prostitution.
This is not what one should expect of Herodotus, and as for me I
look upon him as a real criminal. He who could have told so much
tells us only stupidities. Considering the great number of mistakes
in Herodotus . . . would it not have been better for Egyptology
had he never existed?

The late Sir Alan Gardiner thought better of him. He called
him 'that great genius'; yet even Sir Alan deplored the absence
of any extensive account of Thebes and its monuments, and
admits that other similar omissions, such as reference to the

Sphinx, are to be attributed to his predilection for the marvellous and for the merely amusing stories told him by the temple underlings whom he mistook for priests.

Sir Alan excuses him on the grounds that he was the acknowledged 'Father of History' and the first to distinguish that art from mere poetic romancing. It happened that Herodotus's work was the first comprehensive account of Egypt to survive intact. Had a more factual history been handed down to us through the classical authors, the great mystery of lost Egypt might never have been. As it was, little survived of all that was written about Egypt during the next five hundred years; and it is probable that had it survived none of it would have been any more reliable than the maligned Herodotus. There was more speculation than fact in most of the scraps that have come down to us. Plato, almost a contemporary of Herodotus, contributes a mite of accurate information about the gods of Egypt, but little more. In 59 B.C. Diodorus Siculus went to Egypt, but he draws heavily on previous writers—including Herodotus whom he criticizes—and his entire *General History* is a compilation of uneven value. Strabo, who went as far as Aswan in 24 B.C., was writing a *Geographica* which was a sound work, but his incidental remarks on the history and religion of Egypt share the defects of previous authors, even though he scoffs at Herodotus for his credulity.

In later times, when the cult of Isis spread throughout the Roman Empire after the breakdown of the belief in the gods of Olympus, Plutarch wrote the story of Osiris in his *De Iside et Osiride*, but, as Gardiner says, it bears the unmistakable hallmark of Western speculative ingenuity.

The most useful historian was a learned Egyptian priest, Manetho, born at Sebenithe in the Delta nearly two hundred years after Herodotus's visit to Egypt. He wrote a history of the country for Ptolemy II which might well have been an exception to the rule of general unreliability; but it was lost, and we have only scraps of it transmitted by authors who lived six hundred years after his death. His list of kings, checked and modified against other sources, has formed the framework on which the history of Egypt has been reconstructed.

The Greeks, when they came, never became part of the Egypt they had liberated from the Persians. They were always the occupiers, even when Egypt was an independent country under the Ptolemaic kings. These were, for the native Egyptians, foreign Greek kings; and the Greeks lived in their own cities, chief of them Alexandria, which was totally Greek. Only the administrators went up the Nile among the natives, and the tourists who strolled among the temples and ruins comprehending as little as most tourists do today.

When the Romans replaced the Greeks in 30 B.C. the difference was even more marked. Egypt became a Roman province, in fact the private property of the Emperor Augustus. As such it was thoroughly exploited; but it was also thoroughly administered. A visitor could go anywhere in perfect safety. For two centuries there was an era of tourism that was not to be equalled until the present day. Aristide of Smyrna, a professional rhetorician, eulogized the Roman peace under the Empire in glowing terms:

> One need no longer fear the narrow sandy roads of Arabia and Egypt; no mountain or river is any longer inaccessible, no barbarian nation that one cannot visit. To be secure, one has but to be a Roman.

He might have added that the Empire had created an admirable system of land and sea communication to link East with West. Travellers could go direct from Pouzzolez to Alexandria; or to Carthage and thence by coast road to Alexandria. From there they could continue the grand tour via the Suez isthmus to join the high road to Antioch.

The size of some of the ships on the Alexandria run at the time of the Emperor Augustus is surprising. One great vessel carried the obelisk that now stands in the Piazza del Popolo in Rome. The ship could accommodate 1,200 passengers besides a cargo of nitre, papyrus and 400,000 bushels of wheat.

Post roads were maintained for the Imperial mail. The relay stations were for the use of functionaries, official couriers and the military; and there were private transport contractors to supply horses, donkeys, wagons and oxen for private travellers. If he did not choose to do the journey by boat, a traveller could go from Alexandria right to the frontier of Ethiopia at Hiera Sycaminos by the road along the Nile. And there was a mail route to the Red Sea, from Coptos, the modern Quft. This was known as the New Road of Hadrian, although it had in fact been used by the ancient Egyptians, as their inscriptions on wayside rocks still testify. Its newness consisted of costly maintenance to provide access to the ports of Berenice and Myoshormos. Remains of the staging inns, cisterns and hilltop watchtowers can be seen along this same road by motorists today. A toll tariff for a permit to use the road of the year A.D. 90 has been preserved. The rate for a captain in service on the Red Sea was 8 drachmas; a sailor paid 5; a sailor's wife 20; a courtesan paid 108 drachmas. All paid another 2 obols for sealing. The charge for courtesans seems prohibitive. Egyptologist N. Hohlwein, writing on Roman tourism in the *Chronique d'Egypte*, wonders if this was a rare instance of government effort to protect morals.

There is little evidence of such solicitude at the popular resorts around Alexandria, where all was organized for pleasure and the satisfaction of desires. Gay boating-parties rowed eastward across the lagoon towards Canopus, halting at the inns on the shore to drink the light wines of Mareotis, to dine, and to dance beneath the arbours. The Corpus of Greek Inscriptions preserves for us, under No. 4961, a description of these places:

> This inn is alive with ceaseless banqueting and filled with a crowd of young men. It is not the sound of trumpets that rings here, but that of flutes; it is the blood of animals, not that of men, that stains the floor; we wear graceful clothes, not arms; and here, cup in hand, choirs crowned with flowers sing praise to the eternal gods in night-long song.

Thus in revelry they came to Canopus, where Ptolemy Soter had built a temple of Serapis, celebrated throughout the antique world, whose rites 'made the Romans blush with shame or pale with envy', E. M. Forster tells us. This god was a concoction of Ptolemy Soter's to give the Alexandrians a united cult. Serapis was compounded of the Egyptian god of the Underworld, Osiris, and Apis the bull god of Memphis. Osiris was identified with the Greek god of mysteries and wine, Dionysus; and the synthetic Serapis was quite acceptable to all. He was an unexpected success, and his cult spread around the Mediterranean world, to become the last rearguard of paganism to hold out against Christianity. There is little left today of the Serapis temple, for the military during the last couple of centuries have used it as a quarry. It is difficult to visit now, being within the sacred coastal defence zone. But in the two centuries after Christ invalids flocked there to pray and sleep in the temple, where a cure for their ills might be revealed by the god in a dream.

The delights and entertainments that surrounded the shrine gave Canopus the reputation of being the wickedest spot on earth, and certainly the gayest—a reputation that made sure of its success as a tourist attraction. So sweet were its diversions that Apion, sage of Alexandria, declared that it must be the very site of Homer's Elysian Fields.

Yet Roman Egypt had more to offer than pleasure. It was an unique tourist resort in another way: it clung to its old ways and remained stubbornly itself, unlike other parts of the Empire where people strove to Romanize themselves and become modern with all speed. The Egyptians could thus be viewed in all their native quaintness, dressing their own way, farming their own way, worshipping their antique gods, continuing to build temples and decorating them with hieroglyphs of which their conquerors understood nothing. Roman tourists, satiated with the tumult of Alexandria and Canopus, moved on to Memphis, which was still a living city, and farther up the Nile into the solitude and silence of Egypt which was like no other place on earth, and where they could breathe an atmosphere of the remote mysterious past.

In those times the pyramids still shone with their casing-stones intact, and they must have been a sight much more imposing even than they are today. Possibly the smooth sides bore hieroglyphic inscriptions; certainly they bore the names of thousands of visitors in antiquity who desired to leave a record of their passage. This is no new weakness of humankind; but when the carved name is antique enough it is no longer vandalism; it becomes an historical record. Thus a complete history of tourism in Egypt might have been preserved if the casing-stones had not been removed by the Arabs for building Old Cairo. As it is, no visitor's inscription older than A.D. 1475 is left. But Ludolph von Suchem, a priest who visited the Great Pyramid in A.D. 1336, translated one touching memorial among many Latin inscriptions that he saw carved on it:

> Alone, alas! the Pyramid I see
> And can but weep, my brother dear, for thee.
> Upon the stone I've sadly carved thy name.
> The greatest Pyramid now knows the fame
> Of Annius Decimus who fought for Rome
> With Trajan, and returned in triumph home;
> Who e'en before his thirtieth birthday passed
> Was Pontiff, Consul, Censor too, at last.

Brother Felix Fabri reported the poem again in 1480. It is possible that it was engraved by the sister of D. Titianus, a consul of A.D. 127.

At Memphis numerous monuments and temples could be visited, still functioning, the most striking of which was the Apis sanctuary of the sacred bull. Strabo left an account of his visit to the sanctuary in 24 B.C. The bull-god, he says, was led out at certain times to be viewed by visitors in a special enclosure. Strabo was sceptical about the animal's divinity, yet distinguished persons in later years went to pay their respects. The grandfather of Nero, Germanicus, was among the curious in the year A.D. 19; and the Emperor Titus was present at the consecration of an Apis.

Another wonder that the complete Roman tourist could not miss was the Labyrinth at the entrance to the Fayoum oasis west of the Nile. It was already an ancient monument, being in fact a complex of buildings serving as the funerary temple of 12th dynasty Pharaoh Amenemes III. It had been called 'Labyrinth' by early Greek visitors because they supposed it to be a maze similar to Daedalus's structure in Crete. It was certainly not like any other Egyptian temple. Herodotus described its numberless courts joined by tortuous corridors out of which a man could never find his way. He thought it more marvellous than the pyramids. Strabo echoes his enthusiasm.

Nothing was left of the Labyrinth but limestone chips when Petrie dug there in 1887. Lime-burners had demolished it, living among the ruins for generations while they consumed them.

The pool of sacred crocodiles in the Fayoum was another major tourist attraction which diverted Strabo highly. He described the reptiles taking food from the priests' hands, and

the priests opening the jaws of the crocodiles to show their
teeth. It was a well-established attraction. A circular letter still
exists from 112 B.C. when Roman senator L. Memmius
visited Greek Egypt on a diplomatic mission. It enjoins the
local authorities of the Fayoum to do their utmost to give
the distinguished visitor a warm welcome and to show him the
curiosities of the province, especially the Labyrinth and the
sacred crocodiles. It goes so far as to instruct that cakes shall be
provided for L. Memmius to throw into the jaws of the
crocodiles.

Travelling up the Nile, most Roman tourists went straight
to Luxor—Thebes, as it was then—ignoring the monuments
of Middle Egypt just as tourists do today. They would move
in wonder through the immense hall of pillars at Karnak, and
they would climb the stony trail to the Valley of the Tombs of
the Kings. But like the Greeks before them, their great interest
was in the two colossal seated statues isolated in the so-called
plain of Memnon. Their ardent desire was to hear the northern-
most statue speak.

Ever since an earthquake in 27 B.C., or possibly an earlier
one, had tumbled its top half off, the remainder of the statue
had given forth sounds in the early morning. Strabo was the
first writer to remark on this. He said the sound was like that
caused by a light blow. Others compared it to the noise of a
harp-string parting; and yet others detected a human voice in
it. Strabo the cynic suspected some mechanism operated by the
priests, but there is no doubt that a natural movement of the
stone in the warmth of the sun, or an escape of expanding
air from a fissure, was the true cause of the phenomenon.

For the tourists this was the voice of Memnon, son of
Aurora, the rosy-fingered dawn-goddess, and of her lover
Tithonus. He was Memnon, mythical King of Ethiopia, who
went to Troy to aid his uncle Priam, was slain by Achilles and
rendered immortal by Zeus. The statue was probably identified
with Memnon by very early Greek visitors, just as the Labyrinth had been identified with something familiar to them. It
was in fact, with its mate, a 750-ton effigy of Amenophis III.
The colossal pair stood at the entrance to a grand temple of the
Pharaoh which had already been quarried away by Graeco-
Roman times. Many inscriptions in Greek and Latin cover the

legs of the Memnon statue, bringing back to us the feelings of the visitors who stood there in the pink dawn of an Egyptian day in those far-off times, waiting for the god to speak. Some of the inscriptions are quite moving, written in polished verse by highly literate poets. A complete collection was published in 1960 by André and Etienne Bernand, who remark that the statue develops a personality and a divinity under the progressive influence of those who placed their inscriptions on it. The pre-Hadrian inscriptions are objective: the writers heard the stone speak; it was a strange phenomenon. Thus M. Mettius Rufus, Prefect of Egypt in A.D. 90, came to hear for himself, and bade his official poet engrave the fact on the statue's left foot, in Greek:

> Destroyers have damaged your body in vain; for you emit sounds notwithstanding, as I have personally heard: I, Mettius, O Memnon. These verses are by Paeon of Sida.

Damage to the statue was ascribed to the Persian King Cambyses, who conquered Egypt in 525 B.C. His evil repute was spread by Herodotus, who declared that the King ran a sacred Apis bull through with his own sword. Perhaps a tourist guide told him that. The accusation is questionable, since the sarcophagus of one bull bore the dedication of the King himself.

A little higher on Memnon's left foot is another inscription in Greek:

> I, Aponios, at the first hour I heard. I have engraved this act of devotion in honour of my wife Aphroditarion who I wish were beside me each time you make a sound.

The most interesting inscriptions on the colossus were contributed by two poetesses. One is Cecilia Trebulla, of unknown date, but pre-Hadrian:

> From Trebulla. Hearing the holy voice of Memnon I missed you, O my mother, and I prayed that you might hear him too.

Again, lower, she wrote:

> Cecilia Trebulla, on hearing Memnon a second time:
> until now we heard only his voice, but today we were greeted like friends by Memnon son of Aurora and Tithonus.

Has the stone been gifted with speech and feelings
by Nature, controller of the Universe?

In her third inscription Cecilia Trebulla reports the fancied
words spoken by the statue itself:

Cambyses broke me—me, this stone you see, this statue
in the image of an Oriental king.
Before, I had a plaintive voice that mourned the woes of Memnon,
and that Cambyses took from me.
Today the sounds that I emit in my complaints
are formless and not understood—
poor vestige of my vanished fortune.

Cecilia Trebulla does more than exclaim at the extraordinary
phenomenon. She tries to enrich by myth what the experience
does not explain to her, say André and Etienne Bernand in the
thoughtful essay accompanying their collection of these inscriptions. But the tradition making the statue a god has not yet
grown up. Is he the son of Aurora? Or is the statue of a king of
the Orient, broken by Cambyses? He is at any rate no longer a
mere block of stone; he can be amical or plaintive.

The other poetess is Julia Balbilla who came with the
Emperor Hadrian and his beautiful Empress Sabina on a state
visit. One can imagine the excitement of this august occasion
in that remote corner of the Empire: the gorgeous tentage on
the plain of Memnon; the trains of bullock-carts; the laden
river-boats; the crowd of robed officials around the colossus in
the chilly dawn when the Emperor of the World and his
consort waited for the statue to speak.

Memnon did not utter a sound.

It must have been a very embarrassing moment for all
concerned. So next day, 20th November, A.D. 130, poetess
Julia Balbilla went with the Empress and begged Memnon to
sing:

You who are the son of Aurora, O Memnon, and of the venerable
Tithonus; you who sit before the Theban city of Zeus—or you,
Amenoth, Egyptian king, as the priests declare who are versed
in ancient lore—receive my salutation, and, by singing, welcome
in your turn the revered wife of Emperor Hadrian. Your tongue
has been cut, as have your ears, by a barbarian, impious Cambyses.
Indeed he has been punished by his horrid death, pierced by that
same sword point he used, pitiless, to kill the divine Apis.

But I, I do not believe that your statue will perish, and I have
saved and immortalized your soul for all time by my talent.
Pious indeed were my parents and my ancestors, Balbillus
the Wise, and King Antiochos:
Balbillus, my mother's father, of royal blood,
and King Antiochos, father of my father.
From their race I draw my noble blood, and these verses
are by me, Balbilla the Pious.

At this distance we can forgive Julia her self-adulation,
since she has succeeded in immortalizing the colossus of
Memnon—and herself—for more than eighteen centuries.

Memnon heeded her plea for a musical welcome to the
Empress; he obliged with a song:

Yesterday Memnon received the royal pair in silence, so that lovely
Sabina would be constrained to come back. For you were charmed
by the gracious beauty of our Queen.

Pray give a divine cry on her arrival, lest the Emperor be vexed
with you: too long in your audacity you held waiting his august
and lawful wife.

Thus Memnon, in dread of great Hadrian's might, let forth
suddenly a cry she heard with joy.

I heard, when the stone began to sing. I, Balbilla, I heard the
divine voice of Memnon or Amenoth. I had accompanied here the
beloved Queen Sabina; the sun held its course in the first hour,
in the fifteenth year of the Emperor Hadrian, the month of
Hathyr being at its twenty-fourth day.

The Emperor himself joined them then:

. . . when Titan, flying through the air with his white horses,
held the shadow on the second division of the hours
it was as though one struck a gong of copper,
and Memnon gave once more a piercing cry as a salute.
Even a third time he made a sound.
Then Emperor Hadrian himself lavished salutations upon
    Memnon;
and, on the stone, he left these verses for posterity
to tell of all he saw and heard.
It is clear for all to see that the gods cherish him.

Julia Balbilla was an accomplished poetess. She wrote in
elegiac couplets; she was well-informed and anxious to style her
work with archaic forms and Homeric expressions. Memnon

becomes humanized; the stone, up to now a shapeless thing, is deified and honoured after Hadrian's visit. It has new character and feelings: Memnon is sensitive to feminine charm and to fear. Possibly his human character was accentuated because his divine nature was always vague. Official religion appears not to have given Memnon a precise nature or nationality. Balbilla dared not decide whether he was the son of Aurora or else Amenoth the Egyptian king—as the priests quite rightly claimed he was: Amenoth, or Amenophis III of the 18th dynasty, who reigned 1,535 years before Balbilla's visit. But it is enough, say André and Etienne Bernand, that the colossus was a centre of pilgrimage to the glory of the Emperor and his entourage who received the homage of the singing statue. The poetic background—the victory and death of Memnon, Aurora's tears, the cruelty of Cambyses—behind the mutilated and plaintive statue of misfortune, and the flattery of being saluted by a sign from on high, could only lead pilgrims to the just conclusion that all effort, even victorious, remains menaced, perishable and painful. The pity is that Julia Balbilla should have been tempted to use so lofty a sentiment for personal ends and in an exhibition of her skill.

Cecilia's and Julia's verses are still there on Memnon's left foot, amongst a smother of lesser merit, a little the worse for the weather, yet legible. But Memnon sings no more.

Around the year A.D. 202 Septimius Severus, in the seventh year of his reign, came to hear the god. But the statue remained mute as it had done before the Emperor Hadrian. Seeking to conciliate the god, Severus caused the statue's head and torso to be restored with the blocks of stone we see today. But whatever gave Memnon voice must have been smothered in the process. He never spoke again.

3 The Long Silence

THE Holy Family took refuge in Egypt during the Roman occupation, at the time when tourists were cutting the earlier inscriptions on the feet of Memnon. The well at Mataria near Cairo can still be seen where, tradition says, the Holy Virgin washed the Infant's clothes; and they will show you the crypt at the church of St Serge which contains a grotto where the Family dwelt some time.

Forty-five years later, tradition tells, St Mark converted a shoemaker of Alexandria, Annianus, to the new religion of Christ. It was the beginning of a little group of working-class folk, soon to be joined by thoughtful patricians, who used to meet for discussion and prayer. Seventeen years after that first conversion St Mark was martyred for protesting against the worship of Serapis. His saintly bones lay for eight centuries in the church that was built for them at Alexandria, until they were stolen by the Venetians, who were obliged to conceal them from the Moslem officials in a barrel of pickled pork consigned to Venice.

It was not primarily the decrees of emperors that brought an end to the gods of ancient Egypt. It was the quiet persistence of the little group that St Mark had started. Of that growing yet unfashionable community the Emperor Hadrian is reputed to have written, 'Their one god is nothing peculiar.'

He was wrong. In the end it was the state itself that became Christian. But not before 144,000 martyrs had perished in the cause, according to the estimate of the Egyptian Church which dates events from the year A.D. 284, the 'Era of Martyrs', and not from the birth of Christ. The revolt began by the Christians' refusal to admit the absurd claim of the state that the Emperor was a god. Certificates of Having Worshipped the Gods were compulsory. But the Christians asserted the claims of individual conscience, and chose to be executed sooner than conform. The appalling persecution defeated itself, and in the year 313 Constantine recognized Christianity as an official State religion.

Once that had been done Christianity no longer remained quiet in its persistence, and it was sometimes not gentle. In 397 Patriarch Cyril's wild black army of monks stormed the last of the pagan temples. It was they, most likely, who destroyed the Serapeum at Memphis where Herodotus and Strabo saw the Apis bulls. Most certainly it was they who destroyed the books of the famous library at Alexandria; not the Arabs who came conquering two and a half centuries later under the poet-general Amr, who wrote of Alexandria, 'I have taken a city that contains 4,000 palaces, 4,000 baths, 400 theatres, 1,200 greengrocers and 40,000 Jews.'

But the Arabs did not know the value of their prize in terms of its history and its culture; or of the rest of Egypt. They marvelled at the relics of some mighty past with which the valley of the Nile was sown, and concluded it was the work of giants or of wizards. The natives could tell them nothing: it had been wiped completely from racial memory together with ability to read the hieroglyphs that might have preserved the story. When the State had become Christian and the old rites and the old writing had been forbidden, hieroglyphs soon became inscrutable to the early Christians of Egypt; and the monuments they covered were heathen, therefore evil. The monks busied themselves with hammer and chisel when the idols offended them. The Arabs after them were indifferent to the past which was, after all, not theirs. They used the temples as quarries when they needed stone, or pulled them apart hunting for imagined treasure.

Thus the story of the world's first great civilization became lost for fourteen centuries. For a great part of the time there was no one else in the world to be curious about these things. There was no Europe: not the kind of Europe that would send enquiring archaeologists abroad, at any rate. The France,

England and Lombardy of the Middle Ages were being shaped from the barbarian warriors who had displaced the Roman Empire. In England the invading Saxons had destroyed Chester in A.D. 615, a few years before the Arabs came to Egypt. There were kings of Northumbria and of Mercia, and there were kings in Kent. Hunting, hawking and warfare filled their time; and the Saxon farmers in their villages, compact around the first stone churches, were discussing the merits of the new heavy eight-ox plough, and the change from quern to water-mill for grinding corn.

Scholarship and inquiry were out of place in that robust, practical world. A few monks in monastery libraries handed down surviving copies of the old Roman authors through the generations of the dark years, until the renaissance of learning stirred men to be curious about the ancient world of Rome, Greece and Egypt. But for the time being medieval students had no understanding of the ancient classics in their care. Greek was a dead language; and although they could read the Latin manuscripts, they could not grasp their significance. They were incapable of taking them literally: the medieval mind was too habituated to giving allegorical interpretation to the most straightforward words. Men of the Middle Ages were completely fascinated by visions of a future state of souls. Straight facts written about this world were not communicated to them. They sought always for subtler meanings related to the future existence—for them the only absolute reality.

Thus travellers who went sightseeing in the Middle East in those days were not tourists in our sense of pleasure-travellers. They were pilgrims, and their travel was often long and perilous. People travelled a lot more than we have allowed outselves to suppose, for the Dark Ages were not all that dark. If there was no knowledge of pagan history, there was a lively interest in the holy places where the faith of Christendom had originated, and where Old Testament history had been enacted. And there was an intellectual unity of Christendom, despite its many kinglets and dukes, that was quite different from our world of large, tight national groups and rigid frontiers. Many pilgrims went to pray, weep and exult at the holy sites around the Holy City, and an enterprising few strayed into our Egypt on the way.

One of the very few records of such a journey is a manuscript discovered at Arezzo in Tuscany, in 1883, by G. F. Gamurrini, librarian of a brotherhood long established there. It is the earliest account of ancient Egyptian sites being visited by a traveller from nascent Europe; and the traveller has been identified as the Lady Etheria from Gaul, a nun 'with a bold heart who undertook a journey across the world' to identify the sites she had read of in the Bible, between the years A.D. 379 and 388. Egypt was, of course, a Christian country still, and Etheria records a visit to Alexandria, and to the Thebaid in the desert to the west where many holy hermits were dwelling. She goes on to describe places which modern archaeologists have identified and excavated:

> The City of Pithom, which the children of Israel built, was shown to us . . . at the spot where we entered the borders of Egypt . . . that same Pithom is now a fort. Heroöpolis, which was a city at the time when Joseph met Jacob his father as he came, as it is written in the Book of Genesis, is now what we call a village . . . Four miles from the City of Arabia is Rameses, now a bare field without a single habitation. It is quite plain it was once a big city, built in a circular form and had many buildings. Its ruins, just as they tell, are visible in great numbers to this day. Nothing else is there now but one great Theban stone in which two great statues are cut out, which they say are statues of holy men, even Moses and Aaron, erected by the children of Israel in their honour. A holy bishop told us that Pharaoh with his whole army had entered Rameses and burnt it completely because it was very great, and thence set out after the children of Israel.

The Lady Etheria mentions a sycamore tree planted at Ramses 'by the patriarchs' and describes her journey from the City of Arabia for two days through the Land of Goshen with its vineyards, balsam plantations, orchards, tilled fields and gardens, to Taphnis. This place, she was told, was the birth-place of Moses.

Her eagerness seems to have stirred the imagination of the monks, comments Lina Eckenstein in her *History of Sinai*, which led to decisions as to the localities which were accepted as authentic for centuries. Right up to our own time, in fact. At the turn of the century Edouard Naville identified Ramses with Saft el Henneh where he found Pharaonic inscriptions mention-

The colossi of Memnon. On the right is the singing statue on which the poems were carved. From an engraving in the *Description de l'Egypte*

The Sphinx according to Helferich, 1579

The graceful temple of Kertassi, Nubia, which the anonymous Italian traveler must have seen in 1589. Drawn by Gau, c. 1820

The temple of Kalabsha, Nubia. Drawn by Gau

The Kom Ombo temple, visited by the unknown Italian.
Author's photograph

George Sandys, "poet and traveller."
National Portrait Gallery

Sandys rides to the pyramids. From a woodcut in his book, *Relation of a Journey Begun in 1610*

Sandys's idea of hieroglyphs. He never saw this particular inscription—if it ever existed!

ht: Boullaye-le-Gouz, from a woodcut in his book of travels, c. 1650

ht: Boullaye-le-Gouz, from a woodcut in his book of travels, c. 1650

ow: The Sphinx and the pyramids,
according to Boullaye-le-Gouz

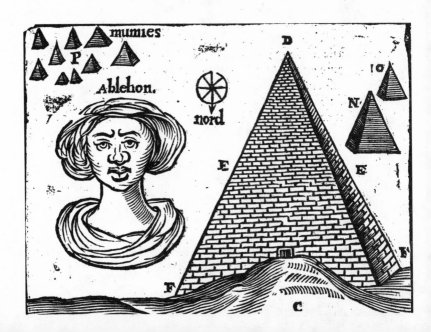

EFFIGIES IOHANNIS GRAVII.
A.D. 1650.
E. M. fec

John Greaves, author of *Pyrami graphia*, in 1650. *National Port Gallery*

Tomb chamber in the Great Pyramid. Drawing by Luigi Mayer, 1801

The Hall of Karnak, from an old engraving

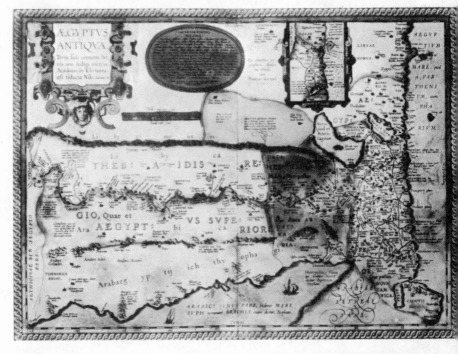

Map of Egypt by Ortelius, in the edition of 1595, showing the true position of Thebes. In spite of this, many travelers passed the site in ignorance until the early 18th century

Benoit de Maillet. From an engraving in his book

Author's photograph of the massive granite ruins of Beybeit, still much as they must have looked to Paul Lucas

The Sphinx according to Pococke, 1743

Norden sails past the ruins of ancient Alexandria. An engraving from his book

The Sphinx according to Norden, 1755

Norden passes the pyramids on his return down the Nile

The temple of Um Ebeida, Siwa Oasis. Sketch by Baron Minutoli, 1821

Entrance to the Valley of Kings, Thebes, which so daunted Bruce's servants

Vivant Denon

The temple of Edfu. Drawn by Denon

Prosper Jollois. Sketch by one of his colleagues during Bonaparte's expedition

Bonaparte's expedition measures the Sphinx. From Deno

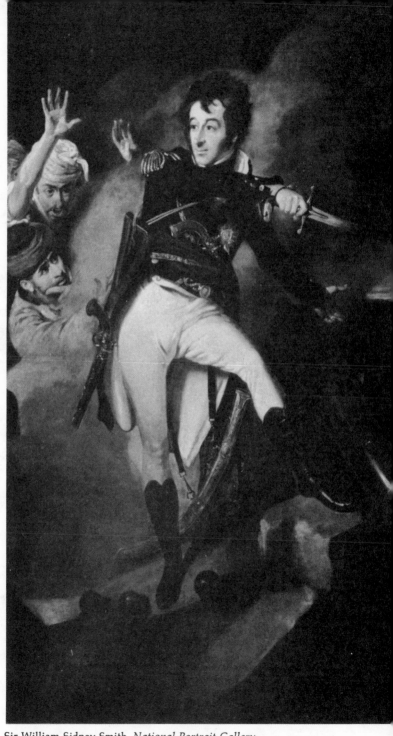

Sir William Sidney Smith. *National Portrait Gallery*

The obelisks at Alexandria. The standing one is in Central Park, New York

The temple on Elephantine Island, Aswan, destroyed after Denon drew it

ing the sycamore tree. Pithom he identified with Tel el Maskhuta on the railway line between Ismalia and Zagazig. It was the first excavation in Egypt undertaken by the Egypt Exploration Fund under Flinders Petrie. Heroöpolis is the Greek name for Pithom. Taphnis may be Daphne, Tel Defenneh, where Petrie uncovered 'Pharaoh's House in Tahpanhes'. So the Lady Etheria was not too far astray in this first unwitting archaeological excursion into Egypt.

In the year 870 Bernard the Wise, with two companion monks and the blessing of the Pope, set out from Rome 'wishing, in the name of the Lord, to see the places of the saints at Jerusalem'. But Egypt was no longer a Christian country, and they had a very difficult time. The voyage to Alexandria from Taranto took thirty days, and on arrival the captain demanded a further six gold pieces to allow them to go ashore. It was six days' sail up the Nile to 'Babylonia in Egypt (Cairo) where once king Pharaoh ruled, under whom Joseph built seven granaries, which yet remain'. He was alluding to the pyramids, and he was not the first to publish this delusion that the pyramids were granaries. It infected many subsequent writers.

Guards led them to the chief man of 'Babylonia in Egypt'; but their letters of identification were of no avail, 'for we were sent by him to prison; until after six days it occurred to us by the help of God to give him 300 Denarii each . . . He then also gave us letters' which saved them from further extortion, but at no place were they allowed to depart without a further document for which they had to pay 1 or 2 denarii. Christians in Egypt had to pay a poll tax. Failing payment, the Christian was sent to prison 'until either by the love of God he is delivered by his angel, or else is brought out by other good Christians'.

Bernard the Wise continued his journey to Jerusalem by land, and records no visit of interest in Egypt. His account may explain, however, why there are so few descriptions of travel in Egypt during the next three hundred years.

Between 1165 and 1171 Rabbi Benjamin ben Jonah of Tudela in Navarre accomplished a remarkable journey, much of it across territory then the scene of fighting between Crusaders and Mussulmans. He entered Egypt from Abyssinia, and he was the first to inform us on the sources of the Nile and the fact that its annual flooding is caused by the seasonal rains in the highlands of Abyssinia. He was for a time Vizier to the last of the Fatimite rulers of Egypt, Adib. Yet the eminent rabbi was still very much a man of his day when he wrote, 'The Pyramids which are seen here are constructed by witch-craft.'

One does not think of the possibility of any of this early, fumbling interest in the remains of ancient Egypt coming from east of Suez. Yet Abdel Latif, an Arab doctor from Baghdad, contributed intelligent and substantial observations which would have been valuable to the West, had their discovery and translation not been delayed until early in the last century. Not being a Christian, he could view the monuments objectively without heed of their connection with biblical history; and Abdel Latif offers a picture of Egypt at a time when the country was rarely visited by Europeans, on account of the fury of the Crusades. He taught medicine and philosophy at Cairo about A.D. 1200.

He wrote that a great number of small pyramids at Giza had been demolished by Karakousch the Eunuch, superintendent of buildings, to construct a stone wall around the old city of Fustat, Cairo and the Citadel. The Great Pyramid was open, and attracted a great many searchers activated by stupid cupidity and chimeric hopes, who followed narrow passages extending to great depths. The most frequented passage led to the upper part of the pyramid, to the square chamber in which there was a stone coffin. The place was full of bats as large as pigeons, and almost blocked by their droppings. Abdel Latif made his way in about two-thirds of the distance, then fainted, and came out, he admits, half dead with fear. The outside still had its smooth casing-stones on, and they were covered with writings 'of an ancient character'. But he met nobody in Egypt who even by hearsay could tell him what they meant. These may have been hieroglyphs, or the names of travellers, or a mixture of both. The Sphinx was apparently undamaged at the time, for he said that the face bore a reddish varnish like new. 'This figure is very beautiful, and its mouth carries the stamp of grace and beauty. It could be said that it smiles graciously.'

He visited Memphis, where our Greek and Roman tourists had wandered the streets of the living city a thousand years

before. Now it was dead. Yet even in the year 1200 the ruins
were still splendid:

> It requires a half-day's march in any direction to cross the visible
> ruins. It is a gathering of marvels to confound the mind. The more
> one looks upon them the greater grows the admiration they
> inspire; and each fresh glance of the eye upon these remains is a
> renewal of delight.

It is interesting to compare with this an account of the ruins
of Memphis as they appeared to Mariette's friend Arthur
Rhoné in 1865:

> A few mounds of earth, a few heaps of bricks crumbling back
> to dust, some peasants' huts under the date-palms, a royal statue
> or two half interred in the mud; and then, far off in the eternal
> sands, a cordon of pyramids great and small encompassing the
> desert plain—that is all that remains of Memphis, of this giant
> city, the most ancient capital of Egypt and perhaps of the world.

In 1268 Antioch fell to the Saracens; in 1289 Tripoli fell;
in 1291 Acre. These losses broke the spirit of the Crusaders.
Upon the conclusion of the Crusades travellers of all kinds,
especially pilgrims, were eager to visit the holy places. Their
movements were hampered by suspicion, but the Sultan el
Nasir of Egypt entered into diplomatic relations with the Pope,
the King of Aragon, and the King of France, and did his best
to protect pilgrims. The journey was usually made in galleys
from Genoa or Venice to Alexandria, and thence, after a visit
to Cairo, by land as Bernard the Wise had done. In Europe
great interest grew up in the Near East, aroused by returning
Crusaders' stories of the marvels they had seen. This in turn
encouraged the publication—through hand-copies still—of
numerous books of travel.

Best known of these 14th-century books was *The Voiage and
Travaile of Sir John Maundevile, Knight,* which purported to be a
guide for pilgrims to Jerusalem, giving the actual experiences
of the author. Of the pyramids he wrote:

> . . . full well made of masons' craft, of the which two be mar-
> vellously great and high, and the tother ne be not so great . . .
> And within they be all full of serpents . . . And some men say
> that they be sepultures of great lords, that were sometime, but

that is not true, for all the common rumour and speech is of all the people there, both far and near, that they be the garners of Joseph . . .

The wonders and adventures in the book are varied and entertaining, and they must have incited many travellers to undertake the journey. However, the *Cambridge History of English Literature* has this to say of it: 'The *Travels* of Sir John Mandeville had been a household word in eleven languages and for five centuries before it was ascertained that Sir John never lived, that his travels never took place, and that his personal experiences, long the test of others' veracity, were compiled out of every possible authority, going back to Pliny, if not further . . . he, or they, carried out the most successful literary fraud ever known in one of the most delightful volumes ever written.'

The author was almost certainly Jean d'Outremeuse, a notary of Liège, who apparently never left his native country.

Other travel books of the time, though genuine, were seldom so entertaining as Mandeville's compilation. They have their revealing flashes at times, though. Ludolph von Suchem wrote of Egypt, 'full of all good things that the heart of man can conceive, and full of everything needful except wine'. He was not the only one to say that. Ludolph was the traveller who recorded the inscription on the pyramid by the sister who wept for her brother. His travelling companion was Wilhelm von Boldinsel, a Dominican monk who also wrote an account of his travels that was cribbed wholesale by Sir John Mandeville— although Sir John opted for the theory of the pyramids as granaries, whereas Boldinsel had classed them as mausoleums. That was in 1336.

Pero Tafur, a Spaniard, who made the journey in 1435, was another who adhered to the strange idea that they were granaries. One would conclude that he actually went to Egypt because of a strange fact which he published, and which he is unlikely to have invented: that the sultan who received him in great style was playing polo. That would be some 400 years before Europeans reintroduced the sport into Egypt.

In 1480 Brother Felix Fabri, of the Dominican Convent of Ulm, was granted audience with Count Eberhard the Elder of Württemberg, who had long ago made the pilgrimage to the

holy places, and who was a Knight of the Holy Sepulchre:
'I asked His Magnificence's advice.' The noble count replied:

> There are three acts in a man's life which no one ought either to
> advise another to do or not to do. The first is to contract matri-
> mony; the second to go to the wars; and the third to visit the
> Holy Sepulchre. These three acts are good in themselves, but they
> may easily turn out ill; and when this is so, he who gave the
> advice comes to be blamed.

Felix Fabri intended to go on the pilgrimage anyhow; so the
non-committal advice mattered nothing. Fortified by a subsidy
from His Magnificence, Felix set off on journeys of which the
record makes one of the most appealing travel books ever
written. The friar carried tablets of wax with him, on which he
jotted down notes as he went along, and his finally compiled
Evagatorium in Terram Sanctam involves the reader intimately as
though he were a member of the band of 15th-century pilgrims
going by sea and land to Jerusalem, Sinai and Egypt.

Although his chief aim was to see the holy places, Felix was
interested in everything, and it is his second voyage that
attracts our attention especially, because it took him to the
monastery of St Catherine in Sinai, and to Egypt. The crossing
to Jaffa from Venice was by trireme with 'sixty cross-benches,
and upon each bench three rowers with their oars'. It was a big
ship, 200 feet long, with a beam of 42 feet and a mast 108 feet
high. The Great Cabin ran the full length of the ship below,
and the pilgrims berthed there, feet to the centre. The bilge
well stank; the privies were around the sides of the ship, and
everything was tarry.

The galley-slaves were bought slaves of the 'Lord of the
Ship', or 'men of low station, or prisoners', exiles, or poor
riff-raff, chained to the benches when there was any chance of
their making an escape. But Felix 'never saw a German galley-
slave, because no German could stand such misery'.

> They are fed most miserably, and always sleep on the boards
> of their rowing benches, and both by day and night they are
> always in the open air ready for work; and when there is a storm
> they stand in the midst of the waves. In general they are thieves,
> and spare nothing that they find; for which crime they often are
> most cruelly tortured. When they are not at work they sit and

play at cards and dice for gold and silver, with execrable oaths and blasphemies. I never heard such terrible swearing as on board of these vessels.

Sometimes among them there were respectable merchants 'who subject themselves to this most grievous servitude in order that they may ply their trade in harbours'. Some were tailors and shoemakers, working in their spare time at their craft. Some hired out as washermen. All had something to trade, under the bench. They even sold excellent wine, bought by the pilgrims.

As for celebration of Sundays and Saints' Days at sea, I declare they are most infamously kept. I have no doubt that the devil takes especial pains to throw hindrances in the way of keeping feast days holy. The holier the day, the harder the work done at sea. It was my custom on board ship to preach a sermon on holy days. During my first pilgrimage a certain son of Belial many times interrupted the Word of God by his laughter, and neither entreaties nor blows would keep him quiet, but he laughed all the more.

Reading Felix Fabri we seem to be part of that ship's company, passing the tedious days as best we may, according to our habits:

. . . wine-drinking, usually done by Saxons, Flemings and other men of a low class. Dice, cards, chess. Singing, lutes, flutes, bagpipes, clavichords, zithers, etc. Discussing worldly matters, reading books, praying with beads, meditation, sitting still. Some pass almost the whole time in their berths asleep. Others run and jump, lift weights. Some sit and look at sea and land and write travel books, which was my daily employment. Finally, there is among all the occupations of seafarers one which, albeit loathsome, is yet very common, daily, and necessary—I mean the hunting and catching of lice and vermin . . . There was one brave knight in our company who would never touch a louse with his fingers, but always took two stones, and used to lay his shirt upon one stone and beat the louse with the other until he had killed it.

When his party of twenty set off from Jerusalem for Mount Sinai their baggage included many jars of wine. One jar broke, and the wine leaked through the hair-sack that concealed it from the Saracens who, they feared, would smell it and break the remainder. 'If we had been deprived of our wine we should not have attempted the pilgrimage to Sinai, nor could we have lived in the desert with no wine to drink.' Horrified to see good wine going to waste, Felix filled his two-quart bottle from the spill.

The Sinai pilgrimage demanded twenty-six days in the wilderness, which only the hardiest pilgrims could survive. On the way they saw ostriches, now extinct, and a unicorn— most certainly extinct—was pointed out to them. Its single horn was all of four feet long,

> wondrous brilliant, and the bone thereof is reckoned as costly as the most precious stones. He is so strong that he cannot be taken by any art or strength of those who hunt him; but it is said by writers on natural history that they place a young virgin in his way, who opens her bosom as he runs toward her, whereat he puts away from him all his fierceness, and lays down his head in her lap and is held thus entranced until he is taken and slain by the huntsmen. He cannot be tamed, and if fettered he straightway dies of vexation. He overcomes the elephant but shows a strange reverence for virgins.

At last they arrived within sight of the monastery:

> Behold, we saw buildings, human dwellings and an oblong church. It was the monastery of the most blessed virgin St Catherine at the foot of the most holy Mount Sinai. We dismounted from our asses, and with great joy knelt and worshipped. It was on that very place that Moses saw that notable miracle, the bush that was burning without its green leaves suffering any hurt.

Felix saw all the sights with enthusiasm, including the Chapel of the Burning Bush, the rock on which the ravens laid food for Elijah, the summit of Horeb where Moses received the tables of the law, and the cleft in the rock

> wherein the Lord placed Moses that he might see the back parts of God (for God had said "Thou canst not see my face, for there shall no man see me, and live"). So out of devotion we laboriously worked ourselves into the hole. But it was of such a height from the ground that a man must let his legs hang outside, together with all the hinder parts of him.

After a long and wearisome desert crossing, the pilgrims came to Cairo, where Felix saw the Well of the Virgin, the

crypt of the Holy Family in the church of St Serge, and the
pyramids, 'marvellous sepulchral monuments of the ancient
kings of Egypt'. At Alexandria, where they embarked for home
on a spice galley, he saw a 'very remarkable column, all of one
stone, yet of wonderful height and width. On the four sides
were carved men and animals and birds from the top to the
bottom; and no one now knows what these figures signify.'
He was, in fact, looking at the obelisk that now stands in New
York. Another, fallen, lay beside it, which now stands on the
Embankment in London. The inscriptions were of Thutmose
III, 1500 B.C.

So brief a glance as we have been able to give to Felix
Fabri's book of travel does scant justice to this lively work.
Though his interest in ancient Egypt was as nothing to the real
purpose of his journey, he is one of the early ones to record an
intelligent curiosity about the heathen past; a curiosity that was
to mature three centuries later. And his descriptions of the
human side of his travels bring alive before us those first
Europeans who stood baffled at sight of the pyramids, temples
and tombs whose mysteries have since been revealed. Often it is
the apparent trivialities recorded by Felix that make his pages
live, as when he caught the drips from the broken wine jar, or
the story of his pretty, tight, expensive yellow leather boots
when he put them on in a hurry for an ascent of the mountains
of Engeddi near the Dead Sea. When he put on the right boot
with a sudden hard pull he felt something moist and half
solid down near the toe. He feared it was a scorpion, toad or
snake, and he felt sure it wriggled. He was in too much haste
to take the boot off again, for his companions were waiting.
So he crushed his foot hard against a stone, mounted his
donkey, and hoped for the best. After a while they came to a
narrow place, where a halt was called. Felix took the opportunity
to inspect:

> When I put in my hand I found some moist stuff, and I learned by
> the smell what I could not learn either by sight or touch. I put on
> my boot again with great indignation, and continued on my way
> downcast and malcontent, wondering who among the company
> would show such disrespect to me and play such a scurvy trick.
> I exercised my mind to decide which of the knights would be so
> irreverent as to put ordure into the boot of a pilgrim and a priest.

There must have been shouts of laughter that evening when he admitted that he had suspected a certain high noble knight of a schoolboy prank—for he found on final investigation that the offensive substance was a ball of horse-manure that some zealous dung-rolling beetle had pushed into his boot 'to become my grist', as Felix neatly put it.

4 Renaissance

MEDIEVAL Europe did not change suddenly as a result of the rediscovery of the culture of ancient Greece and Rome. It was rather that the antique culture began to be studied as a result of the gradual progress away from medievalism. The new learning was a part of the economic and spiritual change at that period of European development. And the change itself was but a phase in the inevitable, continuous adjustment of the social order that is for ever seeking a repose it will never attain. Some of these phases have more marked characteristics than others, and this one has come to be called the Renaissance; for it did look like a re-birth. The decay of the Holy Roman Empire and loosening of the Church's hold over the manner of men's thinking allowed inquiring minds to interpret the old authors more literally, and to follow in fascination the thoughts of the heathen philosophers. The introduction of gunpowder shook feudalism by making the castles of barons no longer unassailable. Use of the mariner's compass and other navigational aids expanded the known world across the Atlantic to America, Mexico, Peru, around the Cape of Good Hope to India by sea. The printing press, strongest agent in all these revolutionary changes, spread the new knowledge among many.

The Renaissance, in so far as the emancipation of the intelligence is concerned, started in Italy, where Francesco Petrarch's scholarship revealed the dignity of man freed from his enslavement to the notion that the world of the flesh was of no significance, and that only the life beyond was real.

Petrarch realized, too, that besides the greatness of ancient Rome that he so admired, there had been a greatness of ancient Greece, and it was imperative to recover the dead Greek language and literature. His friend Giovanni Boccaccio was one of the first to sponsor this work. The growing interest in ancient authors led to the collecting of manuscripts, and the copying of them. Learning became fashionable, and the fashion spread across Europe.

Meanwhile in Egypt, since the disturbance of the Crusades had ceased, Alexandria had been frequented by Mediterranean merchants, especially those from Provence. Venetians were influential there until the end of the 15th century, and Venice was the entrepôt for Eastern goods coming back by the land route across Suez, especially the valuable spice trade. It was on a Venetian spice galley that Felix Fabri returned from his travels.

But the year 1501 marked a decline in this trade, for the Portuguese fleet at Calicut in India sank the Egyptian ships there. Ruthlessly the Portuguese were warring to capture the spice trade for themselves, carrying the goods without transshipment by their new route around the Cape. In 1508 the Portuguese destroyed the Egyptian fleet in the Red Sea, and the Cape route replaced that of the Mediterranean for the India trade.

A few years later, in 1517, Egypt lost the independence it did not recover until the middle of the present century. Selim I, the Turk, invaded. However, he confirmed a treaty signed by the former Sultan Kansou-Ghouri, allowing Catalans and French to trade, and granting them religious protection. Thus it was reasonably secure for travellers to be in Egypt at the beginning of the 16th century, although the voyage thither of several weeks was a risky one on account of pirates, who might be Turks, Barbary or Christian. These pests to navigators remained until little more than a century ago.

Many of the travellers were merchants, and if they left records they were of goods and consulates and conditions of trade, with few observations on history or the monuments. The remainder were pilgrims to the holy places, and some of them went out of their way to see and speculate upon the ruins of ancient Egypt.

Before the Turkish conquest, in 1505, Martin Baumgarten, a knight of Germany, stricken with grief at the death of his wife, who had lost all her children, swore that he would visit the Lord's sepulchre at Jerusalem, the monastery of St Catherine at Sinai and other holy places, 'and what he vowed he quickly performed with great labour and expense', setting out in 1507 at the age of thirty-four.

Martin Baumgarten landed at Alexandria, and thus did the pilgrimage in a reverse direction to that of Felix Fabri. At Alexandria he was shown the same New York obelisk that Felix had remarked on, 'full of figures of living creatures, and other things, which plainly shows that the Egyptians of old made use of such instead of letters'.

Here is no suggestion that the hieroglyphs are anything but alphabetical. The unfounded assertion by some classical authors that they were purely symbolic led many attempts astray in the long search for their solution. Yet Baumgarten, visiting the pyramids, repeats the thesis of Diodorus Siculus when he writes:

> . . . the reason why they were built so great, and so many hands employed, was that the people might have no time to conspire against their kings . . . but none of those kings who designed any of these pyramids for their sepulchre were buried in them; for either the hardship that the people endured, or the tyranny and cruelty of the kings provoked their subjects to that degree, that they either tore their bodies in pieces, or threw them out of their monuments. For which reason they ultimately left special orders with some of their servants, to lay their bodies in some mean and obscure place, that they might thereby avoid the fury of the people.

There is a half-truth here; for the story surely arose from the fact that the tombs were empty from remote times, pillaged not by angry mobs but by stealthy tomb-robbers.

Baumgarten also reverts to the classic tradition by asserting that

> for the magnificence and art that is displayed upon them, they may justly be reckon'd one of the seven wonders of the world, and irresistibly breed admiration in all that behold them . . . the greatest of these pyramids is so large still, that the strongest man that is, standing and throwing a dart strait forwards, can scarce reach the middle of it; which experiment has been oftentimes tried.

The knight proceeded to Jerusalem by way of Sinai and returned home, where, comforted by his pilgrimage, he took a second wife, 'Apollonia, a virgin' who gave him eight sons. It is recorded that he worked with 'minerals'—silver and copper—and one wonders if he was dabbling in alchemy. At any rate this hobby got him into debt, in which misfortune he was much comforted, he writes, by the doctrines and letters of Martin Luther. This is symptomatic of the trend of the Renaissance in Germany, where the revival of learning was channelled into religious reform. At length:

> This pious, honourable and magnanimous knight died in the true acknowledgment, ardent invocation, and constant confession of Jesus Christ, *anno Domini* 1535, in the 62nd. year of his age, when he had fought a good fight, and kept the faith undefiled, together with a pure conscience, and was interr'd in the chapel belonging to the family of the Baumgartens, where he expects a joyful resurrection of his body, renovated into a state of immortality, in the glorious day of the restitution of all things.

The travellers are still bringing with them a strong odour of medievalism, and their interest in the heathen relics is still fleeting, and little more than wonderment. Thus 'the building is not only worthy of being called a marvel but incredible', wrote Jéhan Thenaud of the pyramid which he rightly ascribed to Cheops. Thenaud was guardian of the convent of Cordeliers d'Angoulême, and protégé of Louise de Savoie and her son François d'Angoulême, the future François Ier. She sent Thenaud to pray for her in the holy places of Jerusalem when Louis XII sent Ambassador André le Roy to Sultan Kansou-Ghouri to secure the safety of pilgrims to the Holy Land. This was five years before the Turkish conquest, and Jéhan Thenaud was the last man of letters to see the old independent Egypt, and his *Voyage d'Outremer* contains a charming chapter describing Cairo life and the splendour of the Sultan's reception of the Ambassador; but he is credited with exaggerations.

In this he was no exception. Travellers of his time did not always manage to reach the monuments they described, so they often reported hearsay as eyewitness, or borrowed the accounts of other writers without acknowledgment. The temptation to astound must have been great, because the road was long and hard, so that the risk of being found out was slight. Thus

Greffin Affagart, Seigneur de Courteilles in Sarthe, France, voyaging to the Holy Land, tells a story that one can only wish were true, that beside the well-known column at Alexandria 'called Pompeyan' there was another 'supporting the body of the great King Alexander in a golden case'.

That was in 1533. Thirteen years later a compatriot of his, Dr Pierre Belon, passed through Egypt. His interest was natural history, so he observed the ruins with a more objective attitude than most of the religious tourists. Yet even he was accused of plagiarism in publishing in his name the manuscript of Pierre Gilles, on the nature of animals. He went inside the pyramid of Cheops where he reports seeing 'a vast tomb of black marble', and he contemplated 'the great colossus named by Herodotus Androsphinx, and Sphinge by Pliny, which is a sculpture in front of the Pyramids'. The Sphinx had no longer the stamp of grace and beauty so admired by Abdel Latif in 1200. It had been mutilated by Sheik Mohamed in 1300. This exonerates the artillerymen of Napoleon Bonaparte, who have the popular reputation of having used the nose of the Sphinx as a target.

Pierre Belon makes the useful observation that the third pyramid was in perfect condition as if it had just been built. To this we can add the remark of Jean Chesneau, a secretary to the French Ambassador who was in Egypt about the same time. Chesneau climbed the Great Pyramid and went inside, adding, 'near it are two others, not so large, and not thus made in degrees, and they are without openings'. It would seem certain that only the Great Pyramid had had its smooth casing removed by this time, and that the other two still possessed the greater part of theirs.

Soon after, in 1549, the Chaplain of Catherine dei Medici, André Thévet, made the tour. Credulous, and a poor writer, he is remembered less for his *Cosmographie de Levant* than for the introduction of tobacco into France, which is ascribed to him. Later he became historian and map-maker to the King of France. In front of the pyramids, it is to his credit that he refused to accept them as granaries of Pharaoh, saying 'they are sepulchres of kings as appears from Herodotus . . . since I saw in one pyramid a great stone of marble carved in the manner of a sepulchre'.

He remarked on the 'head of a colossus, caused to be made by Isis daughter of Inachus, then so beloved of Jupiter'—some garbled tale he had picked up—failing completely to identify it with the 'Androsphinz' of Herodotus, whom he had led us to suppose he had studied. With two Venetian doctors he ransacked tombs at Saqqara, burial ground of Memphis, for the mummies dear to doctors and apothecaries of the time.

Vincent le Blanc of Marseilles, writing of Egypt in 1660, said:

'Tis whence the greatest part of Mummy, or flesh buried and rosted in the sand is gotten, which the wind uncovering, the next passenger brings to town for sale, it being very medicinable. Here you see a dead man is often more serviceable to the living, than the living themselves; yet some approve not of the physick.

In the 16th and 17th centuries mummy was one of the ordinary drugs found in all apothecaries' shops, and its importation was a regular trade in which speculators invested, tombs were searched, and mummies pulverized.

Faith in the medicinal efficacy of powdered corpses of ancient Egyptians arose from a confusion of terms. The word mummy is derived from the Persian *momia,* meaning bitumen, or mineral pitch. Sir William Ouseley wrote in the second volume of his *Travels:*

Mummy is a blackish bitumenous matter which oozes from the rock, and is considered by the Persians as far more precious than gold, for it heals cuts and bruises, causes fractures to unite in a few minutes, and taken inwardly, is a sovereign remedy for many diseases.

The resemblance and supposed identity of the natural mummy to the bitumen found in the embalmed bodies of the Egyptians doubtless contributed to maintain its character and to enhance its value in the estimation of the Arabs. The real mummy—*momia,* the liquid pitch from the mountains—possibly does possess some antiseptic qualities, and perhaps the bitumen in the Egyptian mummies reflected them faintly; yet sufferers could scarcely be expected to obtain any extra nefit from the dust of long decayed flesh that would be included in their doses. In *The Works of that Famous Chirurgeon*

Ambrose Parey, published in London in 1634, we are warned that 'this wicked kind of drugge doth nothing help the diseased'.

Few at the time heeded the 'famous chirurgeon's' advice; the trade in mummies flourished as it had been flourishing before the days of Abdel Latif, who wrote in 1200 that he saw *momia* that had been taken out of the skulls and stomachs of mummies on sale. He adds, 'I bought three heads filled with it, for half a dirham. It differs little from mineral pitch, of which it could be used in place.'

The trade in mummies was carried on in Egypt chiefly by Jews. When the supply of mummies became short the Jews were obliged to manufacture them. They obtained the bodies of executed criminals and of Christians who had died in hospitals, stuffing them with bitumen and wrapping them in bandages, then putting them out in the heat of the sun to mature until they resembled genuine old mummies.

There is no call to doubt this gruesome story, for it is related by Thomas Joseph Pettigrew, R.R.S., in his *History of Mummies*, published in 1834: a learned contribution to science, as well as the first purely archaeological work on Egypt to be published in England, according to a recognized modern authority, Warren R. Dawson.

In 1564, relates Pettigrew, a physician named Guy de la Fontaine inspected the stock of mummies in the stores of the chief mummy dealer in Alexandria. He was horrified to find that they were made from the bodies of slaves and others who had died of loathsome diseases.

The fake mummy trade eventually came to an end when a Christian slave, in revenge for ill-treatment, reported to the Pasha the exact nature of his master's trade. Every trader in the country was seized and thrown into prison, not so much, perhaps, because of his horrible occupation, but in view of the opportunity to extort money from him with a comforting sense of righteous indignation. Hampered by the levy which, once imposed, was never relaxed, the production of this cannibal medicine languished and died out.

Johannes Helferich, often quoted and copied by later writers, left an account of his visit to the mummy pits in a book published in German in 1579. The Moors cleared the sand away from deep shafts that led to subterranean chambers with vaulted ceilings, in which the mummies were laid:

> It must be understood that the mummies are the dead bodies of heathens . . . they stay unchanged; they are quite black; the limbs are carefully wrapped in small cloths soaked in costly balsam and thereafter the entire body is enclosed in a wide cloth and bound up just like little children . . . In some of them when they are unwrapped are found within the body little carved men or animals and such like fantasies. The Moors who live hereabouts seek such with great industry which they sell to the merchants in Cairo who in turn resell them . . .

This is an early mention of a trade in curios that was to destroy so much of value to future research through its heedless ransacking of tombs.

Helferich prints a woodcut of the Sphinx so grotesque that it is hard to believe that he could ever have seen it. He elaborates the garbled tale that André Thévet told about the Sphinx when he failed to identify it:

> . . . an enormous head, from one piece carved, standing high, as shown in the figure. The head is the height of three men . . . formerly known as Imago Isidis; it is a portrait of the goddess Isidis originally so called, who is a daughter of King Inachi of Greece whom the Egyptian god Osiris took as his wife—who changed her name to Isis—and after her death she was held to be a goddess, and in her honour this figure was fashioned . . . From afar, under the ground, through a narrow hidden passage, one can pass unseen. By this passage the heathen priests get inside the head and speak to the people therefrom as if the statue itself had spoken. Close by this head are the Pyramids . . . as some people write, the rich courtesan Rhodope built one.

The myth of the secret passage to the Sphinx, and that of the courtesan who built a pyramid, were to be copied by these forerunners of the archaeologists for many a year to come; and Helferich repeats, too, the tradition that the Great Pyramid was the burial place of that Pharaoh who perished in the Red Sea chasing the Israelites.

Not one writer ventures to say that he traversed the secret passage; and Helferich seems to think that the inhabitants were still worshipping the Sphinx. The passage does not exist, yet nobody tried to verify its existence. The state of mind that will accept and repeat unverified facts while actually on the spot was still somewhat that of the medieval acceptance of dogma on faith alone. Circumstantial details of his entry into the pyramid make it certain that Helferich did actually go in there. The air within was so bad, he relates, that for two or three days they were reduced to such a state of feebleness that they could move neither arm nor leg. The Venetian Consul called his doctor to aid them, and in addition:

> The Consul supplied us with tasty food and excellent wine which with God's blessing and human help quickly restored us to our usual selves.

There are few records of English travellers showing interest in the remains of ancient Egypt during this period; but Hakluyt records several voyages that must have been read by William Shakespeare and caused the First Witch in *Macbeth* to exclaim:

> A sailor's wife had chestnuts in her lap,
> And munch'd, and munch'd, and munch'd: 'Give me,' quoth I:
> 'Aroint thee, witch!' the rump-fed ronyon cries.
> Her husband's to Aleppo gone, master o' the *Tiger* . . .

Curiosity as much as commerce inspired the daring *Voyage of M. Ralph Fitch, marchant of London:*

> In the yeare of our Lord 1583, I, being desirous of seeing the countreys of the East India . . . did ship my selfe in a ship of London called the *Tyger*, wherein we went for Tripolis in Syria; and from there we tooke the way for Aleppo.

Aboard *Tyger* was John Eldred. They went overland from Aleppo to the Euphrates, down it in a boat, and on through the Persian Gulf to India. In Mesopotamia they visited the ruins of Babylon and the Tower of Babel, which are described by John Eldred. They were far from our ruins of Egypt, but at least they were Englishmen looking at ruins and not on a pilgrimage.

Three years later we hear of a certain Laurence Aldersey being in Alexandria in the course of his travels:

> . . . my guide brought me aboord a ship of Alderman Martins, called the *Tyger* of London, where I was well received of the Master of the said ship, whose name was Thomas Rickman, and of all the company. The said Master having made me good cheere,

and made me also to drinke of the water of Nilus . . . he brought me first to Pompey his pillar, which is a mighty thing of gray marble, and all of one stone.

The worthy Master showed him all the sights of Alexandria, and he went to see the pyramids at Cairo:

the monuments bee high and in forme 4-square, and every of the squares is as long as a man may shoote a roving arrowe, and as high as a Church. I sawe also the ruines of the Citie of Memphis hard by those Pyramides.

Possibly the very next sailing of the same ship was *The Voyage passed by sea into Aegypt, by John Evesham, Gentleman:*

On 5 of December we departed from Gravesend in the *Tiger* of London, wherein was Master under God for the voyage Robert Rickman (*sic*) . . . The said citie of Alexandria is an old thing decayed or ruinated . . . within the said citie there is a pillar of Marble, called by the Turks, King Pharaoe's Needle, and it is foure square, every square is twelve foote, and it is in height 90 foote. Also there is without the walls of the said Citie, about twentie score paces, another marble pillar, being round, called Pompey his pillar: this pillar standeth upon a great square stone, fifteene foote high, and the compasse of the pillar is 37 foote, and heigth of it is 101 feete, which is a wonder to think how ever it was possible to set the said pillar upon the said stone . . .

There is to the Eastward of this Citie, about three dayes journey, the citie of Grand Cayro, otherwise called Memphis. neere to the saide citie there is a place called the Pyramides . . . one of the nine wonders of the world: . . . the heigth of them . . . doth surmount twise the heigth of Paules steeple: within is a costly tombe . . . made for king Pharao . . . but he was not buried there, being drowned in the red sea.

Also we were at an old Citie, all ruinated and destroyed, called in olde time, the great Citie of Carthage where Hannibal and Queen Dido dwelt . . . to which Citie fresh water was brought upon arches above 25 miles, of which arches some are standing to this day.

By moving Carthage 1,200 miles east, and by placing Cairo east of Alexandria, John Evesham displays some weakness in geography as well as archaeology. His 'Carthage' was probably the old Arab city of Fustat, hard by Cairo, whose remains, including aqueducts, have been excavated recently.

In the National Library at Florence there is a manuscript account by an unknown traveller of a *Voyage made in the year 1589 from Cairo to Ebrim by way of the Nile*, which begins:

> For some years I had a lively desire to see the province of the Saîd as far as the end of the land of Egypt, and my sole reason was to see so many superb buildings, churches, colossal statues, needles and columns . . .

The motive is purely that of archaeology and curiosity, though the manuscript is not that of a learned man. He could not read Greek, and copied only the first words of inscriptions. But his importance is that he is the first true explorer to go nearly to the second cataract, and the first to leave such a detailed record of the monuments. He was certainly the first to visit and describe any of these south of Aswan. Before him the only European travellers to go south of Cairo for any distance had been Anghura in 1395, and Lannoy in 1422, who visited the convents of St Antony and St Paul on the coast of the Red Sea. Later, in 1480, the missionary Ballista da Imola, *en route* to Ethiopia, went from Cairo to Naqada and thence across the eastern desert to Kosseir on the Red Sea.

Our unknown voyager left Cairo on 7th August, 1589, and examined Antinopolis, 'famous and noble city today deserted and ruined'. This was the city founded by Emperor Hadrian in memory of his handsome friend Antinous who was drowned in the Nile at that spot. Our voyager went on to Luxor and Karnak, though without identifying them with ancient Thebes of Egypt. South again, he visited the Esna, Edfu and Kom Ombo temples. At Aswan he saw Philae, and afterwards the many temples as far as Ibrim, the hilltop town on Nile's edge that was invaded in 1173 by Shams ed Daulah, who burnt the Christian church that has recently been excavated by the Egypt Exploration Society of London. When our traveller reached there it was probably inhabited by the descendants of the Bosnian mercenaries whom the Turkish governors of Nubia had placed in the fort they built there about 1520. The courageous unknown had intended to go on as far as Dongola, but failing health, he says, caused him to abandon the idea and return.

Apparently this account of the most daring exploit in the

exploration of Egypt so far was never published. The achievements of other travellers in what little remained of the 16th century are very tame beside those of the unknown Italian. However, his journey seems to mark the transition between the pilgrims who visited the ancient sites as a sideline to their main objective, the pilgrimage, and the antiquaries who came for the sake of the old things themselves. One can scarcely call them archaeologists yet.

The Sieur Villamont, who arrived in Cairo in March, 1590, is thus an early antiquary, for he is credited with being the first and even the only traveller of the 16th and 17th centuries accurately to place the site of ancient Memphis, that had become lost since it was seen by Abdel Latif in 1200. He reported 'sumptuous vestiges where there is still the shape of a city'. Laurence Aldersey—he who was entertained by the Master of the *Tyger*—claimed to have seen these ruins, but we have no more precise placing from him than 'hard by those Pyramides'.

The 17th century opens with the arrival in Egypt, in September, 1605, of François Savary, Seigneur de Brèves, Ambassador of France to Constantinople, where he had just negotiated fresh capitulations and the liberation of Christian slaves of the Mussulmans. He was taken for the usual tourist run-around, and remarks that the pyramids 'terrify by their height'. Entering the sepulchral chamber within the Great Pyramid, he notices that the joints between the huge stones are so marvellously trimmed that 'one could not insert the point of a needle without difficulty'.

His equerry, du Castel, purchased a mummy on his own account, and to his great astonishment found in the body 'on breaking it open, an animal in stone made like a stag beetle'. He had found a scarab, though he did not know what it was, and was no more informed as to its significance than the Arabs who were rifling the bodies in the mummy pits at Saqqara for similar objects to sell as curios. The diplomatic successors of de Brèves were quick to collect scarabs and amulets and to sell them for a good profit in Paris to grace the cabinets of the King.

5 The Antiquaries

A LETTER from Ambassador du Houssay to Cardinal Richelieu reveals the growing interest in classical Egyptian art that was being aroused by the objects taken back from Egypt. It is dated from Cairo, 18th September, 1638:

> Monseigneur, beside the service of the King I could have no more legitimate concern than that of your Eminence. Since the most beautiful monuments of antiquity appear to have survived the perils of so many centuries solely to be judged worthy of a place in your Eminence's libraries and cabinets, may I assure your Eminence that in order to procure for them so glorious a shelter, I have already written throughout the Levant to impose the necessary orders in all places where there are Consuls of France that they seek with great care all such things as may be worthy of this honour.

Not only embassies and consulates were used as agents for collecting curios. Missions consisting of one or two scholars were sent into the Levant especially to seek ancient manuscripts of any kind, ancient coins, and any other antique objects that might interest the royal or noble patron. Since learning, or at least the appearance of it, had become fashionable during the Renaissance, every nobleman who desired to be esteemed was a collector, and the Kings of France were the biggest collectors of all.

The resulting displays of miscellaneous and unrelated antiquities led to some gain in knowledge of the antique world of Greece and Rome, but to nothing of the history of ancient Egypt, for the objects were of course quite divorced from their context, and the inscriptions in hieroglyphic writing were incomprehensible.

Yet the collections were not entirely an idle pastime for the rich and noble; they were a sharpening-stone for the minds of intelligent men and scholars, even if they could not make much of the items at the time. One can see with pleasure that man of universally inquiring mind, de Peirese, councillor of the Parliament of Aix, sheltering from the plague on his property at Belgentier, a village north of Toulon. There he received travellers from the Levant and plied them with questions. We can see him welcoming back Father Minuti about the year 1632, with his boxes stuffed with manuscripts, books in Coptic, papyri, a statuette of Isis and mummies. We can see de Peirese trying vainly to allot symbolic equivalents to the baffling Egyptian hieroglyphs that simply would not render the same meaning twice. And we can see him carefully unwrapping a mummy to ascertain if it held a coin in its mouth as in Greek custom, to pay Charon's fare across the Styx.

For lack of scientific method, scholars were to chase elusive knowledge for a long time to come. But the great private collections were not gathered in vain; they were to become the nuclei of the superb national collections of later centuries, especially those of Italy and France.

In Egypt, as yet, few travellers went curio-hunting south of Cairo. The consuls and ambassadors were kept in the city by their duties, and for the tourists it was dangerous and uncomfortable to go further. They were content with the usual circuit: Pompey's Pillar and 'Cleopatra's Needles' in Alexandria; and in Cairo the pyramids and Sphinx; Saqqara and its mummies; and Memphis, though its placement was uncertain again, in spite of de Villamont. Travel memoirs of the period are monotonously similar, even when the writers are not simply copying one from the other. The picturesque in contemporary Egypt fascinated them. They loved to describe the crowds, the fêtes, the holy men and the slave markets. But they had no interest in the 'false religion' of Mohamed and its mosques, some of them being freshly built then, and much admired now. Christian remains, however, interested them deeply: sites of the traditional visit of the Holy Family; Coptic monasteries and churches; and of course St Catherine's on Sinai.

The Englishman George Sandys was one who did not go beyond the pyramids, yet he included an account of Egypt in his *Relation of a Journey begun in 1610* which went into seven editions. His account is a good measure of the fragmentary knowledge of Egypt at the time. It was derivative and largely inaccurate. Yet Sandys was a literary figure in his day, a poet and an observant traveller. It is simply that, in writing of Egypt, he had no data but what he could see, the tales of others, and the classics.

Youngest son of the Archbishop of York, George Sandys was best known for his verse translation of Ovid's *Metamorphoses*— much admired later by Pope—which he completed in America when he became treasurer to the Virginia Company in 1621. His great journey through the Levant was made early in life at the age of thirty-two. In his dedication to the Prince—Charles I —he deplores the state into which had fallen those kingdoms once 'the theatres of Valour and heroical actions, now through vice and ingratitude become the most deplored spectacles of extreme misery'. Their calamities, he says, are a warning to the rest of the world, 'for assistance wherein, I have not only related what I saw of their present condition, but presented a brief view of their former estates, and first antiquities of those peoples and countries'.

It is this brief view of their 'former estates' and 'first antiquities' as seen by a man of the time of Cromwell and the beginnings of America that interests us. Intelligently he observed that 'Egypt was a See when other parts of the World were inhabited, made manifest by the shells and bones of fishes found in the intrails of the earth . . . by the operation of the River, bringing down earth with his Deluges, and extruding the See by little and little until it caught up with Pharos that was a day's sail off shore according to Homer'.

Nile water, Sandys tells us, 'procureth liberal urine, cureth the dolour of the reins, and is most soveraign against that windy melancholy arising from the shorter ribs, which so saddeth the mind of the diseased'.

Hieroglyphs were invented by Mercury, 'who writ from the right hand to the left, as do all the Africans'. But Sandys failed to notice that the ancient Egyptians did not behave 'like Africans': they wrote their hieroglyphs in either direction, or from top to bottom in columns. 'Hieroglyphics, which consist of significant figures, are hardly to be interpreted,' he asserts; yet he reproduces an example and gives an interpretation based on some imagined symbolic significance: 'O you that enter the World, and go out of it; God hateth injustice.' Unfortunately modern linguists cannot correct his reading because his woodcut bears no resemblance at all to Egyptian hieroglyphs. His figures were 'said to be pourtraicted within the Porch of Minerva's Temple in the City of Sai'. Why did he not copy something that he was sure of? Something from 'Cleopatra's Needle', for example. His illustration reminds us of Helferich's woodcut of the Sphinx in its unlikeness to the original, and it is disturbing to wonder if we too see in things what we are accustomed to see, and not what is there, in spite of our conviction that they had not yet developed the scientific approach that we have.

Sandys lists as his sources of history some of the classical writers: 'Val. Flac. Argon; Lucan; Horace; Homer; Juvenal. Sat.', and his history of early Egypt is vague as this sample:

> At first they were governed by Pharaohs of their own, of whom Sesostris was the most famous and puissant, who entered the Red Sea in Gallies, which he first invented.

Sesostris is a confusion of three kings of the 12th dynasty and Ramses II of the 19th. For the period after the Pharaohs, however, from Alexander onwards, Sandys is more accurate, since many of his sources were then contemporary historians. But of the old times Sandys is satisfied to repeat oft told tales, like that of the well of Syene (Aswan, which he confused with Esna) into which the sun shone vertically at the summer solstice, showing that it was on the tropic—which it is not, by some forty miles. He quotes Homer to describe 'Royal Thebes, destroyed by Cambyses':

> With hundred gates; through each two hundred may
> On chariots mounted pass in fair array;
> Whose houses much hid treasure hold—

The whereabouts of Egypt's Thebes was still a mystery, though the unknown Italian of the Florence manuscript had paused there at Luxor and Karnak without identifying it, twenty-one years before. And Sandys repeats the accusation that Cambyses wounded the Apis bull.

It is obvious that Sandys did not visit Lake Moeris in the Fayoum, but that he uses Herodotus as his source for the old story that the lake was dug by the hand of man—a feat quite impossible, and disproved by geological observation. He mentions the 'two Pyramides, in the middle, on each a colossus of stone, the Sepulchres of King Moeris and his Wife, that Herodotus saw'.

In this he (and Herodotus) was correct. In 1888 Flinders Petrie investigated some huge blocks of masonry at Biahmu in the Fayoum. He wrote from the site to his friend the Reverend William J. Loftie on 18th February (a hitherto unpublished letter, in the possession of John Keane):

> I settled the Biahmu buildings. They are the pedestals of two colossi, with courts around; thus

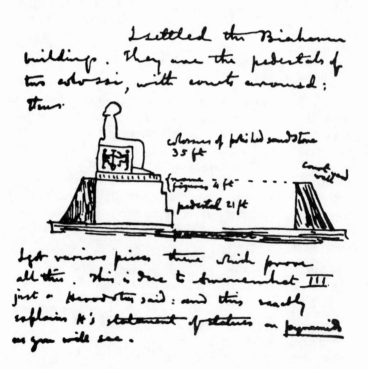

I got various pieces there which prove all this. This is due to Amenemhat III just as Herodotus said: and this exactly explains H's statement of statues on *pyramids* as you will see.

The walls of the court had a sloping face, making it appear that the colossi sat upon a truncated pyramid. 'It shows,' wrote Petrie, 'that he actually saw the figures, though from a distance.'

In Alexandria Sandys went around the usual sights, including the New York obelisk; but he is the first to mention 'another lying by, and like it, half buried in Rubbish'. It was the so-called 'Cleopatra's Needle' of the London Embankment.

His accurate description of the monastery of St Catherine at Sinai inclines one to believe that he actually went there; yet it is difficult to decide whether he was referring to it or to a branch of the monastery in Cairo when he wrote:

> These here made us a Collation, where I could not but observe their gulling in of Wine with a dear felicity; whereof they have their provision from Candy.

Of course he went to see 'those three Pyramides (the barbarous Monuments of prodigality and vain glory)' and quotes Lucan:

> When high Pyramides do grace
> The ghosts of Ptolomies lewd race

to show that they were 'the regal Sepulchres of the Egyptians'. And he brings out again the story of the 366,000 workers eating 'Radishes, Garlick and Onions', and climbs the Great Pyramid, whence he views the Saqqara pyramids far off. Descending, he decides to venture inside; but first his 'Janizaries' discharge their 'Harquebushes' into the entrance 'lest some should have skulked within to have done us a mischief'. This sudden touch brings up a picture of Sandys's period, his weapons and his costume. We realize that he visited the pyramids at the time of the Three Musketeers.

Some of his tales are no less fictitious than those three. He reprints the old favourite: 'Cheops became so poor by the building of the Pyramide that he was compelled to prostitute his daughter.'

The third pyramide was built by Mycerinus. But some say by Rhodope, another of the trade, at first a fellow-slave of Aesop. Her shoe was snatcht by an eagle while she was washing, which let it fall from on high into the lap of the King, who, astonished with the accident, and admiring the form, forthwith made a search for the owner thereof throughout all his Kingdom. Found in Naucretis, and brought unto him, he made her his Queen, and after her death inclosed her in this Monument.

Surely the archetype of all Cinderella stories.

Only the head of the Sphinx was visible in those days, 'though Pliny gave it a belly. By a Sphinx the Egyptians in their Hieroglyphicks presented a Harlot.' The subject seems to obsess Sandys. In fact, a sphinx in hieroglyphs represents a sphinx, and no more.

He describes Memphis at second hand, and confirms that it is 'the regal City' by the mummies, brought thence to Cairo 'some broken up to be bought for Dollars a piece'. He describes the tombs of the mummies from 'what we had heard'. For fear of the Arabs, the night out and the expense of a guard, he did not go there.

All in all, the famous traveller George Sandys did not provide his readers with much that was original regarding the 'former estates' and 'first antiquities' of Egypt. It was mostly a rehash, and he did not improve on his sources. As we have seen, Herodotus, on whom Sandys relies heavily, was himself a purveyor of hearsay; and Homer, whom he quotes as a source, is even more shaky. The poet himself is more than half a myth. 'Homer never saw Thebes,' wrote Bruce, the 18th-century traveller. 'It was demolished before the days of any profane writer.'

Homeric references to Egypt apply to different epochs of Egyptian civilization. When the Homeric poems were written down, about the 9th century B.C., Thebes was a neglected relic. Achilles's description of 'wealthy, hundred-gated Thebes', in the *Iliad*, tells of the capital at its prime under Amenophis III, who was identified with Memnon by the Greeks (the Amenoth of poetess Julia Balbilla). In the *Odyssey*, Egypt is described by Nestor as almost inaccessible, and one concludes that the poet was far from familiar with it. Homer places the Isle of Pharos a day's sail from the coast of Egypt though actually it is joined to it; and the geological structure of the coast rules out Sandys's suggestion that the river's alluvium caught up with the island far out to sea. Homer, in fact, does not know the geography of the Egyptian coast. Helen leaves Thebes laden with presents, the poet's description of which has led people to suppose that it stems from a first-hand knowledge of Egypt. But none of the objects is typically Egyptian: the silver baths; golden tripods; a silver basket on wheels; a distaff of purple wool—all are typically Phoenician.

There is no unreality about the tale Ulysses puts out when wandering in disguise through Ithaca: that he was a Cretan pirate taken by the King of Egypt. But it is no longer the Egypt of Thebes and Amenophis III. It is now a feudal Egypt with a capital on the coast, probably Tanis of the 10th century B.C. The tale was possibly one current in Crete which reached the Ionian poet step by step—just the thing to put into Ulysses's mouth at the moment he was obliged to hide from his friends in his own country, and it was to his advantage to claim origin in the farthest-off Greek country.

The poems that were gathered eventually to become the Homeric epics were composed over a long period of time, going back to the pre-literate Achaeans. The references to Egypt reflect the chronology of the composition of the poems. 'Homer' is for ever divine, but it is poetry, and as a source of history quite useless—at any rate in respect of Egypt.

About 1650 that renowned Catholic Traveller, Sieur de la Boullaye-le-Gouz of Angers, known as Ibrahim Bey, measured the pyramids on his way back from the India of the Mogul emperors, and went inside the largest, followed by a French chaplain. But this priest's 'stomach being larger than his head', he jammed in the passage. 'I believe,' wrote Boullaye-le-Gouz, 'that had he entered brusquely we should have been obliged to quarter him to get ourselves out. I would have felt extreme regret had this misfortune befallen him, for he was a saintly person full of sweetness and charity.'

But Boullaye-le-Gouz himself was not full of charity when he bade farewell to a Jewish friend in Alexandria: 'Dear Rabbi, I love you as a person as much as I abhor and detest your Faith.'

The Catholic Traveller added less than nothing to the study

of ancient Egypt when he ascribed the second pyramid to 'Rodophe daughter of Keope'—the Cinderella-girl of Sandys—and the smallest to 'Caphrin brother of Keope'. But his only sources, the classical authors, were just as much at sea; and he did at least try to be objective by measuring the Great Pyramid, inside and out, down to the nearest inch.

The first truly scientific attempt to balance history against myth in Egypt was published while he was away on his travels. It was made by John Greaves, Professor of Astronomy at the University of Oxford. He was well qualified, for besides being a mathematician he had learned oriental languages and studied the ancient Greek, Arab and Persian writers on astronomy. His approach to the investigation is a great stride in advance of all that had been done before:

> I shall tread in as even a Path as I can, between Truth and the Traditions of such of the Ancients as are still extant: First, putting down the Relations which by them have been transmitted to us; and next, shewing in what manner, upon Examination, I found the Pyramids in the Years One thousand six hundred thirty eight, and One thousand six hundred thirty nine. For I twice went to Grand Cairo from Alexandria, and from thence into the Deserts, for the greater certainty to view them; carrying with me a radius of ten Feet most accurately divided into Ten thousand Parts, besides some other Instruments.

John Greaves's *Pyramidographia*, published in 1646, begins with a critical assessment of the ancient authors, and the correct conclusion that the first pyramid was built by Cheops, the second by Kephren, and the third by Mycerinus. He evaluates the accounts of Arab writers, notes the opening of the Great Pyramid by El Mamoun, son of Haroun el Raschid, in A.D. 820, and publishes a survey of the structure many times more thorough and accurate than any done before. He goes straight to the point when he examines the motives that led to the building of these giant structures:

> Aristotle judges them to have been the Works of Tyranny; And Pliny conjectures that they built them, partly out of Ostentation, and partly out of State-policy, by keeping the People in imployment, to divert them from Mutinies and Rebellions.
>
> But the true reason depends upon higher and more weighty considerations. And this sprang from the Theology of the Egyptians,

> who believed, that as long as the Body endured, so long the Soul
> continued with it

and he concludes that the pyramid was intended as the eternal resting-place for the embalmed mummy of the king.

Greaves set a standard of archaeological investigation that was unfortunately not applied to monuments other than the pyramids until Napoleon's time. Greaves had not, of course, written the last word on the pyramids, but he resolved much that had beguiled the minds of men for centuries.

The purpose of the pyramids had been lost along with the rest of knowledge of ancient Egypt, and as early as the 4th century Julius Honorius had advanced the idea that they were granaries erected by Joseph against the seven lean years. This satisfied medieval pilgrims, with their longing for relics of biblical history, although Denys de Tell-Mahre, Patriarch of Antioch in the 9th century, wrote, 'they are astonishing mausoleums, built on the tombs of Ancient Kings; they are oblique and solid, and not hollow and empty'.

The Arab chroniclers had their own theories. The astrologer Abu Ma'sher Jafer Ben Mohamed Balkhi wrote in the 13th century:

> The wise men, previous to the flood, foreseeing an impending judgment from heaven either by submersion or by fire, which would destroy every created being, built upon the tops of the mountains and in Upper Egypt many pyramids of stone, in order to have some refuge against the approaching calamity.

First exploration of the pyramids was certainly made in Pharaonic times—by robbers. It is not likely that the Arabs who broke into them later found any treasure left. Yet Arab tradition says that when Caliph El Mamoun opened the Great Pyramid in A.D. 820 he found the statue of a man in green stone. It was the cover of a coffin in which lay the body of a man wearing a gold breastplate; on this lay a sword of inestimable value and a ruby the size of a hen's egg which shone like a flame.

Nineteenth-century Egyptologists Mariette and Maspero said they recognized in this description a sarcophagus in its place, a stone cover of human shape, and the mummy of Cheops laden with jewels. It is of course possible that El Mamoun did find the intact burial of Cheops; and if he did, the royal regalia and jewellery must have been magnificent and beyond all price.

It has often been thought that the pyramids were observatories, and the ancient Egyptians have been credited with a profound knowledge of astronomy. In 1693 Carari and de Chazelles both gave their opinion that, besides being tombs, they were built for an astronomic purpose, basing their assertion on the orientation of the structures and the slope of their sides. Paul Lucas, in 1714, suggested that the Egyptians intended them to serve as sundials to mark the changes of the sun at the solstices. 'It appears that rules of an exact astronomy were applied therein.'

There was an interesting confirmation of this theory 139 years later, when Mariette, at the request of French astronomer Biot, observed the vernal equinox at the Great Pyramid in 1853. Biot concluded:

> With or without intention by the Egyptians who built the Great Pyramid, it has, since it existed, functioned as an immense sundial which has marked annually the periods of the equinoxes with an error of less than one day, and those of the solstices with an error less than a day and three quarters.

Since only the Great Pyramid performs this service, it seems that the sundial effect was due less to deliberate calculation than to a chance combination of careful orientation and the slope chosen for the sides after structural and aesthetic needs had been considered.

A purpose far deeper than that of sepulchres has been attributed to the pyramids by numerous people since Kircher in 1666 expressed his opinion that they had a secret, mystic significance. In 1864 the Astronomer Royal of Scotland, Charles Piazzi Smyth, published *Our Inheritance of the Great Pyramid*, and in 1879 he resigned from the Royal Society because it denied him the opportunity to read a paper on his interpretation of the design of the Great Pyramid, which he believed was a revelation direct from the Almighty. Other writers have continued this line of thought, including David Davidson some thirty years ago, whose study of *The Hidden Truth in Myth and Ritual* claimed that the common culture patterns emanated from Messianic Prophecies over 5000 years ago; and that the structural expression of these prophecies is enshrined in the Divine Revelation of the Great Pyramid of Gizeh.

More recently Adam Rutherford wrote in his *Pyramidology*, 'The Almighty arranged for His great and wonderful plan to be portrayed in symbols of stone long before the Bible was written . . . The Great Pyramid was built under Divine inspiration.' Using a scale of Pyramid inches, of which 25 equal one Sacred Cubit, which is one ten-millionth of the earth's polar radius, Dr Rutherford reads the corridors in the pyramid as a chronological representation of the Ages as planned by the God of the Christians. It culminates in the year A.D. 2994 when all evil shall have been removed from our planet. These readings are vastly interesting to those who can believe, by an act of faith, that the Almighty arranged the pyramid thus.

6 The Search for Thebes

SCHOLARS steeped in Homer must have yearned for sight of hundred-gated Thebes; yet those few of the 17th century who went beyond the pyramids walked over the site without knowing it, as did our unknown Italian in 1589. They must have expected to encounter 'sumptuous vestiges' of so great a city, like those of Memphis that Sieur Villamont reported in 1590. But in fact Thebes had been ploughed under or covered by sand. Yet there remained the pylons, obelisks and columns of the vast Karnak complex; of the Luxor temple; of the Ramesseum on the west bank; of the Medinet Habu temple. Several of the tombs of the kings were open; and the colossi of Memnon stood out bold on the plain for all to see. It is amazing that it did not dawn on anybody to connect these plentiful ruins with fabled Thebes before the 18th century. Bossuet half suggested it in 1681. But this was ironical, because Bossuet was using a borrowed account of Thebes written by two men who had not realized that it was the marvellous city sung of by Homer that they had come upon. In his *Universal History* Bossuet says, 'what beauties might we not find if we could reach the royal city, since such wonders have been discovered so far from it'. He did not realize that he had just described the very spot.

Many travellers of the time made no effort to locate Thebes, or even to bother about non-Christian remains; yet one is reluctant to neglect them, for they often make good reading, and they round out our picture of the times.

There is Father Jean Coppin, ex-lieutenant of cavalry, raking up the idea of the Crusades again; of making a holy war against the infidel. He comes to size up the Turkish forces in 1645, and performs his devotions at the holy places on the side. In his *Shield of Europe, or the Holy War*, he tells how he had the eucharist given him in 'the room which was occupied by Jesus Christ and the Holy Virgin', which had become the crypt of St Serge in Old Cairo. It was the same that Felix Fabri saw. Coppin wrote of his visit, 'Although I was tormented to distraction by a prodigious number of fleas that the coolness of the place attracted, I felt a great surge of inner joy.'

Balthazar de Monconys left a vivid diary of his visit in 1647. A scientist who corresponded with Hobbes, he tells how he strolled around the 'tavernes' of Cairo to drink 'cavé', a drink almost unknown still in Europe. He left his monogram on the Great Pyramid, and departed with a variety of souvenirs including a mummy, two crocodiles and twenty-two vipers.

Jean de Thévenot, ten years later in Egypt, is said to have introduced the 'cavé', or café, into France. He prefaces his *Voyage au Levant* with: 'Curiosity and a passion for learning alone prompted me to travel.' He visited many lands, and he is the first explorer of Egypt in the modern sense. With him opens the great era of travellers of the 17th and 18th centuries.

On the way to Egypt a French corsair came alongside his ship. Pistols in hand the pirates stripped the passengers down to their shirts, respecting only the monks, and sent them all back to Acre. Re-embarked on a Cypriot ship, they had barely set off again when two corsair ships came up, this time under Italian command. They put out two armed caiques, and the Cypriot ship quickly ran up the white flag. The pirates took all the baggage, and transferred the passengers aboard the corsair. The ship on which Thévenot now found himself had a crew of 140, with fourteen oars a side. It was armed with twenty-four bronze swivel-guns, four cannons, and it bristled with muskets. There were several Turkish slaves aboard, men, women and children captured in a surprise raid on the Syrian coast a few days before. Provisions ran short, but the pirates did not cut their prisoners' throats, perhaps out of consideration that they were Christians. They even consented not to put them ashore where they might be taken for pirates and burned alive. The pirates hailed a passing ship and put them aboard; and thus

Jean de Thévenot reached Egypt. Being an explorer in 1657 had its special pothers.

Thévenot went to the mummy pits at Saqqara, which he placed, following Villamont, close to where the magnificent city of Memphis once stood; and he boasted of the mummy-powder he obtained. He found the climb up the Great Pyramid so exhausting that he wrote, 'I do not disapprove of those who take with them a little flask of wine.'

Jean de Thévenot was nephew of Melchisédec Thévenot, librarian of the King of France and editor of a celebrated collection of *Voyages*. Melchisédec included in this book a description of a trip to Upper Egypt made by the Reverend Fathers Protais and François, attracted to the region by the Coptic communities, in 1668. Father Charles François wrote the account which is the first in French literature of the ruins of Thebes, the modern Luxor. But the Fathers did not know it was Thebes; and this was the account which Bossuet borrowed so ironically for his *Universal History*. He had lifted it from Melchisédec Thévenot's *Voyages*. Father François wrote of Karnak temple:

> The tradition of the country people says that this was once the dwelling of a king; it has certainly that appearance, for one sees there the great and beautiful remains of a castle with avenues having Sphinxes on either side. The gates are monumental, and rear up beyond all measure and belief, covered with the most beautiful stones it is possible to see. I measured one 35 feet. I could make out nothing of the plan of the buildings, so much in disorder and ruin as they were; besides the short time we had there did not permit us to observe all these things; to examine them piece by piece one would need at least a month, and I was not there more than three hours and a half. I counted some 120 columns in one hall alone, which were five wide-stretched arms in thickness.

That was in the vast hypostyle hall of Karnak that could contain all of Notre Dame de Paris. Re-erected and cared for today, it is surely the most astounding piece of ancient architecture it is possible to see, after the pyramids.

Two miles to the south they saw the Luxor temple,

> in which are 78 columns of a prodigious width. Before the door are two square needles very lofty and quite entire.

The right-hand 'needle' stands in the Place de la Concorde, Paris, now.

On the other side of the river Thévenot mentions the temples and 'the place of mummies called Biban el Melouc'— the Gates of the Kings, referring to the entrances of the royal tombs in the Valley of the Kings (which might be the origin of Homer's 'hundred-gated Thebes', for there is no indication that Thebes ever had a city wall with gates in it). And finally Father François records that 'close to the Nile are two great stone idols seated on thrones'—the colossi of Memnon, which surely should have given a clue to the identity of the place even when royal tombs had failed to do so. After all, Strabo had written about them. But travellers of the 17th century seem peculiarly unable to put two and two together archaeologically, so the mystery of Thebes remained unsolved for another half-century after the visit of Protais and François.

Father Vansleb, relating his second voyage to Egypt in 1672, used the Protais-François account of Karnak and Luxor to describe that part of the river he did not reach. He believed that he had himself discovered the ruins of Thebes, 'which have a magnificent appearance, with a triumphal arch almost complete and several tall columns with Greek inscriptions'. What he actually saw was the site of Antinopolis, Hadrian's city, much farther down.

J. B. Vansleb was a German in French service, and one of the first men to be sent to Egypt with a definite archaeological mission. He had his instructions from Colbert, chief minister to Louis XIV:

> The main object of the voyages which the King commands Sieur Vansleb to make in the Levant is to seek there the greatest possible number of good manuscripts and ancient coins for His Majesty's library. Should he find also among those ancient monuments any statues or bas-reliefs by good masters, he will try to obtain them.

The beginnings of scientific inquiry are seen in further instructions to Vansleb:

> He will make a collection of ancient inscriptions that he finds and try to copy them exactly and in the same language in which they are written, having them read and explained by some interpreter, should he not be acquainted with the characters thereof. He will

find numerous of these inscriptions in the cemeteries and upon the tombs, of which he will also make a description, and of the different manner of burial of divers peoples. These inscriptions will serve him often to ascertain the ancient names of the places where he finds them—these ancient names of persons, of towns, and even of provinces being so effaced from the knowledge of those who live there today that they are scarcely known any more save through these inscriptions.

Vansleb was supposed to penetrate into Ethiopia, but he turned back at Girgeh. It was not far up river, yet farther than anyone else had gone since Protais and François. All the same, one feels that he enlarges on the difficulties he encountered, to justify making no real effort to get to Ethiopia. His reluctance is to be sympathized with, because it was a hazardous journey. Dr Poncet made it in 1698; but Le Noir du Roule was not so fortunate in 1705 when he had managed to get as far as Sennar. The king of the country had him murdered. There were no more of the heroic, imprudent expditions of this kind for more than half a century, when Bruce made his famous journey to discover the source of the Blue Nile.

Vansleb shows the rudiments of an archaeologist's attitude in considering whether the walls of Alexandria were those originally built by Alexander, and in concluding that they were not, because of their similarity with walls of Cairo, known to be the work of the Caliphs. He also took string to measure the bases of the pyramids, and was only prevented from doing so by heaps of sand.

At the Saqqara mummy pits he was let down into the grottoes where there were thousands of earthenware pots containing embalmed birds. Of these he took away half a dozen for the royal library. Whilst in Egypt he sent back some manuscripts, notably two in Arabic dealing with talismans. One was entitled, 'How to find the hiding-places of all the treasures in Egypt, their value, the style of talisman that guards them, and how they can be destroyed'.

The Arabs had been obsessed with the idea of buried treasure ever since they overran Egypt. When Vansleb went to visit Coptic monasteries in February, 1673, he dressed as a Turk for security, and travelled up the Nile in a boat. But near Girgeh rumour spread that he was a rich foreigner who was only going about Egypt to discover the whereabouts of hidden treasure so as to inform the King of France, who would then come and seize their country. He abandoned the trip and returned to Cairo, writing to Colbert of 'the barbarity of the Arabs and the tyranny of the Turkish government', which prevented him reaching the cataracts and penetrating to Ethiopia.

It was not the first of his harassments. On 30th June, 1672, he had set off to visit the desert monasteries of St Macarius, going by boat from Rosetta to Tarane, the usual starting point for the monasteries.

> But before reaching this village I was much insulted by certain young Turks on account of a kilderkin of wine that I had with me. A zealous magistrate with scruples about keeping company with foreigners who drank wine, incited them to come and ask me for some, to gain the pretext, in case I should give them any, of doing me a malice.

Vansleb excused himself, telling them that Moslems were forbidden wine, and that it would cause a scandal; but they became more abusive, threatening to throw his barrel into the Nile. He called the boat-captain to his aid, who was able to pacify the young rascals for the time being. But next morning when Vansleb got into the skiff to go ashore at Tarane, three of the larrikins jumped in too and grabbed his kilderkin to throw it into the Nile. Vansleb snatched it back, took up his gun and aimed at them. His Nubian valet, 'a man of stout heart', seized one of them by the scruff of the neck and dumped him in the river. Then he drew his cutlass and prepared to repel the others. 'When they saw that they had to deal with people who were not afraid of them, they retired to the boat quickly, and in great fury set about the boat-captain with their fists.' Not content with that, Vansleb heard later, they denounced him before the judge in Cairo, declaring that he had drunk wine with a foreigner, and caused him to be fined ten piastres.

Vansleb's precious wine got him into more trouble almost at once. The Arab who carried the kilderkin to the house where he was going to lodge in Tarane found it heavy and was convinced that he bore a load of silver, which he gleefully announced to all he passed, so that soon the village was agog with talk of the rich foreigner who was a consul incognito come to spy out the land, and how they could get hold of his money. He went to the Kachef, the local governor, and begged for an escort to the monasteries; the latter replied that an escort of a few men would not suffice, in view of the plot to ambush him on the road and cut his throat. The Kachef himself would accompany him in a few days' time.

'In vain I told him that I was no Consul but a poor foreigner going to the monasteries to perfect his Arabic; that in this kilderkin there was no silver but only some wine that I had brought with me because I was not accustomed to drink water.' The Kachef insisted that he move out of his poor lodging and stay with him. Vansleb was in great alarm: the Kachef had a bad reputation, and in any case he could never afford the presents it was customary to make to the Kachef's large retinue. He went back to his loft to spend the night thinking of a way out.

At 2 a.m. came a knock on the door. He took up a defensive position and sent his Nubian to find out who it was. One of the grooms of the Kachef had come, whom fortunately Vansleb had tipped well on his visit. The man begged him in the name of the Prophet to get out secretly and smartly because his master was determined to assassinate him. He said the Kachef believed he was a foreigner come to seek the treasures of the ancient Egyptians, and the Kachef was going to take him into the desert on the way to the monasteries and there cut his throat. The groom added that only last month he had had another traveller assassinated in the village for the same reason.

'When I heard this news I had no further desire to sleep,' writes Vansleb—and we do not doubt him. He gave the man the recompense he merited, loaded up, and left. They found a boatman willing to take them, and set off at dawn. They had scarcely left the bank when they perceived the Kachef with thirty horsemen at full gallop in pursuit. 'But he was too late, and in this manner I escaped from his clutches.'

After leaving Egypt Vansleb tarried at Constantinople to finish writing his *History of the Church in Alexandria*. To this, he says, 'I have applied myself with an exactitude and a diligence without equal, in the hope that this Work will render my name immortal'.

Alas, poor Vansleb! He is remembered more, by a few archaeologists, for his failed journey into Egypt. For it was thus regarded when he returned finally to France in 1676, hugging his hope of immortality to his heart. He was censured for not persevering to Ethiopia; for losing time writing his *History;* and, to push him under finally, he was accused of embezzlement, intemperance and low morals. He published the journal of his second voyage in 1677, and dedicated it not to Colbert, but to Cardinal d'Estrées, Bishop of Lyon, possibly in revenge for his disgrace. Two years later he died near Fontainebleau, miserable and discouraged.

With de Maillet, sixteen years French Consul in Egypt, begins the era of international rivalry for the antiquities on a diplomatic scale, that was to culminate in fisticuffs a century and a quarter hence. Benoit de Maillet was appointed in 1692, and contributed more to the knowledge of Egypt than any man of the 18th century. He went inside the Great Pyramid more than forty times, an astonishing record in face of his own description of the horrible ordeal:

> Visitors are half dead when they reach the gallery by dragging their faces over the sand at the entrance. The Arabs pull them up so forcefully, and they are so frightened they think they are going to be stifled. The forty feet they must next pass lying on their bellies, completes their exhaustion. These hardships, combined with the dread of the return, leave them in no mood to undertake the necessary examination of this interior.

De Maillet was the first to establish that the gallery in the pyramid was used to store the stones that would eventually slide down to plug the entrance, and that the well in the passage was included in the construction of the pyramid solely to permit the withdrawal of labourers after blocking all the entrances. He also exploded the myth about the secret passage to the Sphinx, and the orifice through which the figure was supposed to be made to speak.

He noticed mummy bandages with cursive signs different from hieroglyphs, and wrote to the antiquary Rigord:

> It is, sir, an invincible proof that the ancient Egyptians, contrary to universal belief, had characters with which to express themselves, different from the hieroglyphic letters, and, to convince you and to

let you see this rare and without doubt oldest manuscript in any library of the world, I will address to you some pieces of it in a packet.

This was an important discovery. But de Maillet's most interesting contribution to knowledge of Egypt was an outline of a scheme of exploration that was later to be carried out by Napoleon Bonaparte with a thoroughness that resulted in the final opening up of Egypt to archaeological examination. De Maillet wrote to Rigord in 1693:

> We are told that there are still in Upper Egypt temples of which the blue or gilded vaultings are as beautiful as if they had just been finished; there are idols of a prodigious size; columns without number.

He writes of the need for scientific exploration of Egypt 'by persons wise, curious, and adroit', who can travel through the country 'so slowly that they have ample leisure to give to each place the time and attention necessary'. He also recommends the making of an accurate map.

De Maillet's successor, in 1715, was Le Maire, a keen antiquary who had already explored the ruins of Leptis Magna near Tripoli in Libya when he had been Consul there. From Egypt he sent back 'a statue in marble, Greek, of a young boy found in the ruins of a temple in the Delta' and other objects. They were of no earthly value archaeologically, like all objects sent back so far, for the exact location of discovery was not known. But since the science of archaeology was as yet not known either, it made no difference. In any case the consuls were unable to go exploring themselves, even if they had known how. Their duties held them in Cairo, and it was left to more independent travellers to go to the sites.

Among these was Paul Lucas, son of a goldsmith, who voyaged to collect gems, coins and curios for sale. He had made no studies, but had the knack of judging a coin or inscribed stone at a glance, without understanding its meaning. After his first voyage he became official traveller for Louis XIV of France, receiving instructions from the Abbé Bignon, librarian royal:

> Sieur Paul Lucas will proceed to the temple of Jupiter Amon, of which he will make an exact description. Then he will go to the

temple of Jupiter in Upper Egypt to examine the ruins of Thebes, the antiquities near lake Moeris, and the House of Caron, or the Labyrinth. He will also endeavour to open some pyramid in order to find out in a detailed manner all that this kind of edifice contains . . .

These are the first definite instructions to explore by excavation, and they appear to include a desire to know details of the construction of pyramids as well as what else they might contain.

Paul Lucas reached Alexandria on 2nd September, 1716, but he did not carry out all his instructions. He never went to the temple of Jupiter Amon in Siwa Oasis, where Alexander the Great went to consult the oracle. It was a really perilous trip. He did not open a pyramid, see the Labyrinth itself, or examine the ruins of Thebes, which he placed near Aswan. No traveller had so far identified Thebes, although a map by Ortelius, 1584, shows its position clearly. But neither Protais and François, Vansleb, Melchisédec Thévenot, Lucas nor Bossuet appears to have seen this map.

Paul Lucas did not stop at Luxor and Karnak, the unrecognized site of Thebes, because 'the inhabitants were at war with their chief'. But as he drifted slowly past he had time to view 'these vast palaces, magnificent temples, these obelisks, and the prodigious number of thick columns that are still standing'.

He did, however, produce some fresh material of importance: the temples of Armant and Dendera. The Armant temple, near Luxor, has been lost by demolition since his visit, and his detailed description and plan are valuable. And when he stood before the Dendera temple he felt, as so many have felt since, that he was seeing one of the wonders of the world, although it was half buried, and the roof supported an Arab village and all its squalor. He devoted fifteen pages, a plan, and an engraving of the portico to Dendera, which Protais, Vansleb and the rest had seen only from a distance.

Lucas also identified Heliopolis on a visit to Mataria, where the Holy Well is, near Cairo, though there was, and is still, only a single obelisk standing of all the once great city.

One day the Kachef of Giza told him that he had found a deep well down which he had lowered one of his men, who reported a vast complex of passages filled with earthenware pots containing the mummies of birds. For Lucas

> It needed no more to excite the curiosity of a Traveller who has always sought to make new discoveries; this was of that sort; nobody that I know had ever spoken of it.

This is surprising; in fact it is astonishing that Lucas should believe he had made a new discovery; for Vansleb's account had been published nearly forty years before, and surely the antiquarian Le Maire would have heard from de Maillet about the mummified birds, and told Lucas. But perhaps there was a jealous conspiracy of silence. Whatever the reason, these mummified bird pits at Saqqara have a most curious way of being forgotten for years on end, in spite of being in printed books for all the world to see. They were 'discovered' again quite recently, after about a century of oblivion.

Paul Lucas, of course, made an expedition to the bird pits in the grand manner, fully armed, with an escort of a dozen Arabs, a bundle of torches, and

> taking the precaution that Ariadne made her Lover take when he was obliged to go into the Labyrinth of Crete. I had brought with me some string, two thousand yards of it, and we had not reached the end of the Cavern before we ran out of it, so we dared not go further.

It seems an incredible distance underground. Yet his next assertion, if true, is of profound interest. He says that he found an embalmed bull

> in the Catacombs I am describing; this bull was enclosed in a great coffin on which the head was represented; this coffin which was gilded and painted, was surrounded by a fine balustrade about five feet high, likewise all gilded and painted.

Is it possible that Paul Lucas had wandered into some part of the Serapeum a hundred and thirty years before Mariette made his sensational discovery? Lucas himself speculates as to whether this was the place where they buried the god Apis. If he had got in there, it would not be surprising that he ran out of guiding string. The tunnels go for kilometres.

On another expedition he went to see 'the temple of Isis', whom he took for a queen of Egypt, 'situated precisely in the centre of the Delta'. The place was very much destroyed, by an earthquake, he thought. But:

> When one comes to examine these sad fragments one perceives there the precious remains of a magnificence that astounds. One sees there still, low-reliefs of great beauty and an infinity of hieroglyphs which would contain for us, if we had the knowledge, one of the most ancient histories of the world; for I have little doubt that the life and acts of this famous Queen, who reigned in Egypt with her husband Osiris a short time after the Deluge, are recorded there.

These are in truth the inscriptions of Ptolemy II and his successors on the ruins of an immense granite temple at Beybeit near Samanoud, the ancient Sebenithe and probable birthplace of Manetho. Lucas's description is just. This tumbled heap of enormous granite blocks is one of the most impressive sights in Egypt, though few people bother to go there. As one clambers over these overthrown rocks, seeing here an exquisite relief carving, there a flight of steps or a massive lintel chiselled out of the hard stone, the persistent thought is that these are no local boulders, cliff-fallen as they look, but hewn stone from quarries of Aswan, taken out by hand, man-handled on to wooden ships, brought seven hundred miles down the Nile and erected one upon another; then carved to exact dimensions, and relief carvings and hieroglyphs in graceful taste sculptured on every surface, to make what is probably the most magnificent temple ever built. Only a power much greater and more sudden than the slow toil that brought them could have thrown them down thus jumbled. It was surely an earthquake—and what a pity!

Perhaps, one day, men will put Beybeit up again. They could, easily, now. It might be in celebration of the moment when man learns finally the lesson of history: that all his rivalries are lost upon posterity, and his victories are soon forgotten; that only through art can he talk with the future and be immortal.

7 The Great Travellers

I T was the Jesuit Father Claude Sicard who found Thebes. Endowed with a scientific and critical spirit, and a longer experience of Egypt than Lucas, he made many journeys about the country between 1707, when he came to Cairo as Superior of the Jesuit Mission, and 1726, when he died of the plague whilst nursing the sick.

An excellent linguist and perfect Arabic scholar, he was commanded by the Regent, Philippe d'Orléans, to make an exact investigation of the ancient monuments of Egypt. The great manuscript which he prepared was not, unfortunately, published during his lifetime, and was never found after his death. Our information comes from some of his letters, which have been preserved; and the *Bibliothèque Nationale* in Paris has his manuscript map, of remarkable accuracy for the period. It was used by d'Anville for his map of 1760, which in turn was much relied upon during Napoleon's campaign.

Sicard's evangelistic mission obliged him to travel to scattered Coptic communities, among them the desert monasteries of St Macarius, previously heard of only by repute. They were the ones from which Vansleb had turned back when the Kachef had plotted to cut his throat in the desert forty years before. Sicard made the dangerous crossing of the desert, famous and sacred to the memory of the five thousand holy anchorites who lived there in early Christian times. He found four monasteries left, defended by thick walls, each with its tower, drawbridge and mill, entered by a thick wooden door covered by iron plates. A handful of monks lived an austere life there. He shared it, lecturing them on defects of habit or prayer. 'They are worthy souls,' he comments. 'But near to heresy.'

He went to Upper Egypt to convert Copts; yet he also examined the monuments and enjoyed the Nile scenery: the many villages, the acacia groves, sycamores, palms and boats. 'I am not surprised,' he wrote, 'that the Romans had the curiosity to travel in Egypt, to enjoy the pleasure of seeing the various pictures that Nature, more skilled than all the painters in the world, has herself painted in these places.'

At Achmounein he reported 'vast ruins of a great number of ancient palaces of which one can still see the marbles and the granite columns bear witness to its former greatness'. He was much struck from afar by the majesty of a portico of twelve columns. Approaching, he found the work magnificent, delicate, and so complete that 'although it had been put up during the reigns of the Pharaohs (and before the conquests of Cambise, King of the Persians)' it seemed that the workers had only just completed it. 'The architrave is painted on the lower side in golden colour which shines and blinds, and the Firmament is represented on the ceiling. The stars could not be better engraved or the azure appear more fresh or lively.'

This was Hermopolis of the Greeks, Pharaonic Khmounou, a very ancient site. But the portico had not been put up before Cambyses. It was part of a Ptolemaic temple to Thoth, Lord of Hermopolis, set up about 320 B.C., and one of the most impressive ruins of Upper Egypt in the 18th century. Unhappily it did not survive to our day.

Across the Nile was Antinopolis that Vansleb had taken for the site of Thebes—and little wonder, for Sicard found the ruins so well preserved that he could trace the streets, and four city gates standing almost entire. He was especially delighted by the southern gate, a triumphal arch with three great vaulted passages which aroused the admiration of subsequent travellers —but all too briefly, for it was demolished in the eighteen-sixties for the useless construction of powder-mills and factories, soon derelict, during the reign of the princely spendthrift Ismail, along with many other Roman walls and temples. In the main street Sicard found an unscathed column with a Greek inscription that led him to surmise that it was one of

four erected after the victories of the Roman Emperor
Alexander Severus against the Persians in A.D. 233. This alone
should have been enough to make Vansleb hesitate before
deciding that Antinopolis was Thebes, had he observed it.

Here in Sicard is the budding science of archaeology.
Without hesitation he identified Karnak and Luxor as the
capital of ancient Egypt. He had read his Strabo and Diodorus.
He described the colossi of Memnon and the temple of
Memnon, now called the Ramesseum, with its stupendous
fallen colossus that we know to be Ramses II. Especially
interesting is his description of the Valley of the Kings, where he
was able to identify ten of the tombs he had read of in Diodorus
Siculus, who had listed forty-seven a century before Christ.

> The sepulchres of Thebes are tunnelled in the rock, and of
> astonishing depth. Halls, rooms, all are painted from top to
> bottom. The variety of colours, which are almost as fresh as the
> day they were done, gives an admirable effect; there are as many
> hieroglyphs as there are animals and objects represented, which
> makes us suppose that we have there the story of the lives, virtues,
> acts, combats and victories of the princes who are buried there;
> but it is impossible for us to decipher them at present. Should
> it ever happen that someone shall arrive at their meaning, we shall
> have the history of that time which is unknown to us and which
> apparently has never been committed to writing.

Claude Sicard must have visited Beybeit two or three years
before Paul Lucas. He wrote:

> I saw there the remains of one of the most beautiful, vastest and
> most ancient Temples of Egypt; all the stones are of enormous
> length and thickness, all of granite marble. Many of these stones
> are for the most part decorated by sculptures representing in
> demi-relief men and women and all sorts of hieroglyphics. These
> carvings have suffered no damage, neither by time, the sun nor the
> Arabs . . . It appears more than likely that this Temple is the very
> temple of the Goddess Isis mentioned by Herodotus, situated in
> the middle of the Delta near to Sebenithe . . . In these ruins is
> found no brick, no plaster, no cement. We see only great masses of
> granite marble.

Sicard went up the Nile as far as Aswan, where he visited
the temples on the island of Philae. In all he had located, by
1722, twenty-four complete temples, more than fifty carved

and painted tombs, and twenty of the principal pyramids of Egypt. He gathered more knowledge of Egypt than anyone before him, but his writings, dispersed, were little known to the public.

Thomas Shaw, the English traveller who was in Egypt in 1721 while Sicard was far up the Nile, makes poor reading after the letters of Sicard, fragmentary though they were. Shaw, Fellow of Queen's College and of the Royal Society, scholar, antiquary and natural historian, published *Travels or Observations relating to several parts of Barbary and the Levant*. It was a noble example of typography, but the portion devoted to Egypt reveals nothing that he could not have lifted from other authors without leaving his desk. He insists that the pyramids were not tombs but temples for the mystic cult of Osiris, and he repeats the old story that the second pyramid was raised 'from the Money which the Daughter of Cheops produced at the expense of her Chastity'.

Ten years later came Dr Granger of Dijon, who explored Egypt much more thoroughly. Interested in natural science and archaeology, he came to Cairo at the request of his friend Pignon, the French Consul, and set off up the Nile in 1731. At Abydos he came upon a temple not previously seen by Europeans:

. . . almost entire, but buried under the sand up to the roof. I entered by a window after having it dug around . . . all the temple is painted in various colours on an azure ground, decorated with many human figures and hieroglyphic characters.

Dr Granger had discovered the wonderful temple of Seti I with the superb 19th dynasty relief carvings that have come down to us in a state of almost complete preservation. Strangely, the beautiful temple was rarely visited during the century that followed, and it remained full of sand until Mariette cleared it in 1857.

Dr Granger passed through Luxor:

This village is built on the ruins of Thebes; this ancient city, so superb to judge by its edifices, offers to the view today nothing but heaps of stones.

Karnak he does not name, but takes it for a palace, and the hypostyle hall 'a very beautiful salon' supported by six rows of twenty-eight columns. Probably he never went on the west bank, for he speaks of the colossi of Memnon without identifying them, and of the Medinet Habu temple, 'a mile from Karnak', without indicating that they are on the other side of the river.

Esna he confounded with Syene (Aswan) but he noted the temple there. It was so filled with earth that he could not get in. Thanks to this protection, this Ptolemaic-Roman temple is still intact. His journey ended at Edfu, where there is a perfectly preserved example of a late Egyptian temple. He turned back 'because there was a war on—something the Arabs of these parts are almost always at'.

Six years after Granger discovered Abydos the renowned travelling bishop, Richard Pococke, brushed past the temple. One can scarcely call it a visit, for the Arabs

> shewed me a hollow ground from which probably all the stones had been carried away to Girga.

Richard Pococke was an ecclesiastic imbued with a passion for travel. Egypt was only part of an extended foreign tour he made before he became Bishop of Meath. He is regarded as a pioneer of Alpine travel: a boulder in the Chamonix valley was inscribed with his name by the Swiss in 1741.

He landed in Egypt in September, 1737, and set the site of Memphis by a description given by Pliny. At Busiris in the Delta he voices one of the first protests against the destruction of Egyptian monuments:

> They are every day destroying these fine morsels of Egyptian Antiquity: and I saw some of the pillars hewn into millstones.

On a visit to the mummy pits of Saqqara he surmised correctly the use of what were later called canopic jars:

> I saw also several large earthen vases . . . In them was a black fat earth, which made me imagine that the bowels might be preserved in them.
>
>   Returning from visiting the catacombs sooner than was expected, when I unlock'd the door of the room the Sheik had put me in at his house, a little girl about eight years old run out of the room against me; laying hold of her, she cried out, but I had presence of mind enough to let her go, it being a great affront in

these countries for any one to lay hands on the fair sex; and discovering any roguery (which I immediately apprehended) would have caused an embroil in the family, had the Sheik taken my part or not. As soon as I came into the room, I saw a hole had been broke thro' the ceiling, tho' the room was ten feet high, and as I supposed, the mother had let the child down by a rope to rifle my baggage.

Pococke went up the Nile as far as Aswan. Pausing at Dendera, he found the buildings filled up with rubbish, and little houses of mud brick on the roof of the great temple, which, as did every visitor, he greatly admired:

The particular large capital of the pillars has over it a square stone, with a compartment of reliefs on each side, in the best taste and workmanship of any I have seen in Egypt, and are exquisitely fine, insomuch that I conclude they must have been executed by one of the best Greek Sculptors.

In thus taking a shot in the dark at the date of the temple he was nearer the mark than the French antiquaries who came with Napoleon. They based a belief that this was one of Egypt's most antique edifices on a false assumption from a Zodiac ceiling in the temple.

He stopped at Thebes and measured the gates of Karnak; and thence he went to nearby Armant, where he saw a temple whose foundations are all that are left to us now. Of Armant he repeats an old legend that a sacred bull was worshipped there, like the Apis bull of Memphis. This assertion of Strabo was ridiculed by antiquaries and archaeologists for another two centuries, when a chance discovery of a bronze bull in the desert west of Armant by illicit diggers led Sir Robert Mond to excavate the burials of the sacred Buchis bulls in 1927.

Returning down the Nile, Pococke passed in the night, all unbeknown, another renowned traveller, Frederick Lewis Norden.

Norden was a Danish artist and naval marine architect, sent by King Christian VI to make a journey of exploration in Egypt. He attempted to reach the second cataract, but was turned back at Derr in Nubia. Pococke's *Travels* were published in 1743, but Norden's *Voyage,* published in 1755, was the first attempt at an elaborate description of Egypt. No traveller of the time could be expected to add anything to the historical knowledge of Egypt, because the sole sources, the classical authors, had already been squeezed dry. But Norden's description is comprehensive, and his drawings able and interesting.

Like others, he met with trouble through the natives believing that all Europeans were seeking treasure by magic means:

> Travellers here must think themselves happy in being allowed to contemplate the ancient edifices, without daring to stir any thing. I shall never forget what a crowd of people was assembled, while we were mooring at Aswan, in order to see, as they said among themselves, expert sorcerers in the black magic art.

He advises a traveller to

> Begin by dressing yourself in the Turkish manner. A pair of mustachios, with a grave and solemn air, will be very proper companions, by which you will have a resemblance to the natives.

He entered the Great Pyramid 'belly couchant', and advises:

> The first care of the travellers when they come out of the Pyramid must be to dress instantly, cover themselves warmly and drink a glass of generous liquor, in order to prevent a pleurisy.

Norden believes that 'whoever takes the trouble of travelling to Egypt in reasearch after antiquities, is a sober and continent man', but those weak enough to give in to an amorous intrigue found themselves

> so egregiously bubbled in the end, that instead of having enjoyed some high blooded kinswomen of Cleopatra's, they had been the paramours of most abandoned prostitutes, who in order that their dear Strephons should never forget their kindness, had given them a memento indelible by time, place, or mercury.

Another ten years elapsed before another traveller contributed something to the description of Egypt. He was the Abbé Claude-Louis Fourmont, accompanying his friend de Lironcourt, French Consul at Cairo in 1747. Fourmont was interpreter at the library of the King of France, and he wrote a study of Heliopolis and Memphis in which he mapped exactly the famous 'fourth pyramid' on Giza plateau that was re-identified and partly cleared by the Egyptian University in 1932.

Meanwhile rivalry for the portable antiquities of Egypt continued to grow. To acquire antiquities it was not enough now simply to discover them. As soon as an excavation was productive, everyone gathered around: the local inhabitants, the antiquaries, the representatives of foreign powers, the *aga* of the province, each claiming his share under some pretext. The rapacity of the time is reflected in a letter from the French Vice-consul at Alexandria, de Sulauce, to the Minister, Rouille, regarding the despatch to Paris of three statues in 1751:

> The great stir that this discovery has made in the country, in spite of all the precautions taken to keep it secret, prove beyond anything one could say, how much these three statues verily smell of antiquity. The authorities, indifferent to this kind of thing, of which they take no notice ordinarily, have become so annoyed at not possessing them themselves, that they wanted to take them by command from sieur Roboly, the Second Drogman at Alexandria, and it is only by the use of tact, manœuvre and money that he managed to calm their envy.

Thus on the one hand were the sincere antiquaries who braved the hardships of travel, measured the monuments, and wrote useful descriptions of them; and on the other, the despoilers who would damage the monuments and wreck archaeological evidence with no scruples to obtain curios for sale or to please their masters. Naturally the local people fell upon this fresh source of income with gusto, and tomb, temple and pyramid were ransacked without mercy or check, to the grand frustration of archaeologists to come.

Striding across the Egyptian scene now comes James Bruce, the biggest traveller of the 18th century in respect of physique as well as of distance and renown. His transit of Egypt was but one episode in his *Travels to Discover the Source of the Nile*, and on scrutiny it does not appear to have advanced the knowledge or description of Egypt by anything substantial, yet his robust and entertaining narrative has a secure and deserved place in the literature of Egyptian exploration.

James Bruce came of landed people in Stirlingshire, and began to travel after the death of his young wife when he was only twenty-four. He began to study Arabic when he was in Spain, and the possibility of exploring the Nile took a strong hold upon his imagination. To reach its source became the main purpose of his life.

Further to qualify himself for the project, he studied antiquities in Italy, and held the post of Consul at Algiers, where he perfected his colloquial Arabic. Although he was himself a competent draughtsman, Bruce engaged a brilliant architect and artist to help him: Luigi Balugani, of Bologna, who remained with him seven years and died while they were in Abyssinia. Balugani deserved to be better known, and might have been, had Bruce given him his due in the account of his travels. But James Bruce, though a brave, magnanimous man of ability, was filled with self-esteem and the thirst for fame. He could tolerate no rivalry. Physically he was a huge man, six feet four tall. Fanny Burney wrote that his 'grand air, gigantic height, and forbidding brow awed everybody into silence. He is the tallest man you ever saw gratis.'

He reached Egypt in 1768 wearing Arab dress, and sailed up the Nile examining ruins on the way. From Aswan he came back to Qena and went across to the Red Sea at Kosseir, whence he took ship. The perils of his journey are told with racy humour until he came at last, in 1770, upon the mighty Nile 'not four yards over, and not above four inches deep', and stood upon the spot 'which had baffled the genius, industry and inquiry of both ancients and moderns for the course of near three thousand years'.

This was not true. The ancients had never sought the source of the Blue Nile; and Bruce was not the first European to reach this source. The Jesuit missionary Pedro Paez had stood here with Jeronimo Lobo and other Jesuits in 1615. An English translation of Lobo's account had been Samuel Johnson's first publication, and this had been accessible to Bruce; but he attempted to throw doubt on the exploit, revealing the depths to which his love of fame would lower him.

But it is with Bruce's Egyptian passage that we are concerned. He affected to disdain Cairo:

> I never saw a place I liked worse, or which afforded less pleasure or instruction than Cairo, or antiquities which less answered their descriptions.

The last remark was ill-judged from a man who could ridicule the fact that the pyramids were built of blocks of stone. In his opinion they were carved from existing mountains of rock:

. . . anyone who will take the pains to remove the sand will find the solid rock there hewn into steps.

He is correct, however, in agreeing with 'the learned Dr Pococke' regarding the placing of Memphis. Following the description of Pliny relating its position to that of various pyramid groups, he settles for the present-day village of Mitrahina.

His relations with the *reis*, or captain, of his boat are human and genial. *Reis* Abu Cuffi, all dressed up and wearing a red turban, begs leave to go ashore:

I asked him why he did not wear the green turban of Mahomet? He answered, Poh! that was a trick put upon strangers; there were many men who wore green turbans, that were very great rascals; but he was a *Saint*, whatever colour of a turban he wore; would be back early in the morning, and bring me a fair wind.

'Hassan, said I, I fancy it is much more likely that you bring me some aquavitae, if you do not drink it all.'

Hassan Abu Cuffi came back all right, in the night. He could find no spirits, 'and that, to be sure, was one of the reasons of his return'.

Later they struck a bargain for the boat to convey him beyond the point to which it was engaged; 'but, if he behaved well, he expected a trifling premium. "And if you behave ill, Hassan," said I, "what do you think you deserve?"—"To be hanged," said he, "I deserve, and desire no better." '

At Thebes he examines the colossi and comes to the conclusion that they were 'apparently the Nilometers of that town, as the marks which the water has left upon the bases sufficiently shew.'

He speculates on the use of hieroglyphs:

I never could make the number of different hieroglyphics amount to more than five hundred and fourteen. From this I conclude, certainly, that it can be no entire language which hieroglyphics are meant to contain.

The belief that hieroglyphic writing was symbolic and never alphabetic was very firmly established. Many learned men were yet to waste many hours in fruitless guessing.

Bruce went to the Valley of the Kings:

. . . the magnificent, stupendous sepulchres, of Thebes. It is a solitary place; and my guides, either from a distaste at such employments, or, that their fears of the banditti that live in the caverns of the mountains were real, importuned me to return to the boat, even before I had begun my search.

Bruce pushed on, to make his mark of fame in Egypt by the 'discovery' of the tomb of Ramses III—though of course he did not know whose tomb it was. It was henceforward known as 'Bruce's Tomb', yet he made no claim actually to have discovered it, for it was open for all to walk into; but

Farther forward on the right-hand of the entry, the pannels were painted in fresco. The discovery was so unexpected that I was rivetted, as it were, to the spot by the first sight of these paintings, and I could proceed no further. In one pannel were several musical instruments strowed upon the ground. In three following pannels were painted, in fresco, three harps, which merited the utmost attention, whether we consider the elegance of these instruments in their form, and the detail of their parts, or confine ourselves to the reflection that to how great a perfection music must have arrived, before an artist could have produced so complete an instrument. As the first harp seemed to be the most perfect, and least spoiled, I immediately attached myself to this, and desired my clerk to take upon him the charge of the second.

Poor Luigi Balugani—this is one of the few mentions he gets! The resulting drawings are most unlike the originals, however. They have translated the Egyptian purity into full Renaissance classic style, with modelling, muscles and folded drapes.

James Bruce returned to England in 1774, leaving the bones of Luigi in Abyssinia. He did not receive the honours to which he considered himself entitled, and his tales of travel were ridiculed. Deeply hurt and proud, he retired to his acres in Scotland, and it was not until twelve years later that he dictated his memoirs, when 'five massive, ill-arranged, ill-digested, but most fascinating volumes made their appearance in 1790'.

No volumes as readable—or even as instructive—about Egypt appeared during the remainder of the 18th century. The Breton Claude Etienne Savary's *Lettres sur l'Egypte* contain an interesting table comparing the measurements of the pyramids given by authors ancient and modern, and he foresees to some extent the method of deciphering hieroglyphs eventually used by Champollion. Savary was in Egypt for three years after 1776.

The Comte de Volney's *Voyage* between 1783 and 1785 throws no new light on Pharaonic Egypt, but was an excellent guide for army chiefs. Napoleon Bonaparte took a copy of it to St Helena and made notes on a picture of the pyramids. Volney's attitude towards the monuments is that of a contemporary French revolutionary. After his immediate wonder and admiration of the pyramids he hastily returns to the party line:

> But one must admit, another sentiment succeeds this first transport of delight. Afrer rising to so high an opinion of the might of man, when one begins to think about the ends to which it is employed, one looks upon his works only with the eye of regret; one is distressed to think that in order to build this vain tomb, an entire nation had to be tormented for twenty years. One is indignant at the extravagance of despots who commanded these barbarous works; this labyrinth, these temples, these pyramids in their massive structure, are much less evidence of an opulent people loving the arts, than of the slavery of a nation tormented by the avarice of its masters. Whilst the lover of the arts may wax indignant when he sees the columns of the palace being sawn up to make millstones, the philosopher cannot help smiling at the secret malice of fate, that gives back to the people what cost them so much misery, and that assigns to the most humble of their needs the pride of useless luxury.

Indeed, there was little left for the antiquary to do now in Egypt save philosophize. Short of organized excavation or the solving of the riddle of hieroglyphs, he could contribute no more to knowledge. By the end of the 18th century all the principal monuments that were above ground had been located and visited, and some that were below ground whose entrances were known, like the bird pits of Saqqara and the tombs of the kings at Thebes. The next step was organized and scientific examination on a large scale—too much for the lone traveller to undertake.

8 Oracle and Magic

THERE remained one place, however, so remote and mysterious that no European traveller had ever ventured to reach it.

This was the legendary temple of the Oracle of Jupiter Amon in the oasis of Siwa four hundred miles across the desert west of the Nile. The ancient writers tell of the fame of the Oracle that was already so long-established and so great that conquering Cambyses, five hundred years before Christ, sent 50,000 troops towards Siwa with intent to burn the Temple of Amon and enslave the inhabitants. But his army vanished in a sandstorm and was never heard of again.

Pindar the Greek poet sent a hymn of praise to the Temple of Amon at Siwa in the 5th century B.C., carved on stone; and the most renowned of all visits was that of Alexander the Great, the first King of Egypt to visit the priests of the Oracle in person. After a secret audience he wrote to his mother Olympias that he would divulge to her the directions he had received from the Oracle when he returned to Macedonia. What the Oracle told him must have made a deep impression on him, for he wished to be buried at Siwa. His wish was not granted; and he took the secret of the Oracle to the grave with him, for he died far from Macedonia, and Ptolemy, his successor, built a magnificent tomb at Alexandria to receive his body. All he had at Siwa was a stone stela which Ptolemy had placed near that of Pindar.

Hannibal consulted the Oracle at the end of the 3rd century B.C., but Strabo records that the Oracle had much declined in importance by 23 B.C. The last known visitor to Siwa was Pausanias, in A.D. 160. He saw Pindar's hymn of praise and Alexander's stela still in place; and the priests were still holding religious services, and the Oracle was still active. The priests of Amon in Siwa were probably the last in Egypt to make offerings to the ancient gods. The temples there were probably closed down by Justinian in the middle of the 6th century after Christ.

It fell to a London man of means, William George Browne, to be the first European to reach Siwa. This earnest and sedate man studied law after leaving Oxford, but his fate was sealed when he read Bruce's travels, and he resolved to devote his life to the exploration of Africa. He set off from Alexandria on 24th February, 1792, a day fixed by the Arabs as propitious for a good start. Browne accompanied a caravan disguised as a mameluke, and they arrived at Siwa on 9th March. This was not as safe as it sounds. The English geographer who checked his notes afterwards, John Rennell, commented that Browne ran a great deal more risk on his Siwa trip than Alexander the Great did. The fanatical natives of the oasis could not endure the presence of a Christian, mameluke though Browne pretended to be. They reviled him and threw stones at him, and he was in constant peril of his life. However, he did manage to see the ruins of Um Ebeida, though the local people could provide no information to identify the Jupiter Amon temple. Returning from Siwa, Browne, with commendable honesty, expressed doubt that this was the famous oasis of the Oracle at all. Rennell, comparing his notes with all ancient accounts available, insisted that it was.

Six years later, in 1798, Frederick Hornemann, working for the London African Society, reached Siwa with a company of pilgrims. His eagerness to visit the antiquities during the eight days at Siwa made local people suspect that he was not a Moslem. A small army of Siwans pursued the departing caravan and would have killed Hornemann and his servant but for his presence of mind in taking out a Koran and reading it out loud in Arabic.

It was unfortunate the neither Browne nor Hornemann was able to make drawings of Um Ebeida, for it was tumbled in an earthquake in 1811. Buti, a French officer who went to Siwa in 1819, saw it in this state; but he left no useful description. He too escaped alive with difficulty.

Soon after Buti, the French explorer Frédéric Cailliaud reached the oasis under no disguise at all. Perhaps the sheiks were astounded into acquiescence, for eventually they permitted Cailliaud to see Um Ebeida under supervision. But their followers murmured, believing that the long twelve-day stay of the Christian would bring misfortune.

They were right: it came a few months later with the artillery of Mohamed Ali, and the Siwans lost their independence for ever. With this expedition came French Consul Drovetti, the famous engineer Linant de Bellefonds, the painter Frediani, and Ricci the physician. They drew plans of Um Ebeida, and, more important, entered the oasis town of Aghurmi, where they saw an ancient well and some stone walls near it.

The Baron von Minutoli visited the oasis in 1821, and Bayle St John in 1847, but neither contributed more than a fresh description of Um Ebeida. Then in 1852 the Scot James Hamilton came. The Siwans made a night attack on his camp, and Hamilton was sheltered by Yousef Ali, the man who had incited them to do it. It required an expeditionary force from Cairo to rescue him. But then he visited all the sites. He was the first European to enter Aghurmi since Drovetti, thirty-five years before, and he discovered the temple there. This, he said, was the ancient acropolis and its temple, site of the Oracle, and not Um Ebeida, as had been supposed since Browne.

In 1869 Gerhard Rohlfs copied the inscriptions at Aghurmi and showed them to the Egyptologist Brugsch, who agreed with Hamilton. The question was finally settled by the visit of Steindorf in 1900. Aghurmi is the temple of the Oracle, whilst the temple of Um Ebeida is the other one mentioned in the descriptions of the visit of Alexander as being not far from the acropolis and in the midst of the palm tree groves.

Browne visited the rest of Egypt, but there is little to gain from his affected and pedantic descriptions. He recounts, however, that at Dendera he found the local chieftain engaged in blowing up the temple walls with gunpowder in the belief that treasure was hidden there. And at Medinet Habu, at Thebes, he came across a large pool of blood in the temple.

Some labourers told him that the villagers from nearby Gurna had just murdered a Moroccan and a Greek there whose behaviour suggested that they had come to seek treasure by means of magic, in which Moroccans were reputed to have great skill.

After this horrid sight William George Browne would have been well advised to continue indefinitely the life of a scholar and a recluse to which he returned. But after ten years he emerged once more the explorer, bent on reaching Tartary by way of Persia. In 1813, not far beyond Teheran, he himself was foully murdered.

The mania for treasure-hunting with magic was one of the non-biblical plagues of Egypt. Ibn Khaldoun, in the 15th century, wrote that at one time there was so much treasure-seeking that the occupation was classified as an industry and a tax imposed on it.

The results on the monuments were deplorable. Vansleb, on 21st June, 1672, at the foot of Pompey's Pillar, noticed that it was leaning. Eight years before it had been vertical. Arabs with treasure mania had dug under the base, and would have had it over but for the hardness of the stone. Norden, in 1737, writing of the same pillar, said:

> An Arabian dug a hole under the foundation, in which he put a box of gunpowder, in order to blow up the column, and thereby to become master of the treasure he imagined was buried underneath. Unfortunately for him, but happily for the curious, he was a bad engineer.

There was even more faith in magic than in powder as a means of locating and obtaining treasure. Paul Lucas complained, 'It was announced everywhere that I had the secret of seeing by means of my stick into the most obscure places, and even through rocks and the thickest walls, and that I had by this means discovered all the treasures in the mountains whence we came.'

Books were written in Arabic purporting to give directions for finding the hiding-places of treasure and the spells and fumigations for overcoming the talismans that guarded it. One such book was entitled *Book of hidden pearls and precious mystery concerning the indication of hiding-places, findings and treasures.*

The instructions are complex and exhausting to carry out. A purchaser of the Book of Pearls had a run for his money, in a literal sense, and there were many sites to choose from. If you chose to seek 'The road that leads to the Thousand Tombs of Heliopolis':

> When you are at Heliopolis, set off on a Sunday, taking a south-easterly direction for two good miles, until you come near a site named Iahmoum-the-Black, that is placed above a small room. Make fumigations there and go a half-mile towards the north-east with your incense on the flames; you will find an enclosure built of stone and plaster like a circular courtyard, which contains the thousand tombs laid out in ten rows. There are two doors in this enclosure which open, one towards the east, the other towards the south-west. Quite close to it rises a rock and a column on which is engraved the science of geography; it is a talisman that halts anyone who tries to enter the enclosure during the night. When you have seen that, realize that these are the Thousand Tombs, in the seeking of which many persons have perished because they have sought them in an ignorant manner without possessing the requisite knowledge. The tombs are visible to you only if you perform fumigations near Iahmoum-the-Black. Cross, then, the obstacle and fumigate, then dig at the east of each tomb and you will uncover some masonry. Break it, perform continuous fumigation, and you will find a sloping way that will lead you to a chamber containing a corpse covered by a cloth of woven gold and wearing golden armour. Near him is everything that he possessed during his lifetime. The incense should be compounded of agalloche, stigmatas of saffron, dung, carob kernels, sycamore figs. Take a *mithqal* of each of these ingredients, grind them fine, moisten them with human blood, roll them into pellets and burn them as incense whilst walking near Iahmoum; the talismans and the hiding-places will be thus discovered. Take what you need. That is all.

Sometimes the treasures coveted are not gold but the sovereign remedies and stimulants so dear to the Arab heart, such as you may find, if you follow the directions, in the 'Field of Water-melons at Atfih', where there are magic melons that contain cures for blindness, for grey hair, and some which

> enclose a remedy against paralysis. The sufferer can rise and walk with the permission of God (glory to Him) if he takes one seed; if he takes more it will harm him. If you give him three seeds he

will become blear-eyed and blind. If you go as far as ten, he will have a stricture of the urethra and constipation, and he will die three days afterwards. Here you will also see water-melons that resemble gourds, having seeds like the carob; these are aphrodisiacs. If you place one seed in your mouth you will have the energy to conduct carnal commerce as long as you wish, and you will remain in perpetual erection without trouble as long as you keep the seed in your mouth.

Ibn Khaldoun was the first to refute all this nonsense, in the 15th century:

Suppose that a man did want to bury all his treasures and to keep them secure by means of some magical process. He would take all possible precautions to keep his secret hidden. How could one believe, then, that he would place unmistakable signs to guide those who sought the treasure, and that he would commit those signs to writing, in a manner to furnish to men of all centuries and all countries the means to discover those same treasures. It is in direct contradiction to the aim he had in concealing them.

But Ibn Khaldoun's warning was in vain. Treasure-hunters were still at it six centuries later, at the time when Maspero was Director of the Antiquities Service of Egypt. He wrote:

Today still, scarcely a month passes without some professional magician coming to recite incantations or burn perfumes in front of some scene carved on a temple wall or of some isolated tomb, and then attacking it with a pick or even with dynamite to extract the treasure that he believes is hidden there.

Damage to the monuments became so serious that in 1907 Maspero arranged for the Book of Pearls to be published, in the hope that when it was available to anybody for a few piastres, instead of being a rarity, the simpletons who believed in that kind of thing would realize that the treasures described in it must all have been lifted long ago.

Nobody dynamites temples in Egypt today; but this is likely as much the result of adequate policing of the monuments as of any exposé of the Book of Pearls.

9 The Great Expedition

NEWLY graduated as an engineer, Prosper Jollois, aged twenty-two, wrote to his father in Bourgogne on 21st Germinal, year VI of the Revolution (10th April, 1798):

You have perhaps heard talk of a secret expedition, the object of which is completely unknown to the public, and of which I have only the slightest inkling. It is a matter of a very great scientific, political and military venture. It is firmly established that a great number of *savants*, the most distinguished in the various branches of knowledge, will be going on this voyage; and it appears equally certain that the expedition is to be accompanied by 25,000 troops. I forgot to tell you that some politicians claim that it is a question of cutting the isthmus of Suez, to establish communication between the Ocean and the Mediterranean.

And now, putting aside all these conjectures and coming to the point—I have joined this expedition.

I must tell you the reasons that have decided me to commit such a folly, if indeed it is such. First, it is a longing to travel that I have cherished for a long time; then the ardent desire to acquire knowledge, experience; and finally the inmost conviction that I have, that this voyage can be nothing but useful to me.

The voyage was to give young Prosper Jollois knowledge and experience in plenty, and probably it was useful to him in its own way in the end, which was not the dashing, romantic way he surely envisaged when he joined. Already he seems to have had first misgivings when he wrote to his father from aboard the *Guerrier* at Toulon:

I still know nothing of my ultimate destination. One can but hope that the Government will not abuse the blind confidence that a great number of people have in it.

A year later his colleague Etienne Geoffroy Saint-Hilaire was to write from Cairo to his friend Georges Cuvier, the famous naturalist:

The time will come when the work of the Commission of Arts will excuse in the eyes of posterity the lightness with which our nation has, so to say, thrown itself into the Orient . . . Let us await the outcome and resign ourselves to suffer here in patience.

On 1st July, 1798, Prosper Jollois witnessed the landing of French soldiers on the coast of Egypt near Alexandria, as he stood on the heaving deck of *Guerrier*. The sea was rough and the shore rocky. Boats were overturned; a score of men drowned. The troops went ashore in the night without horses, artillery or water-bottles, and walked to the city thirsty, Bonaparte at their head. Next morning from the base of Pompey's Pillar, Bonaparte gave the order to attack. Alexandria was unprepared for even so feeble an assault as this, and by 11 a.m. the city was his.

Next day the scientists and artists, including Jollois, were dumped ashore at the Old Port to find their way to headquarters at Pompey's Pillar, unsure that the city was properly subdued or that the inhabitants were not still firing from windows.

Come what may, I picked my way through unfamiliar streets to the French consul's house, where Bonaparte was lodged. In this short journey I saw enough to disabuse me of the idea I had formed of this superb Alexandria: tumble-down houses falling into ruin, irregular walls, streets of bazaars where the air barely circulated.

He was equally disappointed with the remains of ancient Alexandria, 'heaps of sand and stones'. Wandering towards the Rosetta gate he fell in with 'citizens Dolomieu and Denon'. Dolomieu was a mineralogist who was destined to leave his bones in Egypt. Vivant Denon was an artist and aristocrat whose name had been proscribed by the revolutionaries while he was in Italy. With great courage he had returned to France, and become somewhat of a favourite of Napoleon's. He appears to have been an *ex officio* member of the Commission of Arts and Science with the Expedition, working freelance; because he returned to France before the others and quickly published his own account of Egypt and his drawings. *His Voyage in Lower and Upper Egypt* is a brilliant and even thrilling work that certainly scooped the pool from under the massive *Description de l'Egypte* eventually produced by the official Commission; and Denon's name remains better known than those of many others who endured equal hardships and whose skills were equal or superior to his own.

Entering the French camp, they found the soldiers still on biscuit rations. 'Most of them were glad enough to be ashore, but many were disappointed with the resources of the country, and wanted to be out of it again.'

At sundown they retraced their steps. Near the gate of the town a musket ball whistled past their ears.

Next day most of the Commission members were at Pompey's Pillar, already at work; but all were complaining of being totally abandoned by the authorities. General Caffarelli, whose special charge they were, gave no thought to their welfare. Citizen Dolomieu voiced his disgust that no arrangements had been made for the youngsters, who had been torn from their country, parents and friends with all kinds of fine promises. His tirade had results, says Jollois,

> after five days, during which some were delivered to all the horrors of hunger. They were accorded the rations of private soldiers and quartered in horrible garrets. What a fine subject for a caricature for the French, who laugh at everything, to see the scientists laboriously measuring the dimensions of Pompey's Pillar, and on their return seeking some tank from which to quench their thirst while they waited to satisfy their hunger!

They had, in fact, no means of subsistence, for even money could procure nothing to eat in the town. Jollois and his friends decided to get out of the city with some members of the Commission who had been ordered to Rosetta. But they were refused passage with the flotilla. 'Citizen Fourier,' remarks Jollois bitterly, 'had the adroitness to get himself aboard a galley and to abandon all the young people in his charge to their unhappy lot.' Jean-Baptiste Joseph Fourier is still famous among higher mathematicians.

Eventually they got aboard the *Sans-quartier*, deck passage, and no rations. They had a rough night, and anchored in the midst of the French fleet that Admiral Brueys had taken to Aboukir Bay. On 9th July they were put ashore at Rosetta, forty miles east of Alexandria. The engineers went at once to complain to General Caffarelli. He told them that everything would be fine at Cairo: 'He even bathed them in ridiculous flattery and truly made them swallow a gilded pill.'

Jollois and his friends were given the smallest room in a large, filthy house. For fear of plague they sprinkled everything with vinegar; and they were devoured by fleas and gnats. They spent their days helping the naturalists stuff birds, or completing drawings of houses in Malta and Alexandria which they had measured.

On 28th July, 1798, they had news of the capture of Cairo. On the evening of 1st August Prosper Jollois was walking with companions along the desert edge at sundown. Suddenly

. . . a dull rumble sounded in my ears, repeated a second and a third time. It was unmistakably the sound of cannon. Whence could it come, if not from the fleet? My first impulse was to rush to the square tower of Abumandours; I would have witnessed the combat. But, tormented by anxiety, I went home. All my comrades confirmed that it was indeed the fleet in battle.

I went up to the roof of the house; the night was dark, allowing the many flashes of the cannon to be seen. The ships fired their broadsides; a terrifying noise followed; a fearful carnage went on. Oh, how terrible it was to think of a naval battle! I was absorbed in these painful reflections when a lurid white glow appeared, which gained in intensity. It grew fast, and soon we were certain that a ship was on fire. It did not cease from discharging its broadsides, drifting as the wind willed, until at last when the fire reached the powder magazine, the ship blew up. Nothing more terrifying or more beautiful!

The fight died down, but it started again at dawn and went on all day. Rumours of victory flew from mouth to mouth. They thought they could discern the tricolour flag flying. A whole day passed without news. A despatch-boat sailed into the Nile, thinking itself pursued by the enemy, and throwing its cannon into the river the more easily to cross the bar. The river bank at Rosetta was crowded with French. The captain came ashore. He had seen the conflict from afar. His news was too satisfactory for them to believe it with confidence.

At last official news came from Alexandria, from General Kléber to General Menou:

> It is kept a dead secret. They are afraid to communicate it; then it must be bad. Persons close to the general learn that our fleet no longer exists; that the *Orient* and the *Arthémise* have been sunk. Reports have been brought by a crowd of deserters from the fleet. Sadness and desolation were even deeper than our joy had been great.

On 12th August Jollois describes the beach strewn with corpses of French sailors:

> The stench which hovers over the whole coast for three or four leagues is ghastly. You see piles of six or seven corpses, and here and there a leg or an arm protruding from the sand; it is truly a terrible sight. Since the end of the fight, the Arabs have been building fires the whole length of the coast with the wreckage of our ships; and yet the shore is still covered with timber.

Jollois was moved to Cairo on 18th August. He liked the look of Bulac, had an early morning swim in the muddy waters of the Nile, and went off with his baggage on a donkey, much delighted by this novel form of transport.

Bonaparte was busy forming the Institute of Egypt among the members of the Commission of Arts and Science. Five houses of rich *beys*, with immense gardens, had been requisitioned.

Jollois witnessed a parade in Esbekia Square when Bonaparte reminded his troops of their victories, adding, 'You will all die, like those brave men whose names are inscribed on the altars of fame, or you will return to your hearths, covered with honour and glory.' The discourse ended with the cry, 'Vive la République!' and we are scarcely surprised when Jollois tells us:

> . . . it was nowhere taken up by the troops, so great in general is their discontent. Bonaparte, disposed to gaiety on the occasion, suddenly assumed a very serious air. No doubt it gave him plenty of food for thought.

On 21st October there was an Arab uprising. Mobs roamed the streets, beating any Frenchman they saw to death, and attacking houses occupied by the conquerors. Prosper Jollois and his colleagues at the Institute were not armed, and their guard of grenadiers was removed to surround the great mosque.

Each one of us then wanted to give his opinion, which always happens when non-military men are forced to act militarily. Some wanted to abandon the building; others, moved by consideration of the library and other precious material gathered there, wanted to defend it . . . This last course having been decided on, doors were barricaded and sentinels posted. We had no means of retreat and we would have to die at our posts.

The fight raged in the street outside, but fortunately the Institute was not broken into before the rebellion was quelled.

In the days that followed Jollois and his colleague Lancret were busy with drawings: plans and elevation of the Citadel; a plan of the Ibn Tulun mosque. On 4th January, 1799, he went to the pyramids with General Kléber and a large escort. He came out with his shirt wringing wet, and had a nip of brandy to restore himself before going on to the Sphinx, whose body was being cleared of sand.

At last the great adventure of Upper Egypt came. He set out on a river boat, one of an armed flotilla, under Girard, chief engineer of roads and bridges, to join General Desaix who was then at Asyut. Between the palms, as they passed by, they could see the triumphal arch at Antinopolis. From Asyut they marched with General Belliard to Kena, where they remained all June. He saw the nearby Dendera temple ten times, drawing every aspect of it, fascinated by it like Denon, who wrote:

> . . . all that I had hitherto seen of architecture was insufficient, here, to set bounds to my admiration. What uninterrupted power, what wealth, what abundance, what superfluity of resources must have belonged to a government that could raise an edifice like this, and that could find in its nation men capable of conceiving, executing, decorating and enriching it with all that speaks to the eyes and to the mind.

Jollois reached Aswan on 13th July, 1799, and saw every monument of note on the way, drawing plans and elevations of many for the plates that were eventually published in the great *Description de l'Egypte*. At Philae:

> The inhabitants are defiant; they don't like people visiting their island because they think they go there to look for treasure. Since we have been there three times, they have become very agitated and told us that they will destroy the monuments on their island so that people will not go there any more to bother them.

At Armant they found considerable remains of a temple 'remarkable for the elegance and lightness of its columns' of which only the foundations remain now. Edmé Jomard, in the *Description de l'Egypte*, says that the ceiling blocks were still in place and the interior reliefs almost completely preserved:

> The study we have just made of the temple from its sculptures informs us more about its intention than the passages of ancient authors handed down to us about this ancient town.

He pours scorn on Strabo and Macrobe for saying that at Armant they honoured the sun-bull Pacis:

> These examples alone show how little the old authors knew the Egyptian temples; but one is not surprised, when one recollects that the interior of the temples was always inaccessible to strangers.

We have already seen how the assertion of the old authors was proved correct by the discovery by Sir Robert Mond of the sacred bull cemeteries in 1927.

Jollois spent twenty-one days at Esna on two visits making drawings. Vivant Denon, who was at this temple earlier in the year, called it 'the most perfect remains of ancient architecture'. He was astonished that we should have supinely believed, upon the mere authority of the people themselves, that the Greeks were the inventors of architecture, and that three orders are the only truths of the art. 'The Egyptians have copied nature; they have copied their own; and the Greeks have only added fables to the robberies they have committed on them.'

When Jollois came back to Thebes from Aswan in August, 1799, it was well pacified, and he went everywhere, busy, with his colleagues, measuring and drawing. At Medinet Habu he copied a scene of 'the triumph of a king of Egypt over the Indians' in a naval battle. The king was Ramses III, and his foes were certainly not Indians. Jollois also carved his name on the temple. It is still there, with the date, *an VII* of the Revolution—1799.

Denon had come upon Thebes with the first wave of the advancing army at nine o'clock in the morning on 26th January, 1799, when the soldiers

> suddenly beheld the seat of the antique Thebes, of which Homer has painted the extent in a single word, the hundred-gated Thebes, a poetic and empty expression, confidently repeated through a

series of ages . . . this city, perpetually wrapped in that veil of mystery by which even colossuses are magnified, this exiled city, which the mind no longer discovers but through the mists of time, was still a phantom so gigantic to our imagination, that the army, at sight of its scattered ruins, halted of itself, and, by one spontaneous impulse, grounded its arms, as if the possession of the remains of this capital had been the object of its glorious labours, and had completed the conquest of the Egyptian territory.

Although one is inclined to think that the spontaneous impulse came more from the god-sent opportunity for a stand-easy than from a profound knowledge of ancient civilizations among the soldiery, citizen Denon's lyricism is not out of key. It was a great occasion for those who understood.

Various groups of the Commission of Arts and Science were in different parts of Egypt mapping, studying the natural history, the minerals, the irrigation, the people and the antiquities, while the military tangle in which Bonaparte had involved France was being resolved. When their fleet was destroyed at Aboukir by Nelson on that night when Jollois watched the battle, the French were cut off from home. Everyone knew the expedition was doomed, yet the French managed to remain in Egypt for three years. While General Desaix took his 4,000 men right through Egypt to Aswan, and Bonaparte went with 13,000 to Syria to face the Turks, and General Kléber defeated the resurgent Egyptians at Heliopolis, the scientists and artists of the Commission went on earnestly with their measuring, drawing and recording. Their final achievement was the only fair thing that remained from this sorry, futile campaign.

Voyaging up the Nile or enduring the heat and flies in isolated places, these intelligent Frenchmen must have longed for home and thought long deep thoughts on the motives of human behaviour. Chabrot and Jomard wrote in the first volume of the *Description de l'Egypte* of a storm on the river near the sandstone quarries of Silsila, whence came the stone for the mighty temples of Thebes. The storm drove them ashore against steep rocks. With some surprise they found an old hermit living at the foot of the rocks, thin, impassive, and apparently unmoved by the drama of the shipwreck. They remark that each storm brought a boat against his rocks, so the old man always had some alms in the form of flour or dates from them:

If one sought to see in him a sage retired from the world and living in contemplation, one doubtless deceived oneself. In truth one saw there only a man who, in order to rid himself of the trouble of acting and thinking, had looked for a place where he could live in that idleness and nothingness that is the ideal pleasure of these people. Yet well-to-do people, arrived from Europe after a thousand perils, were chipping the rocks that composed his dwelling under his very eyes, collecting the wild plants that he tore out for burning, sketching and describing this uninhabited place; were they so much more wise than he?

The most valuable contribution to knowledge of ancient Egypt, and the most far-reaching, made during the campaign did not come from a member of the Commission at all.

The *Courrier d'Egypte*, published in Cairo, No. 37, August, 1799, contained a letter describing 'a stone of very fine granite, black, with a close grain, and very hard'. It had been found by Pierre François Xavier Bouchard, an officer of the Engineers, at Fort Jullien at Rosetta. On one face of the stone there were 'three distinct inscriptions separated in three parallel bands'. At the top were the remains of a hieroglyphic inscription; in the middle a text in an unknown script (later recognized as a cursive form of hieroglyphs, and named demotic); and below an inscription in Greek of Ptolemy V, of which the last line prescribed the transcription of this decree in all the temples of Egypt. For the first time we had an Egyptian text in two kinds of writing, the sense of which was provided by a Greek text. The *Courrier d'Egypte* added, 'This stone offers great interest for the study of hieroglyphic characters; perhaps it will even give us the key at last.'

It was the key. And it was fortunate that Captain Bouchard was a man of intelligence who realized that his Rosetta Stone might be important. But it required a wait of twenty-three years before the key was turned by Jean-François Champollion, who was a child of eight and a half when Bouchard found the stone.

10 Withdrawal

JOLLOIS returned to Cairo from his Upper Egyptian journey on 6th November, 1799; but 'the hopes of return to France that we had nursed while we sailed the Nile were quick to melt'. Things had changed. Bonaparte had left his army in Egypt to its fate. The Turks were menacing Damietta, and General Desaix had gone to deal with them. It was not before February of 1800 that General Kléber, now Commander-in-chief, arranged with the British to allow the Commission of Arts and Science to pass their naval blockade and return to France. Full of hope, Jollois and his companions left Cairo for Rosetta on 5th February. On the 9th news came through the British of the change of government in France, and of Bonaparte declaring himself Consul.

The Commission members waited thirty-four days camped on the island of Farehi opposite Rosetta. Kléber thought he should not let them leave before obtaining from the British all possible assurances; but they had to await Sir Sidney Smith. When he came, he said that he must refer back to the Court in London. So the artists and scientists waited another thirty-four days aboard *Oiseau* at Alexandria. But once again events postponed their departure. The celebrated Battle of Heliopolis, at which Kléber routed a Turkish army of 40,000, put the French again in possession of Egypt 'which the notorious insincerity of the English would not allow them to quit save with shame and dishonour', in the words of the exasperated Jollois.

And then on 14th June, 1800, 'the most frightful event took

place, carrying desolation throughout the whole French army. The Commander-in-chief Kléber was assassinated by a fanatic sent from the army of the Vizier.' He was succeeded by General Menou, a small man with delusions of grandeur who saw Egypt as a province of France despite all, and who had become a Moslem in a ludicrous step towards integration, and called himself Abdulla Menou.

A week or so later Jollois and his friend Dubois-Aymé were sent to take levels of the canal near Beybeit, and he was as deeply impressed by the great granite ruins as had been Sicard and Paul Lucas:

> He who rebuilds in his mind's eye this vast edifice, and reflects that all of its enormous mass is granite and that it contains perhaps more of it than one sees in all the ruins of Thebes together; such a man, say I, cannot resist paying a tribute of admiration to the ancient people who raised such remarkable constructions.

He was posted back to Cairo in March, 1801. In the same month the British landed a force at Aboukir. Abdulla Menou attacked them near the ruins of Canopus, lost the battle and retired into Alexandria, swearing that he would resist to the death. On 2nd April General Hutchinson took Rosetta and isolated Alexandria by letting water into the dry bed of Lake Mareotis. By mid-June the armies of Hutchinson, the Turks, mamelukes and bedouins were before Cairo, where the French General Belliard was contending with acute water shortage, raging plague, and the knowledge that his position was hopeless in the long run. It sometimes takes more moral courage in a general to capitulate than to order a fight to the death. Belliard had that courage, and the French marched out with full military honours.

Before the end, Commission members obtained permission to leave the beleaguered city and go to Alexandria. They were poorly received there by Menou, who did not want them. Food was almost unobtainable, even with much money. They shared rations of horse and camel meat with the troops. Menou was still holding out against the British, for reasons of personal pride. He gave Commission members written permission to go aboard *Oiseau* and sail for France, but refused to negotiate a safe-conduct for them with the British. After a month on board, they asked him again to authorize the communication of their passport to the enemy. All he replied was, 'It is permitted that *Oiseau* depart whenever it chooses.'

They chose to sail at dawn on 10th July, 1801, and they were barely outside the port when the British corvette *Cynthia* fired a ball to call them to order. *Oiseau* was still too close to the rocks to go in stays, so they kept on. Another ball, in ricochet, skipping across the water, caused citizen Murat, the captain, to shorten sail and to run the English flag to the mizzen-top, keeping the tricolour also to the breeze—the two flags being the sign that he wished to parley with the enemy. They were escorted to Aboukir, where Captain Murat and citizen Fourier went aboard *Foudroyant*, Admiral Keith's ship. The admiral gave them a letter to General Menou, saying that he refused to let them pass, since no permission had been requested in advance; but he was willing to negotiate.

Sir Sidney Smith, the chivalrous, eccentric defender of Acre, happened to be with the admiral, and he came aboard *Oiseau*, interested to meet so many of France's distinguished men of arts and letters. He spent several hours chatting with them before going on to board his own ship *Tigre*, cruising before Alexandria.

Oiseau got back to Alexandria on 14th July, and was met with an order to moor right under the batteries of the warship *Justice*, and that nobody was to leave the ship. An officer came alongside in a boat from *Justice*:

> His face pale and scared, he called for Captain Murat without coming aboard, and gave him this verbal order which I heard distinctly: 'The general-in-chief orders you to be under sail in a quarter of an hour, otherwise the commander has orders to send you to the bottom.' The officer held his watch in his hand. 'I am in despair,' he added, 'to be the bearer of such an order, but it is my duty.'

The scared officer was too terrified to take their letter from Admiral Keith to the unpredictable Menou; and when they saw the cannons being loaded on the frigate, even the learned passengers of *Oiseau* jumped to the capstan-bars to help the crew get the ship under way. Fuming with rage, General Menou himself walked up and down the quay, watching the operations. Another young officer came in a boat from *Justice*. With tears in his eyes he begged them to hurry: they had an extension of ten minutes. The passengers noticed that the pitiless Menou had posted boats to prevent anyone swimming ashore to escape from this barbarous planned massacre.

A bare few seconds before the deadline, *Oiseau* moved out. A boat overtook them and passed up a letter from Menou. He said that the captain deserved to be hanged for displaying the English flag, and that they had thrown themselves into the enemy's hands instead of 'firing a broadside to maintain the honour of the French flag'. Sententiously he ended:

> I love, I esteem and I honour science and those who cultivate it; I have very special regard for several among you whom I know; I love above all honour and the fatherland. I have given the order that you quit on this instant the ports and roadsteads of Alexandria.

Outside, *Cynthia* rounded them up again, and again they were taken to Aboukir. Sidney Smith came aboard and heard all their troubles. 'Don't leave the admiral,' he advised, 'until you have all you want. You are between the anvil and the hammer.'

Indeed they were. Admiral Keith ruled that since Menou would not have them back, the passengers would be put on shore and *Oiseau* burnt. When the British informed Menou of this decision, he replied that the brig *Oiseau* would be received in Alexandria. Thus on 22nd July, 1801, they were ordered to follow *Cynthia* back to Alexandria once again.

Night fell, and they saw the large pinnace of *Tigre* come alongside. It was Sidney Smith himself, come to try a last-minute chance to take the brig under his protection and get it through. He asked each member of the Commission separately if he wanted to go back. All said no, and Sidney Smith had already given the order to follow *Tigre* when Captain Murat said that he did not intend to go back and face Menou, but he wanted the ship to go back under its own crew. There was uproar from the officers and men, indignant that their captain should desert them in this cowardly manner. The Commission men then decided that if the captain felt like that, nobody should leave the ship. By this time it was late, and Sidney Smith had a sleep on a bed laid out for him on the deck.

Next morning they continued the debate, and the Commission said they would not go back on the ship until a further decision had been sought of the admiral. While this was going on, citizen Thévenin, who had ideas of his own about getting away, took the opportunity provided by a relaxed guard at the companion-ladder to slip down into Sidney Smith's pinnace with two young men of his suite and a couple of trunks.

Perceiving this, everyone rushed to the ladder, citizen Fourier in the lead. Believing, rightly or wrongly, that he too intended to bolt, they all tried to jump in too. Some misjudged and fell into the sea; others got ready to swim if the pinnace pulled out before they got down. In the midst of all the confusion someone shouted, 'To the powder-magazine! They're going to fire the powder!' a cry which struck terror in all, and led to a general rush to the magazine to stamp out any ghastly intention to blow up the ship. Possibly somebody with a sense of the ridiculous had started the cry, for at the magazine they found nobody but the master-gunner, who had been posted guard there in view of the excitable state of all on board. It put an end to Sidney Smith's scheme to get the men of art and letters back to France. The admiral sent them into Alexandria again after a few days; and there the incalculable Menou received them gentle as a dove. A letter reached them even as their anchor rattled down: 'I warned you. You would not listen. But since I knew that you were in a wretched position I have forgiven your misdeeds. You will share our chances, and I assure you they will be those of honour.' This strange man, worried at the brig's non-appearance, had concluded they had been put ashore, and he had even paid the desert sheiks to go and look for them.

The chances he invited them to share with honour were those of dying with their backs to the wall. However, Menou surrendered Alexandria on 30th August, and they were spared this supreme and ridiculous sacrifice.

An article of the capitulation gave the British as prize of war all the antiquities and natural history specimens collected by the Commission. The members rebelled against Menou's weakness in this matter, and they sent a deputation to General Hutchinson. J. Reybaud, in his *History of the French Expedition in Egypt,* says they (notably Geoffroy Saint-Hilaire) did not pull their punches: 'You are taking from us our collections, our drawings, our copies of hieroglyphs; but who will give you the key to all that? . . . Without us this material is a dead language that neither you nor your scientists can understand . . . Sooner than permit this iniquitous and vandal spoliation we will destroy our property, we will scatter it amid the Libyan sands or throw it in the sea. We shall burn our riches ourselves. It is celebrity that you are aiming for. Very well, you can count on the long memory of history: you also will have burnt a library in Alexandria.'

These scorching words, if they were ever uttered, appear to have moved General Hutchinson. The members of the Commission of Art and Sciences departed for home with their collections, notes and drawings intact, save for one object—the Rosetta Stone. The general was very firm about that.

11 *The Spoilers*

THE British did not take over Bonaparte's conquest of Egypt. They gave Egypt back to the Turks. But some British soldiers remained there for a year or so under the command of General the Earl of Cavan, who thought that one of the obelisks of Alexandria—the 'Cleopatra's Needles' so often visited by our pilgrims in past ages—would make a fitting memorial to the victories of British arms in Egypt under Sir Ralph Abercrombie and Lord Hutchinson, if it were erected in London.

He obtained a grant from the Turkish authorities of the fallen needle, which was the better preserved of the two, and his men responded with a will, subscribing money to buy a captured French frigate to transport it, and working parties to dig it out. But for some reason Lord Keith objected, and the scheme was abandoned. Instead, a brass plate was inserted under the top stone of the pedestal of the fallen obelisk, on which was engraved a short detail of the principal events of the campaign. Tribute was paid to the valour of Bonaparte and his troops, with the qualification that 'under Divine Providence it was reserved for the British Nation to annihilate their ambitious designs'.

Thus the two obelisks lay for many years more in the rubbish of the squalid quarter of Alexandria. In 1831 Mohamed Ali reminded the British Government that the needle was theirs for the taking away; but nothing was done. In 1849 the Radical leader Joseph Hume pushed the matter hard in Parliament, but the Government slid out of any action on the advice

of the antiquary Sir Gardner Wilkinson, who said the obelisk
was 'unworthy of the expense of removal'. In 1868 the Khedive
Ismail politely asked the British Government to remove the
obelisk that Mohamed Ali had given them more than once.
Still nothing was moved until 1877, after Dimitri, the Greek
who rented the site, had proposed cutting up the obelisk into
building blocks. Then a wealthy man, Erasmus Wilson, offered
to pay the cost of bringing 'Cleopatra's Needle' to London.
During the journey the special barge containing the 'needle'
broke away, and six sailors lost their lives. The monolith of
red granite, 68 feet long, weighing 180 tons, was erected on
the London Embankment on 12th September, 1878, after a
curious collection of objects had been placed in the pedestal,
including the Book of Genesis in Arabic, a railway guide, a
razor, a box of cigars, hairpins, photographs of a dozen pretty
Englishwomen and a portrait of Queen Victoria. On the south
face are inscribed the names of the six sailors who were drowned.
It is said that the Queen herself asked that this be done.

The obelisk that remained standing at Alexandria did not
remain there long, once London had its 'Needle'. That same
year the Americans obtained the other as a gift from the
Khedive Ismail. William H. Vanderbilt offered $75,000 to
Commander Henry Honeyman Gorringe of the United States
Navy to lower the obelisk, transport it and re-erect it in New
York.

A howl of rage went up in Alexandria from people who never
visited their monument in its surroundings of filth. But
Gorringe worked fast. Within three days of arrival he had a
formal order from Cairo instructing the Governor of Alexandria
to hand over the monument, and before a campaign of opposition against him could be brought to play, his machines were
in place and work was in full swing with the flag of the United
States flying over the site.

The obelisk was safely stowed in a forty-four-year-old
steamer that Gorringe bought, and they set off on a rough and
perilous journey. But nobody was drowned, and they reached
Staten Island on 20th July, 1880. The 'Needle' was landed at
96th Street and the pedestal at 51st Street, and both were
dragged across to Central Park against many difficulties but
with much skill. The foundation stone was laid on 9th October,

1880, by the Grand Master of the Freemasons of New York, with full Masonic rites. Gorringe himself was a Freemason.

When the 220-ton monument stood finally upright and the prolonged cheering had died down, Gorringe remarked laconically that $1,156 was his net profit from the fulfilment of his agreement.

Bonaparte had forced the door of Egypt open for antiquaries. When he left, it was opened by design, from within. In 1805 that remarkable person, Mohamed Ali, took the administration of the country into his own capable hands and welcomed foreigners who could be useful in its development. Not that he thought antiquaries of any direct use. He neither understood the antique monuments of Egypt nor cared what happened to them. But since the cultivation of good relations with foreign powers and their citizens was his interest, he was willing enough to allow those whom it amused to pursue their curious hobby.

Despotic and ruthless though he was, Mohamed Ali was just what Egypt needed at that moment; for he had other qualities besides, of courage, magnanimity, and far-sighted enterprise. And it is scarcely possible to paint the condition of Egypt in colours dark enough to match the epoch. Nominally it was part of the Turkish Empire, which cared nothing for the place so long as the annual tribute was sent in by the Pasha who ruled the province. The peasants were poverty-stricken to the point of fleeing from their land to escape the tax-gatherers. The administration was weak, and its powers wrested from it by the semi-feudal landlords.

Mohamed Ali began life as a penniless orphan in Macedonia. By boldness, cunning and intelligence he rose from a subordinate commander of Turkish troops in Egypt to being named Pasha, or viceroy of the country, virtually an independent ruler. He would have created an empire that included Turkey itself if the British had not prevented his doing so. Although grasping for power, he used it for the good of Egypt. At a time when Arab science was in complete decadence and the wisdom of the ancient Egyptians forgotten, he introduced European methods to construct canals and irrigation barrages, and to start new industries.

Henry Salt, who was later to be British Consul, saw Mohamed Ali in 1803, and described him as 'a little man of

intelligent countenance, with a reddish brown beard of moder-
ate dimensions' which he stroked continually. He would have
been thirty-six years old then. But the Baron von Minutoli,
eighteen years later, described him as 'well built, medium size,
with black fiery eyes which are always in movement'; and
Edward de Montule, about the same time, said he 'possesses a
physiognomy characteristic of his conduct; it is cold, like that
of the Turks, but noble, majestic, and worthy of the dignity
which he has attained. He is addicted to the pleasures of
women, and his harem is composed of more than five hundred
females.' Of this aspect of him the Baroness Minutoli wrote:
'He has two legitimate wives, one of whom resides at Cairo, the
other at Alexandria. The number of his concubines is immense;
there are above two hundred in his harem at Alexandria.' She
had seen them there, for she and her husband were given
quarters at the palace at Alexandria during the plague. Edward
de Montule also gives an instance of the astute knowledge
of his people that Mohamed Ali had. At a time when Cairo
was in revolt, his sixth sense told him immediately how to
end it:

> He asked for four resolute men, who were produced, Mustapha, my
> interpreter, being one of them. They were ordered to enter the
> city, break into the first shops that presented themselves, and
> commence a general plunder. This they executed; consternation
> spread, and the revolt terminated; after which the Pasha paid for
> all the damage which had been occasioned. I believe few sovereigns
> ever made an application so just to the known character of their
> subjects.

In another part of his *Travels* de Montule says:

> One fact is certain, which is, that the government of the Pasha
> knows much less how to profit by the antiquities of the country
> than even the Arabians; he permits every thing to be taken piece-
> meal, and by different individuals, while the whole enterprise
> might be confided to a single company, which might propose the
> formation of a grand Museum at Cairo or Alexandria.

This is one of the earliest references to the idea of a museum
for Egypt; and a good thirty years' devastation of the antiquities was to come between the writing of those words and the
realization of the dream. De Montule describes the monuments

of Thebes as he saw them in 1819; but, he says, the present natives of Gurna, the village on the west bank there,

> the most independent of any of the Arabs of Egypt, and greatly superior to them all in cunning and deceit, live in the entrance of the caves, or ancient sepulchres. They prefer, to the labours of agriculture, the more profitable but disgusting employment of digging for mummies.

Baroness Minutoli remarks casually:

> Being in want of wood, the Arabs supplied us with a considerable quantity, consisting of the remains of mummy cases, among which were some very valuable pieces which my husband saved from the *auto da fe*. The grave inhabitants of ancient Egypt certainly never suspected the use which would be made of their last abode.

Giovanni Finati, the Italian traveller, found Henry William Beechey the artist living in the vestibule of one of the tombs of the kings, and Belzoni the explorer living in another that he had just discovered. Finati observed 'that the antiquaries could inure themselves to imitate the natives in applying to common purposes the wooden fragments and morsels of antiquity that abound, especially the mummy cases, as seats, as tables and shelves, and even as fuel.'

The great Belzoni left a vivid account of his underground explorations in the dark, stifling passages crammed with painted coffins from floor to ceiling:

> . . . and when exhausted I sought a resting-place, and found one: my weight bore on the body of an Egyptian, and it crushed like a band-box. I naturally had recourse to my hands to sustain my weight, but they found no better support, so that I sunk altogether among the broken mummies, with a crash of bones, rags, and wooden cases, which raised such a dust as kept me motionless for a quarter of an hour . . . The purpose of my researches was to rob the Egyptians of their papyri.

But the ancients did not sit up and tell the hulking Belzoni what they thought of him. The spirit that could make Khaem-wase believe that Nenefer-ka-ptah and Princess Ahura could do just that to him when he went to rob their tomb was gone for ever.

Jean Jacques Rifaud, a mercurial Marseillais who beat his Arabs for not understanding Provençal, was a sculptor and excavator who spent more than forty years in Egypt, where he went in 1805 with the sole object of acquiring portable antiquities. Sometimes he carved his name and the date on the statues he found. 'The Arabs laugh at excavators,' he wrote:

the trouble and expense incurred seem absurd to them, and each has his own explanation of the antics of European antiquaries. Some take them for pagans who push infamy so far as to caress statues. They have seen statues being moistened with the tongue to see what kind of stone they were made of, and they have concluded that the statues were being kissed. According to others the marbles that we take from them contain gold, that we alone have the secret of extracting.

Sir Frederick Henniker, Bart, gives a lively though derisive picture of the rapidity with which Egypt was being stripped of its portable antiquities during the first half of the last century. Sir Frederick was more of an athlete than archaeologist, being the first recorded European to have climbed the second pyramid, a dangerous attempt now prohibited. He reached Alexandria on 17th October, 1820:

I have been on shore; the very stepping stones at the water's edge are a mass of antiquities about to quit their native country, with strong letters of recommendation from Messrs——and——(the consuls) to the respective governments of England and France; defaced hieroglyphics and noseless statues sent for no visible reason, unless for ballast. Who would imagine that such things are to be paid for? If such are the pieces of the gorgeous palaces that are worth carrying away, there will scarcely be left a wreck behind! I may return to Rome to look at obelisks, and to London and Paris for all else of Egyptian labour.

His farewell to Egypt has nothing to do with the case, yet it shows at least that there yet remained some staunch British resistance to the glamour of Egypt's call:

Adieu to the Nile, the least romantic but most useful of rivers; the waters of which are the dirtiest but most beneficial in the world; on whose bank there is scarcely one spot that would attract the attention of an artist, nor an object of antiquity comparable to the Parthenon and Colisoeum.

The artist Nestor l'Hôte, in the fifth of his *Letters from Egypt*, dated October, 1839, says that what was left of the Ramses II temple at Abydos after the invading sands and the barbarians had done with it had been cruelly finished off by 'speculators in antiquities, consuls and others, who in this respect have no reason to envy the vandalism of the Turks or the unhappy renown of Lord Elgin'. The famous chronological Table of Kings had been in this temple. The twelve-foot-long relief carving had given a list of fifty-two kings, and was of immense historical interest. It had been removed by the French Consul Mimaut, on whose death it was sold to the British Museum. 'It seems,' wrote l'Hôte, 'that when taking out this stone, they did not want to leave anything of the room that contained it; three of its walls have almost vanished, and the fourth retains only the bottom half of the figures of divinities that decorated it.'

Ernest Renan, the French philosopher, wrote in *Revue des deux Mondes*, in 1865:

> For more than half a century Egyptian antiquities have been pillaged. Purveyors to museums have gone through the country like vandals; to secure a fragment of a head, a piece of inscription, precious antiquities were reduced to fragments. Nearly always provided with a consular instrument, these avid destroyers treated Egypt as their own property. The worst enemy, however, of Egyptian antiquities is still the English or American traveller. The names of these idiots will go down to posterity since they were careful to inscribe themselves on famous monuments across the most delicate drawings.

Purveyors to museums were not the only destroyers of antique buildings. The administration used them as handy quarries with ignorant disregard of their significance. In 1859 Vivien de Saint Martin gave a list of some of the monuments that had suffered in this manner since the Great French Expedition:

> Elephantine has been stripped of its lovely temple which exists only in the great work of the Commission. Armant has yielded to a sugar refinery the most beautiful half of the portal. The small temples of Esna, El Kab, the Typhonium of Edfu, the great tomb of Onnofre at Saqqara, half of the hypogeum of Lycopolis are lost for ever. The ground excavated unceasingly by the *fellahin* has given up to them an enormous quantity of precious objects, which have been sold, broken up, melted down, dispersed to the four winds.

And what was the attitude to all this of the ruler of it all—the man to whom Father Géramb had lightly said that it would be scarcely respectable to return from Egypt without a mummy in one hand and a crocodile in the other?

Mohamed Ali, when urged to save the antiquities, retaliated by saying, 'How can I do so, and why should you ask me, since it is the Europeans themselves who are their chief enemies?'

12 The Conservators

ALL was not destruction, happily. There yet remained disinterested travellers with loftier purposes than to stuff their luggage with saleable antiquities. One of those who came to see, to enjoy, and to record was the Swiss, John Lewis Burckhardt, who had studied Arabic at Cambridge. He affected Arab dress and travelled under the name Sheik Ibrahim; but not always successfully. A native of Amara, far down in Nubia, who had seen Burckhardt there, said of him, 'He was not one of the true believers. Instead of giving thanks to God after eating, he only put a small piece of bread, which remained over, into his pocket, contrary to the practice of the true Mussulmans, who never use on the next day what is left on the preceding.'

Burckhardt discovered the ruins of Petra, in north-west Arabia; and in Nubia he discovered a site whose name has become even more widely known than that of Petra in recent years. On 22nd March, 1813, he passed the village of Ballana and ascended a steep sandy mountain:

. . . on the west side the mountain bears the name of Ebsambai. I left my guide with the camels, and descended an almost perpendicular cleft, choaked with sand, to view the temple of Ebsambal, of which I had heard many magnificent descriptions. It stands about twenty feet above the surface of the water, entirely cut out of the almost perpendicular rocky side of the mountain, and in complete preservation. In front of the temple are six erect colossal figures, representing juvenile persons, placed in narrow recesses. The temple was no doubt dedicated to the worship of Isis.

What he had just seen was the smaller of the two temples at what we now call Abu Simbel. The 'juvenile persons' were figures of Ramses the Great—Ramses II—and his wife Nefertari, for whom he built the temple in honour of the goddess Hathor. Reports of this beautiful little temple had already filtered through, as Burckhardt said. His great discovery was to follow by mere chance:

> Having, as I supposed, seen all the antiquities of Ebsambal, I was about to ascend the sandy side of the mountain by the same way I had descended; when having luckily turned more to the southward, I fell in with what is yet visible of four immense colossal statues cut out of the rock, at a distance of about two hundred yards from the temple: they stand in a deep recess, excavated in the mountain; but it is greatly to be regretted, that they are now almost entirely buried beneath the sands . . . The head which is above the surface has a most expressive, youthful, countenance, approaching nearer to the Grecian model of beauty, than that of any ancient Egyptian figure I have seen . . . I suspect, could the sand be cleared away, a vast temple would be discovered, to the entrance of which the above colossal figures probably serve as ornaments.

Burckhardt did not live to see the vast temple. He died in the same year that Giovanni Belzoni found the way in—1817—the same brawny Belzoni who had crashed through the coffins in the tombs at Thebes. This former professional strong-man had been engaged by the British Consul, Henry Salt, to carry out various archaeological excavations and removals, and now he was to explore the Abu Simbel temple that Burckhardt had reported. Even the great Belzoni was taken aback by the mightiness of the task:

> On approaching this temple the hope I had formed of opening its entrance vanished at once, for the amazing accumulation of sand was such that it appeared an impossibility ever to reach the door. I calculated, that the doorway could not be less than thirty-five feet below the surface of the sand, and to attempt to make an aperture straight through it to the door would have been like making a hole in the water. Besides, the natives were wild people, totally unaccustomed to such labour, and knew nothing of working for money; indeed they were ignorant of money altogether.

And that was not all; the Kachef was a local tyrant, and opposed to the operations unless he was heavily bribed by the foreigners. Accompanying Giovanni Belzoni was Salt's secretary, the artist Henry William Beechey, who was later the biographer of Sir Joshua Reynolds. Also with him were two other Giovannis in Salt's service, Giovanni Finati and Giovanni d'Athanasi. On the way up they were fortunate to encounter two British naval officers, James Mangles and the Honourable Charles Irby, who joined their enterprise. Fortunate, because when the Kachef had seen to it that they were short of labour, the artist and the captains took off their jackets and shovelled sand. That was on most of the twenty-two days of hard labour in the hottest month of a scorching Nubian summer.

Belzoni wrote in his *Researches and Operations in Egypt,* that in the last days of July, 1817,

> we discovered a broken cornice, the next day the torus, and of course the frize under, which made us almost sure of finding the door next day. Early in the morning of the 1st. of August we went to the temple in high spirits, at the idea of entering a newly discovered place. We soon made the passage wider, and entered the finest and most extensive excavation in Nubia. It was evidently a very large place, but our astonishment increased, when we found it to be one of the most magnificent of temples, enriched with beautiful intaglios, paintings, colossal figures, &c.

The temple of Ramses II at Abu Simbel was in fact unique, a superb feat of ancient architecture and engineering. World-wide interest was aroused in Abu Simbel when the water of the lake behind the High Dam, constructed during the 'sixties of this century, threatened to submerge it. A bold scheme to raise the entire temple in one quarried-out block, by means of hydraulic jacks, was abandoned because sufficient money was not subscribed in response to an appeal by U.N.E.S.C.O. It was finally decided to cut the temple into large blocks, transport them to higher ground above, and reassemble them there.

Burckhardt, on his way up river to discover Abu Simbel, met an English Member of Parliament, Thomas Legh, on his way back after penetrating as far as Ibrim—a feat which no European had accomplished since the unknown Italian traveller of 1589. Accompanying Legh was his friend the Reverend Charles Smelt, and as guide they had an American named Barthow, whose qualification for the job was fluent Arabic and no more. Legh says he 'had traded many years in the Red Sea'.

The M.P. and the parson travelled for curiosity and adventure, yet they were not above taking a mummy or two if they came upon them. This led to one hair-raising adventure, the outcome of which did not reflect at all to their credit. A Greek had told them about a mummy-pit near Manfalut; and on the morning of 30th March, 1813, they ferried across the river there and approached four Arabs to be their guides. These men consulted together, and Barthow overheard them 'muttering something about danger' and thought he heard the expression, 'If one must die, all must die.'

'This excited our suspicions,' says Legh laconically; but 'I had by me a brace of pocket pistols, which I concealed in my trowsers.' Three of the Arabs went with them into the underground tunnels, torches blazing, while the fourth remained above with the boat crew. The intricacies of the winding galleries resembled a labyrinth, and the place was full of bats, flying and hanging from the roof. Legh accidentally scorched one when he raised his torch at the entrance.

> We had not gone far before the heat became excessive. I found my breathing extremely difficult, my head began to ache most violently, and I had a most distressing sensation of fulness about the heart. We felt we had gone too far. At this moment the torch of the first Arab went out; I saw him fall on his side; and I heard a rattling noise in his throat—he was dead. The Arab behind me advanced to his assistance, and stopped. I observed him appear faint, totter, and fall in a moment—he also was dead. The third Arab came forward, and made an effort to approach the bodies, but stopped short. We looked at each other in silent horror. The danger increased every instant; our torches burnt faintly; our breathing became more difficult. There was no time to be lost— the American, Barthow, cried to us to "take courage", and we began to move back as fast as we could. We heard the remaining Arab imploring our assistance, and upbraiding us with deserting him. But we were obliged to leave him to his fate. To stay was death.
>
> Our appearance alone without our guides naturally astonished the Arab who had remained at the entrance of the cavern; and he anxiously enquired for his friends. To have confessed they were dead would have excited suspicion, he would have supposed we had murdered them, and have alarmed the inhabitants to pursue us and revenge the death of their friends. We replied therefore they

were coming, and were employed in bringing out the mummies we had found. We lost no time in mounting our asses, and passed hastily by the village to regain the ferry.

Unfortunately for the travellers the third Arab did not die down there. He got out and spread the alarm. They were haled before the Kachef by a menacing crowd armed with swords and spears. Luckily the Kachef was so frightened of Mohamed Ali Pasha, whose *firman* for travel they held, that he felt obliged to protect them. And luckily, too, the brace of pistols had never been produced. The Kachef asked the Arab who had remained on the surface by what means these unarmed infidels could have been supposed to kill his friends in the vaults:

He replied, *by magic*, for he had seen me burning something on our first entrance. This was the bat I had accidentally scorched. Our cause now began to wear a better complexion: part of the crowd, who treated the idea of magic with contempt, believed us innocent, and the rest probably dreaded the imaginary powers with which we had been invested.

It was finally agreed that they should pay two Spanish dollars to each of the widows, and the same as a present to the Sheik of the village; after which they were allowed to resume their voyage.

One is surprised that Thomas Legh, M.P., should include such an infelicitous tale in his published narrative, especially as it is clear that no pains were taken to ascertain whether the men were really dead. And the story told at the pit's mouth to the poor Arab who remained there put the finishing stroke to their callous conduct. It may reflect an attitude towards 'natives' that has not yet been surmounted by Westerners.

Our Member of Parliament also possessed a black Nubian slave, given him by the Kachef of Derr, and went to some pains to smuggle him out of Egypt, whence the export of Negroes was forbidden. At the hour of siesta,

when the soldiers and officers of the custom-house were asleep, my servant walked with the boy into the desert to the west of the town (Alexandria), and a boat from our ship conveyed them on board, without the least suspicion.

We are left to wonder how the boy from the Nubian wastes fared in early 19th-century England, for that master of

chicanery, Thomas Legh Esquire, M.P., never mentions him
again.

One of my favourite travellers is Edward de Montule, who
sat his camel wearing a top hat, with his dog in a basket by the
saddle. He retained his top hat when descending the mummy-
pits on the shoulders of an Arab, and surely wore it when he
climbed the second pyramid on 31st January, 1819. This was
just before Sir Frederick Henniker's climb to the top. De
Montule dared not go beyond the edge of the coping at the
south-east angle, on which he 'subscribed' his name.

Soon after his arrival in Alexandria he made a drawing of
Pompey's Pillar, and then descended to the canal,

> which my dog approached, who only smelt at the water and retired;
> I tasted it and finding it agreeable, drank copiously, from which,
> at night, I became so disordered, that a dose of physic would not
> have proved equally powerful in its effects. I was very ill the ensuing
> day. I had recourse to a remedy almost uniformly efficacious with
> me, I ate raw onions.

At Silsila, de Montule believed he had made a first discovery
of the vast sandstone quarries 'from which were probably drawn
the greater part of the monuments of Egypt'. In this last
supposition he was perfectly right, but he had not read his
Denon, else he would have known that the French had been
there before him. This was the place where Jomard and
Chabrot had found the old hermit when their boat was driven
ashore on the rocks. Their account in the *Description de l'Egypte*
had not, of course, been published before he left France.

De Montule found the lovely temple at Abydos, that Dr
Granger discovered in 1731, 'so buried in the sand as to present
no favourable point of view for a drawing. By means of some
researches made under the orders of M. Drovetti (the French
Consul) you penetrate beneath the ceiling of the temple.'

Knowing Drovetti, we suspect that his 'researches' were in
truth searches. He was an avid collector of portables. At any
rate de Montule got in and observed that 'what renders this
building peculiarly curious, are vaultings, or arcades, sculptured
in blocks of stone 25 feet in length, which must have produced
a very singular effect in Egypt, and fully proves that the
architects were not so completely bound to adopt determinate
rules as is generally conceived'.

At Hermopolis he saw the superb portico of twelve columns that had aroused the admiration of Claude Sicard a hundred years before, and of many travellers since, including the enterprising Denon. De Montule writes sadly:

> The Europeans frequently complain, without reason, of the barbarity of the modern Egyptians. An Italian whom I ought to name in order to signalize him for a Vandal, and who is employed by the Pasha, wishes to abolish this portico to make lime.

And lime the Italian made of it. Within five years this most impressive monument had gone for ever.

Top-hatted Edward de Montule and his dog visited the colossi of Memnon on 29th December, 1818. He would have nothing of the Memnon myth. He was an astute observer who might have made a good archaeologist fifty years later, when hieroglyphs were understood. He wrote:

> These two statues, still erect upon the plain, have never served but as guardians of a palace or temple situated in their rear. The columns of the temple are sunk to the capitals, near one of which we found a flat stone, broken into two pieces, and covered with hieroglyphics: it was either an altar or a tablet of the law, being 12 feet wide and 30 feet long.

He was right about the temple. It was a vast mortuary temple of Amenophis III, 1405 B.C., of which the foundations were sufficiently excavated by Dr Herbert Ricke, of the Swiss Institute of Cairo, in 1963, to give the plan. The 'tablet of the law' was in fact a stela containing a dedication of the temple, and it stood at the usual 'station of the King' against the rear wall of the holy of holies. It can be seen today, mended and re-erected by the Egyptian Antiquities Service.

'The two pyramids of Dashur,' wrote de Montule, 'interested me the more from a curious statement respecting them, which was made by M. Drovetti, being as follows:

> "During the first years of my residence in Egypt," said he, "I never thought or dreamed of any thing but antiquities. One night in particular, I imagined that I had penetrated into a pyramid, which had not yet been explored. I proceeded for some time along a corridor, dark and silent, when, on a sudden, I conceived myself to be in a vast chamber, from which a narrow passage led to a second, at the top of which, at about twenty feet from the soil, I

saw an opening. As time and space count for nothing in a dream, I sent for ladders, and perceived, in the middle of another apartment, a carcase extended upon a bed; near which burned a sepulchral lamp. This vision struck me so forcibly, that I resolved to visit the pyramids of Dashur, the interior of which was not yet known. I caused the rubbish from the first passage to be cleared away, and on viewing the first chamber my astonishment was excited, being precisely similar to that figured to me in my dream; out of this a passage presented itself, into which I crawled with pain, and found a second, when raising my regard, how was I stupefied on beholding, at the summit, a square aperture precisely similar to that my dream had depictured. I sent for a ladder, and got into the corridor, which conducted me to a third apartment, but as to the bed, the lamp, and the body, not a vestige of either appeared."

'On reciting this adventure, M. Drovetti still seemed astonished, and almost displayed symptoms of terror at the similarity of his dream with the actual contemplation of facts. The pyramid in question is precisely what he described it to be.'

13 The Rivals

BERNARDINO Drovetti, who dreamed of chambered
pyramids, was the doyen of the diplomatic corps in
Egypt. He had served as a colonel during Bonaparte's
Egyptian Expedition, and served as Consul-General of France
for most of the ensuing thirty years. He had a high reputation
as an antiquary. The Baroness Minutoli wrote:

> None is better acquainted with the monuments than he. It is
> much to be desired, that he would communicate to the learned
> world the fruits of so many years' study and observation.

The learned world would have been but little enriched by
anything that Drovetti was capable of publishing. Forty years
later Henry Rhind the Scot, one of the first true archaeologists,
was to write sadly of the disordered state in which the consuls-
general of France and England had left the tombs at Thebes
which he himself was trying to examine scientifically:

> . . . the mode of procedure was by no means of a satisfactory
> nature. Nearly all their explorations were conducted under the
> supervision of agents whose instructions, while it is only just
> to believe that they had in some respects broad scientific ends in
> view, would seem, by some oversight, to have been to attend
> to the accumulation of relics, rather than to the circumstances
> under which these were found. At least we look in vain for
> sufficient accounts of the latter.

Rhind was a gentle and polite man, or he would have said
bluntly that to ransack tombs without giving any description
of their pristine state, and to sell the objects pillaged from them

without noting where they came from, contributed nothing whatsoever to knowledge.

The French-naturalized Piedmontese Drovetti was not only the representative of a friendly nation, but also the confidant of the Viceroy Mohamed Ali. Thus he enjoyed special privileges by which he profited to excavate the soil of Egypt in every direction. De Montule, who often talked with him in Thebes in 1818, wrote, 'I envy the fate of M. Drovetti, who is daily the witness of fresh discoveries. The Arabians, by whom he is adored, uniformly convey to him the result of their labours. In the midst of the ruins of Karnak, the finest of Thebes, the most splendid of Egypt and the world, rises a portal sixty feet high, where M. Drovetti has caused an earthen house to be constructed, from whence he appears to command the precious relics of antiquity that surround him.'

Henry Salt, the British Consul, was granted plenty of *firmans* too, and put on a fine display to impress the local people. Forbin wrote in his *Voyage au Levant:* 'Salt, English consul, was established with a numerous suite, under tents in the Valley of Kings. He presided at the excavations that the Society of Antiquaries of London was having made at the most important points of Thebes. Plenty of money, plenty of presents have won for him the affection of the Arabs.'

The privileges extended by the Pasha to these two, and the liberty he gave them, aroused in both an avidity and a rivalry so intense that they were obliged to come to a gentlemen's agreement about the areas which each would recognize as the exclusive zone of operation of the other. Between them they staked out the whole of the Nile valley, and saw to it that any newcomer was warned off by the local Kachef, or if persistent, was left without any labourers for his excavations.

Henry Salt fancied himself as artist and literary man. He had studied painting under Joseph Farington, R.A., and was something of a draughtsman; but as a poet he was no great shakes:

> Egypt, renowned of old, demands my song.
> High favor'd Land, where Nilus sweeps along
> His course majestick, with full flowing stream,
> And back reflects to-day the Sun's bright beam;
> Sweep on in triumph, noble River, sweep

> Thy welcome waters to the thirsty deep . . .
> Oh! how I love along thy banks to stray,
> And watch the fish that on thy bosom play.

Salt accompanied Viscount Valencia to Abyssinia in 1803 as secretary and artist, and afterwards journeyed there on his own, writing a book about it. In 1816 he arrived in Egypt as Consul-General, with some reputation as an antiquary for having found a Greek inscription at Axum. 'He undoubtedly got it into his self-important head that he was a valuable contributor to nascent Egyptological science,' wrote H. R. Hall in the *Journal of Egyptian Archaeology, 1915.* 'But his contributions to Egyptology were as valueless as his poetry.' Salt believed that he had the clue to decipherment of the hieroglyphs; but 'Salt's claim to originality is only fit to set up in the region of Humbugia,' wrote Sir William Gell to Thomas Young in 1826. 'For I have myself sent to Egypt all the inventions of yourself and Champollion as fast as they came out. I understand that Salt went crazy on the subject of *his own inventions,* and told them all that you and Champollion knew nothing about it and that he was the only real discoverer. Whenever Champollion has not published, Salt is generally wrong, which corroborates the proof of his having seen what was printed.'

As his chief agent in the field, Salt engaged the 6 foot 8 inch Giovanni Belzoni, who was too proud, however, to consider himself in any respect Salt's servant. Belzoni's first task was to move the colossal head of Memnon—actually Ramses II—from the Ramesseum at Thebes to the river and get it down to Alexandria for embarkation, a labour that only a Hercules of muscle and determination like Belzoni could have performed. The rose granite head is 2·67 metres high and weighs $7\frac{1}{2}$ tons. Belzoni had it dragged on rollers, inch by inch, across the soft fields and dykes nearly three miles to the Nile. It was sold to the British Museum by Salt and Burckhardt in 1817, and is still one of the most impressive pieces of the Egyptian section.

Salt's interpreter was the Greek, Giovanni d'Athanasi, known to all as Yanni, who wrote a rather waspish *Researches and Discoveries under the Direction of Henry Salt Esq.* Of Belzoni he said, 'Mr B. was not long in meeting with difficulties, for besides the disadvantages of an impatient and intractable temperament, his interpreter was a drunken Copt, who, unable long to brook the bad treatment he experienced with Mr B., did not serve him with zeal and fidelity.'

He says also that Belzoni's famous opening of the second pyramid at Giza took place when Salt had sent him back to Cairo to deposit some heavy antiquities dug up at Thebes. Instead of returning at once to Thebes, where Salt awaited them, Belzoni obtained permission to make 'slight excavation round the pyramids' by misrepresenting his relations to Salt during his absence. This was at the time when Belzoni discovered the finest, deepest tomb in the Valley of the Kings, that of Seti I, builder of the temple at Abydos. Belzoni made a model of this tomb which he exhibited in Europe in 1819, much to d'Athanasi's envy:

> Without the name of Mr. Salt, and without his money, Belzoni could never have gone into Upper Egypt, nor even to France for his amusement. I declare Mr. Belzoni was but the servant of Mr. Salt, and all he has published in his name was done in Mr. Salt's name and moreover by direction of Mr. Salt.

Mr and Mrs Belzoni made themselves a comfortable residence in the Seti tomb while work was going on there. Edward de Montule doffed his topper to enter when they made him welcome at Christmas, in 1818.

> The various chambers were successively and brilliantly illuminated by rows of candles stuck on boards and carried by men who moved from place to place as required. One can give no idea of the splendour of this subterranean palace lit up in this manner. In a small apartment known as the side board room, our repast was served.

This word-picture was drawn by Dr E. Hogg, a Glasgow M.D. practising in Naples, who did not in fact pass through Egypt until 1832, long after the Belzonis had gone; but the description of a festive occasion underground was still valid. Dr Hogg was using the Belzoni tomb to return hospitality of neighbouring tomb-dwellers, Robert Hay and his artists, whom we shall mention shortly.

Tomb-dwelling was not unusual for antiquaries of the period, and modern archaeologists still find them handy for temporary homes. In 1960 I was guest of Dr Ricardo Caminos of Brown University in a rock-cut shrine at Silsila which he was publishing. We could not have been more comfortable, with the work table at one end, the dining table in the middle, and the wine cellar at the other end.

R. de Buissierre describes another troglodyte of Thebes in 1824:

> Wilkinson lives in one of the tombs of the Libyan chain; to reach it we climbed for half an hour among steep tracks. Eventually we arrived at our tomb; it is arranged with taste, furnished in the Egyptian style, distributed among several chambers decorated with frescoes; a pleasant coolness reigns there.

The Wilkinson he went to see was Sir John Gardner Wilkinson, one of the greatest names in early archaeology of Egypt. He was one of the serious and constructive archaeologists who now began to appear in Egypt. Wilkinson published material on the early study of hieroglyphs, and his great *Manners and Customs of the Ancient Egyptians*. The three volumes of *Manners and Customs* were compiled from a study of the wall paintings in Egyptian tombs at a time when scarcely anything could be understood of the hieroglyphic inscriptions, yet its fine woodcuts of scenes that have since been lost are still consulted by archaeologists, who pay respect to their accuracy.

Another serious visitor to Egypt was the landed gentleman, Robert Hay, who devoted his life and wealth to making drawings, plans and copies of inscriptions in Egyptian monuments. His papers and drawings are in fifty-eight volumes in the British Museum, and they are of the greatest value today in view of subsequent damage to the monuments. On two of his trips he took the artist Joseph Bonomi with him. Together they made plaster casts of battle scenes in the Beit el Wali temple in Nubia, and of one of the colossal heads of Ramses II at Abu Simbel. When Amelia Edwards, founder of the Chair of Egyptology at the University of London, went to Abu Simbel in 1873, she was so distressed to see flakes of plaster still mottling the handsome countenance of Ramses that she ordered gallons of strong coffee to be brewed, with which the sailors of her boat stained the plaster to match the stone.

But the deeds of sage men generally make plain reading,

unhappily; and when we have paid them the respect that is due to them, we turn back to the foibles of Salt, Drovetti and Belzoni for the drama of human failings.

During this time Salt had added to the gaiety of nations by getting married, writes Bryn Davies in the *Bulletin* of the Faculty of Arts, Cairo, May, 1934. There was certainly an international flavour about this unusual romance. According to the Count Marcellus, a French traveller, continues Bryn Davies,

> an Austrian merchant in Alexandria had told his agent in Leghorn that if he could find a young girl with nothing better to do in Europe, he might send her to him in Egypt. Three months later a Venus of seventeen landed in Alexandria, whom he greeted with joy and decided to marry as soon as a convenient time had elapsed. One day Salt passed under her window, was struck by her beauty, proposed, and was accepted on the spot. The Austrian was furious and complained to his Consulate . . . The question at issue then resolved itself into two heads: *a*) Whether the laws of commerce contain any stipulation that allows of Paul seizing merchandise consigned to Peter while that merchandise is still in bond; *b*) If so does not Paul owe Peter what he has laid out on the article in question. After a prolonged exchange of notes a third Consulate was called in as arbiter and decided in favour of Salt on payment of the costs. Marcellus lunched at dawn with Salt and his wife in Cairo and found her a charming blonde well worth a law suit.

It seems a peculiar time to have lunch; however it did not deter the blonde Venus from entertaining them after lunch with 'Tanti Palpiti' and other airs of Rossini on the grand piano that Salt had imported from Europe. She made him a devoted wife for the few years they were together, for she died in childbirth five years later.

Shortly before the marriage, which took place in 1819, Belzoni describes a conference between Salt and Drovetti at which he was present, to settle the respective spheres of operation of the two rivals.

> Mr. Drovetti, with all the complaisance possible, invited the consul and myself into his habitation among the ruins of Karnak. We were regaled with sherbet and lemonade, and our discourse turned on our next expedition to the Isle of Philae; when I happened to say, that, as I had to take the obelisk from that island down the cataract, I feared it was too late in the season, as the water would

not serve at the cataract to float and launch down a boat adequate to support such a weight. On hearing this, Mr. Drovetti said that those rogues at Aswan had deceived him; that they promised many times to bring down the said obelisk for him, but that they only promised to do it to extort money from him.

The obelisk was one of which Belzoni had taken possession in 1815 for Salt, who had a *firman* from the Pasha. Salt had ceded it to the scholar and Member of Parliament William J. Bankes, who intended to have it removed to England, and who had asked Belzoni to get it down the river for him. They told all this to Drovetti, who, nursing his fury, grandly ceded the rights he still maintained he had in it to Mr Bankes. 'This was not a compliment to our consul,' comments Belzoni, who believed that the gift was prompted by Drovetti's realization that he could never get the great thing out himself:

> I thought this was another present, made to Mr Bankes like the cover of the sarcophagus made to me, which was so far buried among the rocks of Gurna, that all their efforts could not prevail to take it out.

He may well have been right. The obelisk was twenty-two feet long, and it weighed about six tons. It had been set up in honour of the goddess Isis of Philae by Ptolemy IX and his wife Cleopatra, according to Sir E. A. Wallis Budge, about 240 B.C. Salt and Drovetti would not of course have known this, because the hieroglyphic inscriptions were not understood. But, says Wallis Budge, the obelisk has special interest in connection with Egyptian decipherment, for with the help of a Greek inscription painted on the pedestal, William Bankes was able, in 1816, to identify the cartouche that contains the name of Cleopatra. It was some years before Champollion claimed to have deciphered this queen's name.

There were three inscriptions in Greek on the base of the obelisk, the longest of which is a complaint to the king that

> those travellers who visit Philae, generals and inspectors, and royal officials, and scribes, and chief officers of police, and all the other officers who are in the service of the Government, and the armed guards who are in their following, and the rest of their servants, compel us to pay the expenses of their maintenance while they are here.

The King's order that the temple be relieved of this crippling imposition is also painted on the base.

Even the mighty Belzoni had some trouble loading the obelisk on the boat at Philae:

> . . . the pier appeared quite strong enough to bear at least forty times the weight it had to support; but, alas! when the obelisk came gradually on from the sloping bank, and all its weight rested on it, the pier, with the obelisk, and some of the men, took a slow movement, and majestically descended into the river, wishing us better success.

Belzoni and his men fished it out of the mud, and eventually the obelisk reached England. But it was not until 1839 that it was finally set up at William Bankes's country seat, Kingston Lacey, Wimborne, Dorset, in the presence of the Duke of Wellington.

But Belzoni had not finished with the disputed obelisk when he sent it on its way down river. Returning to Thebes, he went to look over some of the ground allotted to Salt for excavation in the temple of Karnak. When he had finished, and was leaving:

> We met an Arab running towards us, crying, from having received a severe beating from our opponents, merely because he served, and was faithful to us, as far as an Arab can be. This would have been another motive to create some altercation, but it had no effect; I took no notice of it, and was going on straight to Luxor. I was about three hundred yards from the great propylon, when I saw a group of people running towards us; they were about thirty Arabs, headed by two Europeans, agents of Mr. Drovetti. On their approaching, Mr. Lebulo was first, and the renegado Rossignano second, both Piedmontese, and countrymen of Mr. Drovetti. Lebulo began his address to me, by asking, what business I had to take away an obelisk that did not belong to me; and that I had done so many things of this kind to him, that I should not do any more. Meanwhile he seized the bridle of my donkey with one hand, and with the other he had hold of my waistcoat, and stopped me from proceeding any farther; he had also a large stick hung to his wrist by a string. By this time my servant was assailed by a number of Arabs, two of whom were constantly in the service of Mr. Drovetti. At the same moment, the renegado Rossignano reached within four yards of me, and with all the rage of a ruffian, levelled a double-barrelled gun at my breast, loading me with all the imprecations that a villain could invent; by this time my

servant was disarmed, and overpowered by numbers, and in spite of his efforts, took his pistols from his belt. The two gallant knights before me, I mean Lebulo and Rossignano, escorted by the two other Arabian servants of Mr. Drovetti, both armed with pistols, and many others armed with sticks, continued their clamorous imprecations against me, and the brave Rossignano, still keeping the gun pointing at my breast, said, that it was time that I should pay for all that I had done to them. The courageous Lebulo said, with all the emphasis of an enraged man, that he was to have one-third of the profit derived from the selling of that obelisk, when in Europe, according to a promise from Mr. Drovetti, had I not stolen it from the Island of Philae. My situation was not pleasant, surrounded by a band of ruffians like those, and I have no doubt, that if I had attempted to dismount, the cowards would have despatched me on the ground, and said that they did it in defence of their lives, as I had been the aggressor. I thought the best way was to keep on my donkey, and look at the villains with contempt. I told Lebulo to let me proceed on my way, and that if I had done anything wrong, I should be ready to account for it; but all was to no purpose. Their rage had blinded them out of their senses.

While this was going on, I observed another band of Arabs running towards us. When they came nearer, I saw Mr. Drovetti himself among them, and close to him a servant of his, armed with pistols. On his arrival before me, Mr. Drovetti demanded, in a tone not inferior to that of his disciples, what reason or authority I had to stop his people from working. I told him I knew nothing of what he meant, and that I found myself extremely ill used by his own people, and that he must answer for their conduct. In an authoritative tone he desired I should dismount, which I refused to do. At this moment a pistol was fired behind me, but I could not tell by whom. I was determined to bear much, sooner than come to blows with such people, who did not blush to assail me all in a mass; but when I heard the pistol fired behind my back, I thought it was high time to sell my life as dear as I could.

It seems that the pistol-shot gave Drovetti a jump too, and made him realize that the fracas could end in tragedy with serious consequences to his diplomatic self. He changed his tone, smoothed everybody down, and said no more about the obelisk. But Belzoni was completely disgusted. 'What an idea of European civilization such an event must give the Arabs,' he concluded sadly, and soon afterwards he left Egypt for good.

Salt died in Egypt in 1827, and Drovetti died in a mental asylum at Turin, in 1852. It is ironical that a large and important part of the antiquities collected by Salt, who worked for Britain, was bought by the French Government; while one of the great collections made by Drovetti, who worked for France, is the principal part of the great collection at Turin; and another collection of Drovetti's was acquired for Berlin.

14 Extraction of a Zodiac

I N the spring of the year 1820 M. Sebastien Louis Saulnier
sat in his Paris office, 32 rue de Rivoli, pondering on the
great number of imposing yet rather uniform monuments
that were already beginning to clutter the collections of Europe.
He thought that the time had come to look beyond these
meaningless copies of the same kind of thing, and to aim at
some object of recognized importance, something individual
and even unique. Saulnier was a man of substance, a Deputy,
and a collector of antiquities which he was proud to turn over
to the nation, in the interest of science, at a profit.

After long reflection his choice rested on the great planisphere, the Zodiac relief on the ceiling of a room above the
temple of Dendera. He would cause it to be transported, he
wrote, 'to the bosom of intellectual Europe'.

It was a handsome piece of carving: two concentric circles
nearly 8 feet in diameter, showing what appeared to be a plan
of the heavens in symbolic signs including those of the zodiac.
The central disc was supported by the standing figures of four
women and eight kneeling hawk-headed gods. Likely enough,
thought M. Saulnier, the Zodiac served in the celebration of
Mysteries, when it was revealed to the initiates that the
divinities they adored were only symbols of the heavenly bodies.
Study of it might confirm the established belief that the ancient
Egyptians knew of the sphericity of the earth, the obliquity
of the ecliptic, the causes of eclipses: in fact that they were
scientific astronomers in remote antiquity.

That its antiquity was not so great as he supposed was an

ignorance shared by all the antiquarians of the day, for the decipherment of hieroglyphic writing was another two years in the future, and there was no one to tell him that this Zodiac ceiling was a product of the latter end of Egyptian history. Yet for all that it was an unusual piece, sure to bring him a high price. Its removal should be just possible, although it was an enormous stone, 12 feet long, 8 feet wide and 3 feet thick, weighing quite 60 tons.

Despite its size, it had remained modestly unperceived in its room up there on the roof of the temple through a long succession of centuries. It had suffered little damage; and keen-eyed travellers like Pococke, Bruce and Norden had passed that way without taking note of it. The patriot Saulnier proudly observes that it was first spotted by General Desaix during one of the most brilliant epochs of French military history, when he was pursuing the remnants of Murad Bey's army across the solitudes of the Thebaid. And it was Denon, whose enthusiasm for the arts had led him to share the perils and fatigues of the campaign, who was the first to draw the planisphere of Dendera. And it was the French scholars accompanying the Expedition in Egypt who made known to the world the importance of the moment. 'In fact,' concludes Saulnier, 'it had in a way become a national monument; and I felt sure that on its arrival in France it would be considered so and welcomed as a trophy of the army of France in Egypt.'

His decision was final: the great Zodiac of Dendera must be brought to France. A friend, master mason Lelorrain, who shared his enthusiasm over the project, agreed to take charge of the enterprise.

At the beginning of October, 1820, all was ready, and Lelorrain embarked with his equipment. Unfortunately when he arrived in Cairo the notorious Drovetti had been reappointed French Consul-General. This was a nasty setback, for Drovetti and his British rival Henry Salt had assumed to themselves an unwritten right to just about all that remained of the Pharaohs, and they saw to it that every sort of obstacle, legal or physical, was put in the way of any stranger who dared venture on their preserves.

Lelorrain realized that he would have to use cunning to succeed, and that it was of first importance to keep the true object of his voyage a complete secret. Fortunately the nature of the project was so unusual, and the difficulties of accomplishment so great, that it would have been hard to guess what he was after. He allowed everyone to suppose that he was bound for Thebes where most amateur diggers tried their luck.

He had no trouble in getting a *firman* of safe conduct from the Pasha, who wisely took no sides in the France-versus-England scramble for antiques, and who may have taken a malicious pleasure in helping fresh contestants into the fray.

He hired a boat and left Cairo accompanied by a janissary of the Pasha's guard and an interpreter who deserves more than the anonymity in which M. Saulnier passes him down to history, for he proved to be the saviour of the enterprise.

It was a whim of fate that on the eve of departure, even as Lelorrain was loading the boat with equipment to purloin an ancient monument of Egypt, a babe was being born in France, at Boulogne-sur-mer, rue de la Balance, who was destined to put a final stop to this free-for-all lifting of Egyptian relics. It was 11th February, 1821; and the babe was christened Auguste Ferdinand François Mariette. His day was thirty-five years off, when he would rule the antiquities of Egypt; yet Lelorrain was soon to have his first taste of opposition from the uncrowned kings of the Nile of his own day.

About halfway to Dendera all hands were called to manœuvre the boat through a difficult passage. Watching anxiously, Lelorrain noticed one man sitting alone on deck doing nothing at all. He asked the fellow angrily why he was idling at a time like that; to which the man replied blandly that he was not a member of the crew. He had been assigned by Salt to accompany the expedition as observer. Lelorrain, touched though he was by such solicitude, took the precaution of putting the candid emissary ashore without a moment's delay.

They arrived at Dendera in the middle of the night, and were made welcome by the Sheik of the village with oriental if rustic hospitality.

Lelorrain was up at first light, eager to set eyes on the great temple he had come so far to see and to despoil: the temple so imposing that rough soldiers of General Desaix's division halted unbid, stared and clapped their hands at sight of its portico of twenty-four enormous columns, surmounted by sculptured heads of the goddess Hathor, in those days still rich with the original colours of the Egyptians.

Centuries of accumulation had heaped debris so high around the temple that it reached nearly to the roof. Within, the stairway in the thickness of the wall that leads up there was hidden by rubbish. So Lelorrain toiled up the slope, and presently stood on the wide stone-flagged roof. But he did not pause to enjoy the early sunshine of the March morning. He strode immediately to a small building containing three rooms, went straight to the centremost, and looked anxiously at the ceiling.

There it was, the circular Zodiac, the priceless relic that he had come so far to find, still safe and sound in its place. He might so easily have found the sky glaring at him through a hole instead.

He examined its position carefully and satisfied himself that, thanks to the mound of debris, it would be possible to slide the disengaged monument down from the roof. But on one point he had been misinformed. The chamber was roofed by three huge slabs of stone; and the Zodiac did not occupy merely one of them, as he had been led to suppose, but spilled over a quarter of the centre slab as well. Dismay at being faced with cutting and transporting two stones instead of one was soon followed by another problem that demanded instant decision. He discovered that he was not the sole visitor at Dendera. Some English travellers were already camped there, making drawings, and they told him that they intended remaining there some time longer.

He realized that if he started operations now these people would be sure to talk about it when they moved elsewhere, exposing him to all the tricks of his experienced rivals in the antiquities trade. There was nothing for it but to maintain the mystery of his intentions. So he went on a tour.

He stopped off at Thebes but did not try to make any excavation, even as a blind. It was plain to see that the agents of the monopolists Messrs Salt and Drovetti had such influence on the lesser officials of the district, sometimes through presents and sometimes through pressure from above, that the men of Gurna village were intimidated and dared not offer even their labour for fear of reprisals, so that when Lelorrain arrived at

Thebes he could not have hired one man to turn a spade for him had he fancied to make an excavation.

With difficulty he acquired a couple of decorated coffin-lids and a few other objects of no unusual interest. They served to give a good impression that his mission in Egypt had been frustrated to the satisfaction of all, and as he slipped down the river towards Dendera he shuddered to think what would be in store for him there if his secret had leaked out. Just to make things more secure, he let it be known that he was bound for the shore of the Red Sea in order to make a collection of sea-shells. This ruse was a little too successful, for it was quickly relayed to the Consuls-General in Cairo and Alexandria with the additional embroidery that Lelorrain had been taken ill and forced to lie up in some village of the Thebaid.

M. Saulnier, back in Paris, received this disquieting news with the speed, he remarks drily, that envy and other vile passions of the human heart never fail to give to evil tidings. He had no means of communicating with his intrepid envoy, and the brave Lelorrain dared not write to him for mistrust of those through whose hands the letter must pass. Thus M. Saulnier passed his days in self-reproach for risking the health of his friend, and a considerable capital, in an enterprise of which he could now see only the inconveniences and the danger. Yet all the while Lelorrain was proceeding quietly down the river in excellent heart and carrying out the plan that was behind schedule only because of the interruption by the English artists.

He arrived at Dendera again on 18th April, 1821, when the weather was warming up, and learned to his satisfaction that the English had really gone. Now was his moment. He recruited twenty Arabs under a head man and led them, with his interpreter, to the ruins.

His first move was to build a scaffold up to the ceiling to support the stone when it was disengaged. Then straight away he was faced with the difficulty of making a hole through three feet of stone, through which to introduce the saw. He could not use his chisels for so formidable a task, else there would be none left for reducing the thickness of the stone, and hence its weight, when it was taken out. There was nothing for it but gunpowder, with all its risk of irreparable damage to the monument. He used it with infinite precaution, testing the strength of the powder until he had the right dose for making a succession of delicate blasts. But it took him two days in the blazing sun with a shade temperature of forty degrees Centigrade to get through to the chamber without hurting the Zodiac in any way. With a sigh of relief he imagined that the battle was won. But it had scarcely begun. He soon discovered that the saw could cut only one foot in a day; and since the three sides to be cut measured 24 feet in all, it was going to be a long job. Too long. He was in a hurry. His operation would not remain unperceived for many days more; and if he were discovered before he had finished, all would be lost. So he made two more holes with his gunpowder, and in this manner he could keep three saws going at once.

His Arabs, stimulated by promise of a generous reward, worked with incredible ardour; Lelorrain did not leave the job for an instant, so that he could keep constant watch on the movement of the saws. Then suddenly the great heat of the sun was too much for him. A terrible fever burnt him and it was impossible for him to move. It went on for a week, during which he would not send for the doctor at Farshut else all would have been discovered. Meanwhile it was of prime importance that the work go on; and this is where the interpreter proved his worth. He took his master's place, and there was not a minute's interruption to the work. A kindly Arab dosed Lelorrain with native remedies and he recovered his strength gradually.

When the sawing was finished the stones were at last hoisted clear on to the roof of the temple. It had taken twenty-two days to free the Zodiac.

The job of hauling it down to the Nile was quite as gruelling as the first part of the operation; for the nearest point at which Lelorrain had found suitable mooring for the boat was more than four miles away. They did well the first day, dragging the sledge with the large stone clear of the ruins; and next day they covered more than a mile. But by then the crushing weight had chewed up the wooden rollers he had brought to such an extent that they were useless.

Next day they replaced them with the few logs obtainable in the village. They were in a pulp before the day was out.

After that it was only by means of his tackles, his levers and the muscles of fifty Arabs that they could move the sledge at all. Day by day the ground covered became less until at the end they were taking twelve hours to advance sixty paces. The Arabs were exhausted by the heavy work for hours in the stifling heat, and often Lelorrain, though convalescent, was obliged to haul on the ropes himself. It required sixteen days of toil to drag the precious rock to the edge of the Nile.

It was the season of the Nile's fall, and the delay had created a vertical cliff twelve feet high above the boat. Lelorrain was obliged to have his men make a ramp of earth down to it. The sledge was hauled to the brink, anchored to a palm tree by a cable, and thirty men held ropes to check its descent. Lelorrain placed soaped planks on the ramp, and all was ready for the triumphal moment of embarking the Zodiac at last. But as soon as the sledge engaged the slippery planks the inert monster they had wearied themselves to move for so many days appeared to spring to life. It shot down the ramp like a thunder-bolt, spinning the rope-men into the air and snapping its cable like wool. Fortunately it did not land on the boat or it would have gone through the bottom like a torpedo. It toppled sideways off the ramp and plunged into soft mud six feet from the water's edge.

Lelorrain surveyed this last disaster in despair. But his Arabs were not dismayed. He had always treated them kindly and paid them liberally. In this moment of crisis they set to right away to rescue the ponderous stone. Within hours they had dug it out, and seemingly by sheer determination had inched it up and into the boat.

But they had scarcely wiped the sweat off their brows before a fresh peril set them moving fast. The boat was sinking. Water was entering by cracks that the intense heat had opened above the water-line. When the stone had been put aboard these cracks had been pushed below the surface. The valiant Arabs rose to the occasion once again. While some bailed ship frantically others tore off their gowns, jumped into the Nile, and began to caulk the leaks. With the amazing gift for improvisation that the Arabs have, the boat was soon soundly afloat, and it was safe to load the smaller stone.

The time had really come to say goodbye to his friends,

and this he did with real feeling of regret, for respect and affection had grown on both sides. Then he gave the order to cast off; but nothing happened. The owner of the boat refused to budge, saying that the waters had gone too low. Lelorrain knew that this was nonsense.

Angered yet even more puzzled, he cast around in his mind for the real motive. He remembered then that the news of his operations must have reached Cairo, because an American named Bradish had called at Dendera while they were still going on; and next day his interpreter told him that in an off-guard moment the boat-owner had boasted that an agent of Salt had offered him a thousand Turkish piastres to delay the departure of the Zodiac for three weeks.

Lelorrain sent an offer to the owner, of the same amount as the bribe, if he would leave immediately. The man fell on his knees swearing that his fidelity would never swerve again, and cast off without further ado.

Some days short of Cairo they were hailed by an approaching boat aboard which Lelorrain recognized a European, one of Salt's men. This envoy waved a document and called out that he was bearer of an order signed by Kaya Bey, the Grand Vizier, forbidding Lelorrain to take the Dendera Zodiac. Our Frenchman's reply was to run up his country's flag, declaring that his authority came from the Pasha himself and that anyone who tried to deprive him of the Zodiac would have to board a French ship by force and take the consequences. This bold front had its effect, and after a few minor threats to save face, the British agent sheered off.

In Cairo Lelorrain heard why this piracy had been attempted. The news had been brought back from Dendera by the American Bradish as he guessed it would be, and Salt was wild with rage because he had been on the point of attempting the Zodiac himself. His friend William Bankes had just sent him all the necessary equipment from London—the same Bankes for whom Belzoni had removed the obelisk from Philae. Salt hurried off to lay complaint to the Pasha; but the prince had no time to listen: he was foiling a plot to massacre all the Christians in Alexandria, and was preparing to go there in person to stop it. So Salt applied to Kaya Bey, an old friend, with the result that we have seen.

When the river hold-up failed, Salt followed the Pasha to Alexandria, where he had the impertinence to claim that the Zodiac was rightfully his because he had conducted excavations at Dendera long before Lelorrain had ever seen the place.

Maybe the Pasha was irritated by the greedy Englishman's persistence. He asked only one question: was Lelorrain's research authorized by himself? On being answered yes, he gave the Zodiac to Lelorrain, while some Turks in his entourage expressed astonishment that so hotly contended a case could be raised over two stones in a country where there were more than enough of them for all.

The liveliest interest marked the unloading of the stones at Marseilles. 'It was scarcely out of the ship,' wrote the correspondent of the *Journal de Paris,* 'when the divisional general, the prefect of the Department, and the mayor ran on to the pontoon where it had been placed . . . It was with an almost religious awe that I approached this antique monument.'

There was no wagon in Marseilles strong enough to carry the stones to Paris, so a special one had to be built. It delivered them safely in the first week of January, 1822.

Among the many distinguished visitors who came to see the Zodiac were Jollois, whose adventures with Napoleon's Expedition we have followed, and Devilliers who had been his co-artist in drawing the Zodiac for the *Description de l'Egypte* some twenty years before. What their feelings were, and their comments on seeing the mighty Zodiac thus laid low, were unhappily not recorded by M. Saulnier; but he marshals five pages of argument to justify its removal, the most persuasive being that the Zodiac would otherwise have fallen into English hands, for was not Salt practically on his way to get it when Lelorrain forestalled him?

The Zodiac remained on show pending disposal, and the public flocked to see the object of art, age and mystery. M. Saulnier, who liked to do things in the big way, hired François Gau to make a copy of the monument. Lithographs of this were run off quickly while interest was hot, advertised at five francs each at all print shops. Gau was already renowned for the albums of his Egyptian travels, and is better known to posterity as one of the famous architects of France.

Within the year the precious monument was acquired by King Louis XVIII for 150,000 francs, an enormous sum in those days. It remained in the royal library—which was later the *Bibliothèque Nationale*—until 1919 when it went to the Louvre, where it was placed in the Grand Gallery on the ground floor, No. D.38. Its neighbour was, ironically, the rose granite sarcophagus of Ramses III acquired from Salt in 1826. The Zodiac is now on the stairway.

Savants of the early 19th century were stirred to emotional controversy by the Dendera Zodiac. Some saw it as an astronomical document showing by the order of its signs the great antiquity of the edifice from which it had been taken. Others saw it correctly as an astrological monument of a late period. In fact the planisphere of Dendera dates from the end of the Ptolemaic or even the Roman period; and we can draw no conclusion whatsoever from it that the Egyptians were different from other ancient people of the East who believed that the sun turned around the Earth inside a circular Zodiac in twelve parts comprised of the twelve constellations that the sun appeared to cross in a year. This notion is represented on the Dendera Zodiac in a quite literal way. The circular zone—the sky—is supported by the four cardinal points—the standing women—and four pairs of kneeling genii with heads of hawks. Around the circumference march the thirty-six genii of the thirty-six decades of the year; for the Egyptian year of 360 days was divided into ten-day periods. Within these are the twelve signs of the Zodiac to which are added symbols of the fixed planets and a number of stars and constellations. The whole appears to be a map of celestial Egypt, which the Egyptians conceived to be in certain respects a replica of terrestrial Egypt with the same nome divisions. There were more nomes, or provinces, than the twelve Zodiac signs, so they were augmented by the planet and star symbols.

Visitors to the Dendera temple today will see little difference from what Lelorrain surveyed on that bright anxious morning a century and a half ago. The imposing building has suffered little damage since. Only the mound of earth down which he brought the stones has been cleared away, and you can wander at will among the tall columns inside, in the mysterious light of the almost intact building. And you can mount, by the clean-swept stair in the thickness of the wall, to the roof, to the little room where Lelorrain and his Arabs sweated over their saws: and there in the ceiling you will see the Zodiac, looking just as Lelorrain's eager eyes saw it—only it is a copy in plaster of what he took away.

15 Decipherment

IT was all very fine to extract great stone monuments by stealth or diplomacy and to haul them across land and sea to rival collections; but it advanced the knowledge of ancient Egypt very little. In fact all the discoveries in Egypt so far had led the antiquaries but few steps further than the classical authors had taken them. Places mentioned by the old writers had been located, but this was mere confirmation; it was nothing fresh. Something of the nature of the ancient Egyptians could be estimated from beholding their works; much of their mode of life was illustrated by the pictures on the walls of tombs; but of their history, of the names and order of their kings, of their conquests and of their religion nothing was gathered that had not been supplied already by the Latin and Greek historians whose surviving writings were often fragmentary, copied from earlier, now lost, works, and informed on hearsay.

The compilation of history requires documents—names, dates, acts and facts—from which to extract the story. In the case of Egypt those are what the classical historians did not pass on in sufficient quantity and quality. Of historical research there was none. Sources of history were not checked, and the work was often padded out with trivia in the manner of Herodotus. As the 'Father of History' he was vastly inexperienced. At the same time it is unreasonable to expect otherwise of a period when history had not yet untangled itself from epic and legend. Thus the little our antiquaries knew of Egypt set them yearning to know more of the mysterious past whose splendid ruins they could do no more to than measure, admire and wonder about.

Yet all the while, everywhere around them, inscribed on almost every stone of those very monuments were the missing names and acts, the accounts of gods and conquests for which they yearned, writ plain for all if only they could read. And for all the antiquaries knew the whole fabulous wisdom of the Egyptians was written up there too. Through the centuries of discovery in Egypt the sad lament went up time and again when some inquiring mind gazed baffled and longing at the mute hieroglyphs, as when Paul Lucas stood before the tumbled granite of Beybeit, 'the precious remains of a magnificence that astounds', and sighed over 'the infinity of hieroglyphs that must doubtless contain one of the most ancient histories of the world, if we had knowledge of them'.

Many attempts were made, of course, to come by that knowledge. But none had the slightest success before the Rosetta Stone was found. Nearly all was guesswork, miles wide of the mark, misdirected right from the start by the obstinate belief that hieroglyphs were precisely what the word means, and nothing more: pictures with a symbolic meaning, as when we draw a hand on a signpost with index finger pointing. Its accepted meaning is 'this way', and we do not have to know any language to understand it: the idea flashes direct from the ideograph. Had we spelled out *THIS WAY* instead of drawing the finger, a Chinese wayfarer without any English would require an alphabet book and a dictionary before he could proceed.

It occurred to only one of the early investigators that he would have to compile an alphabet and a dictionary to read the Egyptian language written in hieroglyphs. The others did not consider the possiblity that the hieroglyphic signs might convey the sounds of words through an alphabet; they could never have guessed that, when the signs were employed as ideographs and did convey an idea direct to the mind, it was only to determine a word that had already been written out in alphabetical hieroglyphs.

It was all much too involved for beginners who had no clue to the alphabet or language of the ancient Egyptians, and who had been put off the scent by authorities they supposed reliable, such as Horapollon and Chaeremon, Greek writers who spread the fatal belief about hieroglyphs being figurative symbols and not letters.

No wonder, then, that the celebrated Jesuit scholar of the 17th century, Athanasius Kircher, made translations that are more obscure for Egyptologists today than the texts themselves. The late Sir Alan Gardiner tells us that Kircher, studying the inscription on the Pamphilian obelisk in Rome, submitted this rendering of what we now know to be the Roman title *Autocrator:* 'The originator of all moisture and all vegetation is Osiris, whose creative power was brought to this kingdom by the holy Mophtha.'

'The holy Mophtha,' remarks Sir Alan, 'still remains a mystery to Egyptologists.'

Henri Gauthier, the French Egyptologist, once drew up a list of forty-four authors who published some sixty works between them on Egyptian hieroglyphs, during the period between the invention of printing and the decipherment of the Rosetta Stone. Jan Pierre Valérian's *Hieroglyphica* of 1556 went into seventeen editions. In 1564 the English mathematician, John Dee, tried his hand at the subject; and between 1643 and 1676 Athanasius Kircher, of 'holy Mophtha' fame, published at least six works on it. He was the most extravagantly imaginative of all these self-styled interpreters of hieroglyphics, who refused to see in this form of writing anything else but symbols, says Gauthier.

The one and only writer who got out of this rut was the English clergyman, William Warburton. He alone recognized that the hieroglyphs truly constituted a written language, in his *Essay on Egyptian Hieroglyphs,* of 1738; and he was the first to tread the true path that could have led to decipherment. But his successors fell back into the error of symbolism made fashionable by Kircher. By 1764 French Orientalist Joseph de Guignes and others were back at the old game of trying to find similarity between Egyptian and Chinese symbols, and of proving that China was a colony of Egypt

A similar effort to prove the identity of Chinese and Egyptian was made in 1761, in a book by an English Catholic divine and scientist, John Turberville Needham, based on the inscription on a black marble bust, supposedly of Isis, in Turin Museum.

To defeat critics, Needham persuaded a committee of learned men in Rome to sign an attestation that they had seen a large part of the signs in a Chinese dictionary.

This was probably true, but it raised the indignation of English clergyman, William Stukeley, M.D., who had written of hieroglyphs and Chinese characters back in 1743. At once he wrote two papers that were read before the Society of Antiquaries in 1762, to show that the Egyptian characters on the bust had meanings totally different from those of the Chinese characters they resembled. He expressed in addition the opinion that Egyptian hieroglyphs concerned religious matters exclusively: he was therefore satisfied that true know-ledge of them would never be forthcoming; and thus he had said the last word on the matter.

Seeing that William Stukeley was a true follower of Kircher, his guesss at the meanings of the symbols was no more reliable than Kircher's 'Mophtha'. The whole discussion was in fact earnestly futile: even more deliciously futile when we realize that the 'bust of Isis' was an obvious local forgery, and its 'inscription' did not even resemble Egyptian hieroglyphs—something that Needham would have done well to observe in the first place.

The manuscripts of the Rev. William Stukeley's papers are in the possession of British Egyptologist, Warren R. Dawson, who tells us also that our learned divine was a man of original opinions, even eccentric. On one occasion he postponed a church service to give his congregation the opportunity to observe an eclipse of the sun. Doubtless he was dying to see it himself. After his funeral at East Ham in 1765 the grave was levelled off, and no monument marks the spot, at his request.

William Stukeley was secretary of the first Egyptian Society on record. Like many societies of this kind, its origin was a dinner: this one at Lebeck's Head Tavern, in Chandos Street, London, on 11th December, 1741. Lord Sandwich presided, and among those present were the celebrated travellers Pococke and Norden. The President's staff of office was a sistrum—the hand-held instrument of music with rattling discs that was shaken in time with sacred chants. The Rev. Stukeley delivered a learned discourse on the sistrum, which was used, he told his audience, to scare off birds during a sacrifice.

The first Egyptian Society endured but a couple of years.

This, then, was the tangle of ignorance, prejudice and habit of thought out of which investigators in the early part of the last century had to climb. Bonaparte's Expedition had made Egypt more accurately visible to scholars, but that was all. The learned dissertations of two hundred years gone by did little but obscure the view.

When the Rosetta Stone reached England as part of the spoils of war in 1802 the inscription in hieroglyphs at the top was regarded in the traditional manner as purely ideographic; and since it contained the same decree as was written in Greek at the bottom, it was expected that the idea symbolized by each individual hieroglyph would soon be apparent, and that the reading of all Egyptian inscriptions would then be easy. But it did not work out like that at all. The scholars were baffled. They could not make any sense out of it. Each hieroglyphic sign appeared to have a different meaning each time it was used. And no wonder; it was as though we assigned to each letter of our alphabet an idea in place of a sound, then wondered why we got nothing but a string of disconnected ideas.

Scholars turned then to the inscription in the middle, written in the unknown script described in the Greek as the 'writing of the books'. This, they thought, was probably alphabetic, in the language of the ancient Egyptians. The guess was very nearly correct, for the language was late Egyptian written in demotic, as we call it now—the writing of the people. But it was not purely alphabetic: it was a combination of phonetic and ideographic symbols just as the hieroglyphic inscription was. In fact, demotic and hieroglyphic are one and the same, except that demotic is a running form of hieroglyphic that has developed so far from it in appearance that there seems to be no connection between the two. This small error of judgment was to cost the scholars much midnight oil.

The name of Jean-François Champollion is so wrapped up with the Rosetta Stone and the decipherment of Egyptian hieroglyphs that one might readily suppose him to have been the first and even the sole scholar to have tackled the task. But in fact this would be to expect a little too much of this prodigy, astonishing though he was; for Champollion was a child of eleven when the first copies of the Rosetta inscriptions were passed around among scholars in 1801. No doubt young Jean-François saw a copy in this year when he was taken to see the mathematician, Jean Baptiste Fourier, who had been a member of Napoleon's Commission in Egypt. Fourier showed him pictures of the monuments of Egypt, and he must have talked imaginatively of the lost wisdom of the Egyptians locked up in the unreadable inscriptions; for the visit sparked off an ardent desire in this unusual child to probe the mystery of the hieroglyphs, and from that moment he gave himself up to acquiring the equipment for the task. Before he was seventeen years old Champollion had learnt Hebrew, Arabic, Syriac, Chaldean, Sanscrit, Zend, Pali, Parsi, Persian, and studied various ideographic texts such as Mexican and Chinese. Believing that Coptic, still surviving in the ritual of the Egyptian Christian churches, might have retained something of the ancient language, he studied that too. And he also took in his stride the modern languages he knew would be necessary for his researches: English, German and Italian.

Right from the start Jean-François Champollion's life has the charm of legend, beginning even before his birth. His father-to-be was a bookseller of Figeac, in the Department of Lot, whose wife was an invalid in such declining health that the doctors, one after another, gave up her case as hopeless. Since there was nothing to lose after that, a renowned sorcerer was called in, Jacquou by name. He looked at her, then gravely announced that she would soon give birth to a child. In view of her feeble condition it seemed as though the sorcerer was as useless as the doctors; and since she was forty-eight years old and had not had a child since her son Jacques-Joseph ten years before, it looked as though Jacquou were crazy as well. But he dosed her with simples and recited his words, and to the astonishment of all except the sorcerer himself she recovered her health. Soon afterwards there were signs that a child was coming. Then the sorcerer predicted, 'It will be a boy, and he will be a light of the centuries to come.' He could well have added that he would be a light to the centuries past also; for what he said came true. On 23rd December, 1790, Jean-François Champollion was born, one of the most brilliant scholars the world has known.

At the age of five Jean-François identified, in a missal of his father's, the prayers that his mother had taught him to recite by heart; and by this means he taught himself to read. We have already reviewed his accomplishments by the time he was seventeen. In that year, 1807, he went to Paris to study with the Orientalist Sylvestre de Sacy, living an undernourished student's life because his father's means were too slender to spare sufficient for his basic needs. Champollion's tutors often advised him to turn to some other pursuit: there was no future in the study of ancient Egyptian scripts; more seasoned men than he had failed. Yet he remained faithful to his vow to conquer the hieroglyphs. His sole supporter in this apparent folly was his brother Jacques-Joseph, whose confidence in the youngster and whose affection for him never swerved.

It is not surprising that everybody else believed that the tutors' advice was sound. The Rosetta Stone, hailed as the key to lost writings of Egypt, had lain there in England since 1802, yet nobody had succeeded in turning that key more than a tiny uncertain fraction. All who fancied themselves as masters of ancient languages had pored over the Rosetta scripts. The cranks tried to prove that they were extracts from the Bible; Count Gustaf de Pahlin declared that ancient Chinese hieroglyphs were identical with Egyptian; and the wise ones kept quiet. In 1812 we find Matthew Raper complaining on behalf of the Society of Antiquaries, 'Seven years having now elapsed since the receipt of the last communication on this subject, there is little reason to expect that any further information should be received.' Work on the stone had obviously bogged down.

Translations of the Greek text were made, of course, very soon after the stone was found, and the French have the credit of being first to announce the purpose of the inscriptions and the kind of writing used for the Egyptian texts. That information was in the Greek. But during the first twelve years of the stone's availability only two informed voices were raised to announce results of study of the Egyptian scripts.

One of them was Sylvestre de Sacy, the Orientalist, who was to teach Champollion five years later. In 1802, right after the stone was brought to Europe, he pointed out what he thought must be the sign-groups in the demotic text corresponding to the names of Ptolemy, Alexander and Alexandria in the Greek.

In the same year Jean David Akerblad published a *Lettre à M. de Sacy* saying that he had also identified these names, and sixteen other names and words besides. In addition he had tried to work out a demotic alphabet which had some success with the proper names but none with the rest of the demotic inscription. Akerblad, a Swede, was a good scholar who had studied Coptic and worked on Phoenician and Runic inscriptions, yet the Rosetta Stone stumped him, and after making no more progress by 1815, he gave it up.

De Sacy had done no better in the time, and this seems to have soured him against his former pupil Champollion, who, in 1814, brought out two volumes on the geographical names of ancient Egypt in which he claimed that he could read the demotic inscription on the Rosetta Stone with almost complete success. De Sacy called this 'nothing but charlatanism' in a letter to Thomas Young, a newcomer to the field.

Champollion was no charlatan, as events were to prove. With the over-confidence of youth he had jumped to the conclusion that Coptic and ancient Egyptian were so alike that a Coptic scholar would be able to read the demotic script as soon as he had worked out a demotic alphabet. He was only twenty-three years old, and he had yet to find out that Coptic had drifted a long way from its parent Egyptian, and a lot of other things besides. Yet the bold claim must have irked the older man, who warned Thomas Young against letting Champollion see his results lest he appropriate them and claim priority.

Thomas Young was a physician with a wide range of original investigations in natural philosophy, mathematics, mechanics, languages and medicine. He is famed for his great contribution to theoretical science, the wave theory of light. He did not take up work on Egyptian scripts until he was forty-one years old, when his interest was aroused by a papyrus that his friend Sir W. Rouse Boughton had bought in Luxor. Young secured a copy of the Rosetta Stone texts and set to work trying to fit words in the demotic inscription against words that should correspond to them in the Greek. It was guesswork and calculation with uncertain results. But it led to a significant discovery that some of the demotic characters bore a strong resemblance to signs in the hieroglyphic inscription. He became convinced that the demotic was a cursive form of the hieroglyphic—a running hieroglyphic handwriting.

This was extremely important: it meant that the demotic was not entirely an alphabetic script, as had been supposed, but that it must be at least partly symbolic. He checked this theory carefully against material published in the *Description de l'Egypte*, the magnificent volumes of the Commission of Arts and Science with Napoleon's Expedition that were just now appearing. Finally Young's conclusion that he had 'now fully demonstrated the hieroglyphical origin of the running hand' was set out in a letter dated 2nd August, 1816, that was circulated among scholars at home and abroad.

The obvious next step was the hieroglyphs themselves, seeing that they were the originals. Young examined a group of signs enclosed in an oval 'cartouche' situated in the hieroglyphic text at about the same place as the name Ptolemy occupied in the Greek. On the assumption that the Egyptians might have been forced to give phonetic values to some hieroglyphs in order to write foreign names, he gave the values of the Greek letters in Ptolemy's name to the hieroglyphic signs within the cartouche: he was hazarding an identification of the letters. He did the same with a cartouche that was expected to contain the name of Ptolemy Soter's Queen, Berenice, by reason of a Greek inscription nearby. The only symbol common to the two cartouches was that to which he had assigned the value 'I'. It fitted in the right place, which was encouraging.

From a total of thirteen signs occurring in the two names he got six right, three partly right, and four were wrong. But indeed one can say that he did read phonetically Ptolemy's name almost correctly from this very limited and shaky 'alphabet'. However, it was insufficient for him to *read* the Berenice name. He had only two letters correct in that, and would never have deciphered it but for the hint from the Greek inscription. In 1819 the *Encyclopaedia Britannica* published his article on Egypt, which contained the history and customs of the ancient Egyptians as far as it was known; an account of his reading of the name Ptolemy in hieroglyphs; and his suggested alphabet.

Meanwhile Champollion had published little on the demotic script and nothing on the hieroglyphic. It was not until 1821, two years after Young's *Britannica* article, that he published an essay on Egyptian writing, *De l'écriture hiératique des anciens Egyptiens*. In this he took a stand that appeared to be exactly opposed to Young's findings. He affirmed that none of the Egyptian writing was alphabetic, and that in demotic and hieroglyphic alike, the characters were 'signs of things, and not sounds'.

Yet within a year, Thomas Young, visiting Champollion in Paris, found him making 'gigantic' strides in deciphering foreign names expressed phonetically, and compiling a hieroglyphic alphabet. For this reason opponents of Champollion have accused him of stealing Young's ideas.

The Belgian Egyptologist, Jean Capart, during an address at the Centenary of the Decipherment of Hieroglyphs in 1922, gave a dramatic account of Champollion on the morning of 14th September, 1822, poring over some hieroglyphic copies fresh arrived from the Abu Simbel temple, in his study on the top floor of 28 rue Mazarin in Paris. He had by then collected some twenty-five phonetic hieroglyphs by deciphering Ptolemy, Cleopatra, and other foreign names. With these he could read back a large number of foreign names and titles even without a Greek crib.

Examining one of the cartouches newly copied from Abu Simbel, Champollion saw that it contained a circle possibly representing the solar disc; next, a sign to which he had given the value 'M' (it was actually 'MS'); and finally two signs to which he had given the value 'S' in his alphabet. He perceived that by giving the sun-disc its Coptic sound 'RE' and at the same time identifying it with the god Ra of the classical authors, he had the Biblical Pharaoh Ramses, one of the 19th dynasty kings in Manetho's list.

Greatly excited, he tackled another cartouche. It contained the picture of an ibis, sacred to the god Thoth, and the same 'MS' sign as in the first cartouche. Obviously Thothmes.

In that instant the hieroglyphs dropped their shroud of insoluble mystery. In one blinding flash it was revealed that they were used phonetically not only as an expedient to convey names foreign to Egypt, but also to write those of native kings in bygone epochs.

Champollion checked and re-checked his discovery until he

was perfectly certain of it. Then he rushed to find his brother. Throwing a mass of notes on the table he cried, 'I've got it!' and fell in a dead faint. He was worn out by months of ceaseless research.

His brother understood instantly that Jean-François had made a major break-through: for had he not given him confidence and encouragement for twenty years? Anxiously Jacques-Joseph nursed him through a nervous collapse so prostrating that Jean-François did not open his eyes for five days. But two days after that he was up and discussing the text of his announcement of the discovery with the *Académie des Inscriptions*.

At the session of 27th September, 1822, he read portions of his now famous *Lettre à M. Dacier, secrétaire perpétuel de l'Académie royale des Inscriptions et Belles-Lettres, relative à l'alphabet des hiéroglyphes phonétiques.*

In this Champollion does not acknowledge any help from Young. He credits de Sacy, Akerblad and Young with drawing first conclusions from the demotic text of the Rosetta Stone, but goes on to announce 'an important series of new facts' as though his own work owed them little or nothing: 'It is from the same inscription that I deduced the series of demotic signs . . . expressing the proper names of persons foreign to Egypt . . . I naturally concluded that since the signs of this popular writing were, as I have shown, nothing but a hieroglyphic shorthand . . . there must exist also a series of phonetic hieroglyphs.' He demonstrated the use of these for reading Greek and Roman names, but at this point dropped only a hint of the evidence that they were used for writing names of native kings from earliest times. In a footnote he makes it quite clear that he does not regard himself as having taken up where Young left off: 'Dr Young . . . has done work analogous to that which has occupied me during so many years.' Champollion was making it perfectly plain that he had obtained his results by original research and his own method. But publication of the *Lettre à M. Dacier* was the starting-gong for an academic fracas around the names of Young and Champollion that at one point took on almost the appearance of an international incident, and that lasted long after their deaths. Indeed its bitterest tussling was thirty years after the *Lettre*, when John Leitch published Volume III of the *Works of Dr. Young*, in which Leitch dealt with Champollion as Mr Serjeant Buzfuz dealt with the 'systematic villainy' of Mr Pickwick. He accused Champollion of appropriating Young's discoveries, and wrote: 'His charlatanerie and literary dishonesty are acknowledged by the most eminent of his countrymen, such as de Sacy and Letronne.'

De Sacy's remark about charlatanism was uttered in a private letter before Champollion had published any of his discoveries. After becoming acquainted with Champollion's work he wrote very differently in the *Journal des Savans* of March, 1825, where he credits Champollion with 'the honour of having found the road that can lead to the knowledge of the ancient written monuments of Egypt'. Letronne too came around to recognizing Champollion's merits.

Another accusation was that Champollion, after reading Young's *Encyclopaedia Britannica* article with its 'supposed alphabet', had tried to suppress his own publication of 1821, *De l'écriture hiératique*, because he had said in it that hieroglyphs were 'signs of things, not sounds'. This was a mischievous false statement that misled those who did not look at the documents themselves. For Champollion repeated the assertion, word for word, on the first page of the *Lettre à M. Dacier* before developing the theme about the spelling of foreign names. Thus there would have been absolutely no point in suppressing the first publication. Both he and Young in fact still believed that hieroglyphs were 'signs of things, not sounds'—except in the case of proper names.

Thomas Young naturally supposed that Champollion had continued from where he himself left off. But Champollion maintained to the end that he had arrived at his conclusions by independent study. The quarrel was never of Young's making. He never accused Champollion of borrowing or of dishonesty, and their relations, if at times a little strained, remained always cordial. It was obvious that Champollion had the capacity to arrive at results independently, after his reading of many names without help of Greek parallels. All Young claimed was credit for first reading the hieroglyphs. Those who grudge him this say that his was more of an identification than a reading: he knew beforehand that it must be Ptolemy's name; and his 'alphabet' would not decipher any other name besides Ptolemy—and that not correctly. Champollion, after collecting more abundant material, worked out a proved alphabet which could be applied to all inscriptions.

A very fair judgment on this unfortunate dispute was given in 1954, in a book which should have no prejudice in favour of Champollion's claims: *Thomas Young*, by Alexander Wood and Frank Oldham. 'We need not claim that Young's work rivals or even approaches in importance that of Champollion. But we do less than justice to Young if we do not claim for him substantial contributions to the study of Egyptology while that subject was still in its infancy . . . and if we do not reiterate the claim for him on the tablet to his memory in Westminster Abbey that "he first penetrated the obscurity which had veiled for ages the hieroglyphs of Egypt".'

In 1824 Champollion published his *Précis du système hiéroglyphique*, in which he revealed that the secret of Egyptian writing was the combination of ideographic with phonetic signs. Once he could read the language he found grammatical elements identical with Coptic, and he progressed with disconcerting speed. Success and recognition came to him fast. In the same year he went to Turin to study the Drovetti collection just established, and at Leghorn he acquired another of Drovetti's collections which became the basis of the *Musée égyptien* at the Louvre. In 1826 he was appointed a conservator at the Louvre. In 1828 a joint French and Tuscan mission, led by Champollion and his pupil Rosellini, landed in Egypt. Each of them was accompanied by six architects and artists. They went the length of Egypt and Nubia, the first ones to copy the inscriptions with the knowledge that they would be read and understood.

The letters in which Champollion reported back were like those of a man landed on an unexplored shore: in the world that Champollion had just opened up he was for the moment the only one who could see and understand, for none of his companions could properly read the monuments. But it meant that he expended too much energy trying to be everywhere at once. The doctor of the expedition found him on one occasion lying in a dead faint among his papers in the Valley of the Kings.

Honour and position awaited Champollion on the return of the expedition in December, 1829, with portfolios bulging and many antiquities: he was elected member of the *Académie des*

Inscriptions, and the following year the Chair of Egyptology was created for him at the *Collège de France.*

Our sketch of Jean-François Champollion has of necessity been much too brief to portray a man so unusual. We could only follow the single thread that led him towards Egypt, passing by his political and religious convictions, his friends and foes, his loves, that brought crisis and drama to a life intensely lived—a story fortunately captured by the devotion of Fraülein Hartleben, who published two packed volumes of his life in 1906, followed by his letters and journals. The late Professor F. Ll. Griffith wrote of him in *The Times* of 2nd February, 1922, the year of the Centenary of Champollion's discovery: 'He was no dry-as-dust scholar: he showed himself lively in companionship, playful and fond of children, a leader among his comrades, and considerate to his subordinates; sarcastic in controversy unless checked by his brother, confident and magnetically persuasive in personal intercourse.'

On 13th January, 1832, he was taken with a sudden *attaque d'apoplexie.* He had no illusions as to the outcome of his illness. 'It is too soon,' he lamented. 'I have so much more to do.' It was indeed too soon: he died on 4th March, aged only forty-two.

16 The Garden of Antiquity

THE tremendous significance of Champollion's decipherment of Egyptian writing was not confined to Egypt. It
changed the whole concept of historical science. The
reading of the hieroglyphs alone tripled the number of
centuries in which history could be founded on written documents. The story of mankind was thrust back to ages incredible
even to 18th-century scholars, who believed that beyond
Homeric Greece there had been nothing but primitive bar-
barism. Now it was revealed that the heroic days of Greece were
lived at a time when great empires of the more ancient world
were declining after millennia of splendour. Through his discovery we look back across vast regions where in the past lived
races and people whose very names were forgotten.

In his centennial discourse Jean Capart repeated what
Champollion wrote a century and a half ago, in a flash of
marvellous intuition:

> Historians will see in the most ancient times of Egypt a state of
> things that the course of generations has not perfected, because
> that could not be: Egypt is always herself, at all her epochs,
> always great and powerful in art and enlightenment. Going back
> up the centuries, we see her always shining with the same brilliance,
> and nothing lacks us to satisfy our curiosity but knowledge of the
> origin and growth of civilization.

Bonaparte's Expedition to Egypt had perhaps only one
durable result, the wresting of the Rosetta Stone from the soil.
The bones of this greatest conqueror of modern times rest at
one end of the avenue de Breteuil in Paris. At the other end is

the monument to Pasteur, who made the greatest conquests against death. Would it not be fitting, remarks Capart, to add a monument to Jean-François Champollion, who made his conquests against a power that men fear often more than death itself—oblivion?

But Champollion needs no monument of stone. His unfinished works were edited by his devoted brother, who published his grammar and dictionary, and later the big volumes of drawings from the voyage to Egypt.

Niccolo Ippolito Rosellini, Champollion's first student and colleague on the Franco-Tuscan voyage, had not the capacity to carry on the scientific work thus begun. But by 1837 the German Karl Richard Lepsius had shown himself worthy of the task; as did also the Vicomte Charles de Rougé, who was eventually to occupy Champollion's Chair of Egyptology at the *Collège de France*. Later, Karl Heinrich Brugsch, born five years before Champollion's death, was to continue building the knowledge of the Egyptian language with his demotic grammar and hieroglyphic dictionary. But, as Richard Lepsius wrote, all was founded on the astonishing progress of Champollion in the eight years following publication of his work on the hieroglyphic system.

One of the artists Champollion chose for his team on the Franco-Tuscan voyage to Egypt of 1828 was young Nestor l'Hôte. Son of a Customs officer, Nestor had been an imaginative child who used to re-create ancient Egypt in his garden by embalming dead pets and erecting pyramids to them. He wanted to be a painter, and studied seriously, but when he was eighteen his father put him into the Customs. This was in 1822, the moment when Champollion's discovery was announced. Greatly excited, Nestor got himself posted to Paris and made the acquaintance of Champollion, who encouraged him to study Egyptology.

As a member of Champollion's expedition Nestor l'Hôte was a mixed blessing. His enthusiasm, his ability to draw with accuracy the hieroglyphic forms to which he was accustomed, made him the hardest and fastest worker; but his fine-strung temperament often aroused dispute and discontent in the group when conditions were gruelling and all were tired. The combined expedition went up river in two *dahabias*, the cabined

sailing-boats of the Nile, copying inscriptions and works of art
from the temples and tombs. After three months in Nubia the
dahabias came downstream again and pulled into Thebes.
The Luxor temple carvings were recorded, and they crossed the
river to the Valley of the Kings to take up residence in the
tomb of Ramses V, known today as that of Ramses VI because
the later Pharaoh usurped it. Here Champollion and Rosellini
spread their beds, surrounded by their young companions.
Here the two leaders would exchange impressions after the
day's work; and one seems still to hear the din of mirth and
repartee that echoed back from a baker's dozen of intelligent
young Frenchmen and Italians camped in those ancient
corridors.

Nestor l'Hôte gathered 500 drawings and 400 pages of
notes; but he was fagged out and declared that he was finished
with hieroglyphs and desired nothing better than to return to
the routine of the Customs. Back in France in 1830, he did so;
yet he did not drop his Egyptology. The death of Champollion
two years later plunged him into grief and a remorse that
appears to have matured him. In recompense, he went alone on
a nostalgic expedition in 1838 to fill in what had been left
undone on the first. He reported back in a series of letters to his
sponsors, in one of which he writes from the Valley of the
Kings,

> where, eight years ago, I passed two months in company with the
> illustrious and so regretted Champollion. This valley, where so
> many precious memories are reborn for me, seems to have taken
> a forsaken air, a tinge of more austere melancholy, deeper than
> ever. I have put my bed in the place that was occupied by his, and
> my fancy has been happy to make his image live again; if only I
> could also evoke the genius that has immortalized him!

After wandering attentively throughout the Valley of the
Kings he records his conviction that there remained still many
unopened tombs. But who, he asks, will undertake such
immense works, which would rival that of the monarchs who
caused the tombs to be hewn?

Little did he know that only a few feet beneath the tomb of
Ramses VI, the very spot where he wrote those words, lay the
unparalleled wealth of Tutankhamon.

Nestor reported, too, on the destruction of monuments

ceaselessly going on under the Turks, grinding the stones for the production of saltpetre. 'At the rate they are carting off the two pylons at Karnak,' he wrote with deep concern, 'I doubt not that the ruins of Thebes will disappear within a few years.'

But it was not only the Turks. Visiting the remains of the temple of Ramses II at Abydos, he wrote the fifth of his letters—one we have already seen, in which he castigates 'speculators in antiquities, consuls and others, who have no reason to envy the vandalism of the Turks'. It will be recollected that he was referring to what is known as the second Abydos Table of Kings, dating from 1330 B.C. It was discovered in 1819 by William Bankes—whose obelisk Belzoni transported from Philae—and removed by the French Consul Mimaut.

After a third voyage to Egypt Nestor l'Hôte began arranging his drawings and notes for publication; but he did not get very far with it. Enfeebled by his privations when his servants had stolen his provisions and left him short of water on the shore of the Red Sea, he died in 1842, still a young man of thirty-eight.

Shortly afterwards his father was transferred to a Customs post at the seaport of Boulogne-sur-mer—an event that might appear of too small consequence to chronicle here. Yet it was to have the most profound and far-reaching effect on the destiny of the antiquities of Egypt, in a manner quite unforeseeable.

Meanwhile the antiquities lay there unprotected in the sun and wind, whose gentle fretting was, however, less to be feared than the heartless pillage of Turks and tourists. Indeed there was much force in the argument that it was an act of mercy to remove such as could be moved to the safety of a museum, lest a worse fate befall them.

The first Christians hammered out and plastered over painted sculpture that might show the origins of their religious ceremonies; the Arabs, Koran in hand, obliterated as dangerous all that it did not command them to preserve; these are the barbarians: but France, snatching an obelisk from the ever heightening mud of the Nile, or the savage ignorance of the Turks, who have not hitherto respected these soaring needles except through fear of their falling and the impossibility of cutting up the pieces; France, by doing this, earns a right to the thanks of the learned of Europe, to whom belong all the monuments of antiquity, because they alone know how to appreciate them. Antiquity is a garden that belongs by natural right to those who cultivate and harvest its fruits.

So wrote Captain de Verninac Saint-Maur, commander of the expedition that transported from Egypt the obelisk that now stands in the Place de la Concorde, Paris. There was a good deal to be said for this line of reasoning at the time.

We should not be shocked. then, to know that it was Champollion himself who recommended one of the obelisks that stood in front of the Luxor temple for removal to Paris. This was in a letter to his brother written from Egypt on 12th March, 1829. And after his return to France he wrote to the Minister of Marine:

It is not without astonishment that the foreigner traverses our capital without finding anywhere one single monument that recalls, even indirectly, our astonishing Egyptian campaign. No kind of monument is more fitting to perpetuate the memory of this great expedition than one or several Egyptian obelisks.

He insisted that the first to be moved should be the Luxor obelisks, with priority to the right-hand, or western one. They were much better, he said, than the Alexandria 'Cleopatra's Needles', of which the prone one was the property of England, and the standing one had been given to France at the request of Louis XVIII. Neither France nor England, as we know, had done anything about moving their weighty gifts.

Unfortunately for the French, Mohamed Ali had just presented the two Luxor obelisks to Britain at the earnest request of the British Consul, John Barker, successor to Salt. On 31st May, 1830, the French Consul Mimaut and the Baron Taylor, representing France, had audience with Mohamed Ali who was astute enough to satisfy both parties by offering Barker the great Karnak obelisk of Hatshepsut if he relinquished the two at the Luxor temple to the French. He agreed, rather foolishly, for it was probably impossible to have moved the 97 foot monster through the ruins to the river.

The option on it has presumably lapsed through failure to shift it, otherwise Britain is still the proud possessor of the largest obelisk in Egypt.

Now France possessed three obelisks, and the Baron Taylor,

in his enthusiasm, was convinced they could all be transported to France forthwith. The transport ship *Dromedaire* in fact arrived at Alexandria on 25th June, 1830, and the obelisk there would have been taken, if all the timber needed for the job had been on board. The delay led finally to the project being abandoned. The gift lapsed, and this 'needle' stands, as we know, in Central Park, New York.

Meanwhile a quite unusual ship, the *Luxor*, had been built in France, capable of carrying an obelisk down the Nile, across the sea, and up the Seine, passing under its bridges, to Paris. *Luxor* drew less than two metres, and it had five keels so that it would not split under the 236½ ton obelisk that would be slid aboard while *Luxor* lay beached at low Nile. To get the obelisk down and on to the ship was the task of diminutive naval engineer, Apollinaire Lebas, whose short height and fitting name were in inverse ratio to his skill and zeal. Mohamed Ali, when Consul Mimaut presented Lebas, pretended he could not see the little man, and jested, 'Where then is your engineer?' But, ever ready to admire unusual and risky enterprises, he declared, 'I regard your project as though it were executed in my own name and for my own glory,' and ordered every facility to be made available.

At Cairo little Lebas was received by herculean Krali, director of Nile navigation, in a tented pavilion on the river bank. Krali said he had once been sent by the Pasha to bring 'the king's stones' to Cairo; but had recoiled in face of the impossible task of moving the huge obelisks. He added to this discouragement by pointing to a tent-pole with a split extending a third of the way up it. 'The right-hand obelisk has a similar fissure,' he said. Aghast, Lebas hoped he was mistaken, or that he had used some tiny crack as an excuse to the Pasha for not moving the stones; for nobody had ever mentioned a fault in the obelisk before—neither Champollion nor even the great *Description* had recorded it.

But Krali was not exaggerating, At Luxor, Lebas's Italian mason Mazacrui tapped the monument with his mallet and listened. 'It is split,' he diagnosed. 'Yet the sound is healthy. I think it is not broken right through. We can take it, provided it is lowered very gently.'

Poor Lebas! He went back to the boat,

walking like a drunken man, and repeating ceaselessly: 'it has a fissure that no work on Egypt makes mention of.' My sole thought was that I might be accused of breaking the stone while getting it down or dragging it on board.

His usual buoyant spirits soon returned, however, and the fissure only added to the challenge. By ingenious care, using beams, pulley-blocks and capstans manned by sailors of the *Luxor* and Arabs of Luxor town, the great monolith was at length brought gently down and stowed safely aboard the ship. The troublesome fissure was in the stone all right. It had been there since the obelisk was first hewn. When Lebas had the monument prone, he found that the ancient Egyptians had inserted two fantail tenons of sycamore wood in the base to keep it from splitting more. All Lebas had to do was to replace the powdery remains of the old wood with new.

This was the first of vast difficulties and delays, from the plague to months of waiting for the rise or fall of Nile or Seine; but Lebas overcame all. To the sound of bugles he raised his 78 foot obelisk in the Place de la Concorde on 25th October, 1836, in the presence of Louis Philippe, King of the French, his Queen and 200,000 roaring citizens—with man-powered capstans.

A steam engine of forty horse-power had been prepared to provide the lift; but, reported the *Journal des Débats* of 16th October, 1836,

> It is much to be regretted that sufficient precautions were not taken to ensure this engine working satisfactorily . . . It would have been well to associate the monuments of antique art with one of the finest productions of the inventive mind of modern times.

Another visit by *Luxor* to pick up the left-hand obelisk had been Baron Taylor's intention, but it never came about. Probably the French preferred quietly to forget it after the half-million dollars it cost to get the first. Today a wide park has been laid out to set off the approach to the Luxor temple; but its imposing pylon gate will always have the bereft appearance of an elephant with one tusk missing.

As though to balance the extraction of a precious monument from Egypt, Jean-François Champollion had addressed a notice about the preservation of monuments to the Chief Dragoman of Mohamed Ali. He wrote of the increasing number of Europeans who were visiting Egypt with no commercial purpose, but simply to view the ruins they heard so much about. He dangled the ever-enticing bait in respect of Egypt's interest to attract visitors who spent money, and deplored the wide destruction of the ancient monuments. ('It is well known,' he was careful to say, 'that these barbaric demolitions have been carried on against the enlightened views and intentions of his Highness.')

He names seven sites recently destroyed, including the pillared portico of Hermopolis, so feared for by Edward de Montule on account of the Italian who wished to burn it for lime. It was lime by now. Included, too, were two temples near Esna, three at el Kab, and two on Elephantine Island opposite Aswan.

Champollion then suggests that it be made an offence to move any stone or brick from an ancient building, and that indiscriminate excavation be controlled, and a check put on the exodus of antiquities abroad.

It is ironical that at this time the French, at Champollion's suggestion, were helping themselves to one of the largest pieces it was possible to carry away.

The idea that this notice planted in Mohamed Ali's mind bore fruit in the Ordinance of 15th August, 1835—the first move towards protecting the remains of ancient Egypt.

The Ordinance drew attention to the passionate acquisition of antiquities by European souvenir-hunters, collectors and museums, to such an extent that there was real danger of 'seeing these monuments, pride of past centuries, soon vanish from the soil of Egypt, down to the last one, to enrich foreign countries'. To prevent this it was ordained:

1. that the exportation of antiquities was prohibited;
2. that all antiquities already in the possession of the Government, or acquired by it in future excavation, be brought to Cairo, and 'a museum constructed in the manner of those of Europe';
3. that not only was it strictly forbidden to destroy any antique monument, but that the Government would take measures to conserve them everywhere.

Jussef Zia Effendi was nominated Inspector of the Museum, and one of his functions was to make several tours of inspection annually through Upper Egypt.

The Ordinance did not prohibit excavation; it merely stopped what was going on—or tried to. A *firman* could be obtained from the Pasha by an individual. But objects found did not automatically belong to the holder of the *firman*.

It all looked fine on paper, but of course it was impossible for the overworked Jussef Zia Effendi to have any real control over digging or damage, single-handed in a huge area without any guards to post. But the Pasha was trying. He had not suddenly become an archaeologist overnight. He was interested in the antiquities because the Europeans spent time and money on them. If they had museums in Europe, then Egypt should have a museum, and they could come to Egypt to look at the stuff. And spend money. The museum was in fact started in the Ezbekia gardens in Cairo, but it did not last very long after Mohamed Ali. Various sovereigns gave away the best pieces to distinguished visitors, the last of whom was the Archduke Maximilian of Austria. He was offered what remained in the museum.

The most substantial control provided by the Ordinance was over the export of antiquities, making it less attractive to cut large chunks off the monuments for sale. Limited though its implementation could be, the Ordinance of 1835 was the extremely important beginning to that progress whereby de Verninac's 'garden of antiquity' belongs at last to the Egyptians of today 'by natural right'.

But there was yet a long way to go before the Egyptians were to appreciate it, cultivate it, and gather its fruits.

17 Karnak by Moonlight

SWEEPING through Egypt's 'garden of antiquity' at this time came proud Achille Constant Théodore Emile Prisse d'Avennes—restless, independent, outspoken, irritable and courageous—and withal a very able man. He claimed descent from an old Welsh family, Price of Aven, with armorial bearings in reward of their reckless valour on the Lancastrian side in the Wars of the Roses. His branch of the family had migrated to Flanders to avoid persecution from Charles II.

Prisse d'Avennes, at the age of nineteen, was no sooner out of art school than he was designing a grandiose monumental fountain to commemorate the heroism of French soldiers in India, their bitter disappointments and the injustices done them. Prisse was always champion of the oppressed. The City Fathers were not. They returned his design.

> Administrative intrigues wearied him, and since his frank, generous nature, so loyal, proud and independent, refused to bend to the demands of petty employment, he resolved more than ever to give sway to his artistic tastes and his leanings towards exploration.

Thus writes his biographer, his younger son Emile, who claims no prejudice in publishing his father's life. It is simply to record what he did for science, the arts and his country, and to tell of the 'cruel vicissitudes against which he struggled to the very verge of the grave'.

That is nonsense. It becomes quite evident that young Emile is playing up the noble exploits of his father in the hopes of preferment or a state pension in his memory. Yet I doubt if he

over-coloured the picture of his sire. Achille Constant Théodore
Emile Prisse d'Avennes was quite a fellow.

In 1826 his chivalrous nature took him off to fight for Greek
independence. In 1829 we find him in Egypt, in the service
of Mohamed Ali as civil and hydrographic engineer, and
teaching topography at the military school at Heliopolis.

The Governor of the school, Abdullah Bey, made him give
special lessons to high-ranking officers after his normal hours.
This he put up with; but when the Bey sent for him and told
him to lithograph copies of the regimental music-sheets he
declared that it was an insult to a skilled artist and cartographer
to be expected to copy band-music, and he refused. Abdullah
Bey ordered him to be clapped into irons. His impassive and
unflinching manner in face of this threat so irritated the *bey*
that he ordered a thousand lashes of the hippo-hide whip, the
courbash: more than enough to kill a man. Upon this Prisse
drew his sabre and made to carve the Governor up. But he was
surrounded and seized. Resistance was impossible, says his
biographer, and he agreed to obey the order.

He went home, wrote his resignation to the Minister of War,
despatched it to Cairo, stuck a dagger and a brace of pistols in
his belt, marched back to the Governor's office, threw a copy of his
resignation at his feet, and declared that he was now a free French
citizen, and if the *bey* lifted a finger to order his arrest he would
blow his brains out. Leaving Abdullah Bey gaping, he marched
out, mounted his waiting horse, and galloped off to Cairo.

He may have taken a calculated risk in staging this piece of
melodrama, knowing that the Minister of War was the *bey*'s
uncle, who would not want the story of his nephew's treatment
of a foreigner to reach the Pasha's ears. Prisse obtained double
pay and a public apology from the Governor before returning
to duty 'with all the honours due to him'.

Still full of the enthusiasm of his twenty-two years, Prisse
designed further grandiose projects: an irrigation dam below
Cairo; a Cairo-Alexandria canal; the drainage and cultivation
of the lakes of Lower Egypt; a hydraulic machine to water all
Alexandria. But the Pasha thought him too young to carry out
these important works. A scheme for lowering and transporting
the Luxor obelisks was ignored by the French Minister of
Marine. These repeated disappointments 'in a country where

they neither appreciated nor used his talent', decided him to try no more, but to search for rare documents to take to France and publish. He resigned his job in 1836 and studied hiero-glyphs 'in which, later, he became the equal of Champollion'.

Prisse became a professional traveller, adopting the Mohammedan dress and leading 'the adventurous life of a true artist', with no resources besides his drawings, his pen, or some help from the family. He 'drew, described and published' from Turkey to Abyssinia; and his biographer claims that he visited Mecca. In 1840 he appears to have settled for a while at Luxor, where he bought a slave and named him Abdullah with charming irony before giving him his written freedom.

One day the director of the saltpetre factory between Luxor and Karnak ordered the removal of the mound wherein were buried eight crew members of the obelisk-ship *Luxor*, who had died of plague nine years before. Prisse d'Avennes believed that he was doing this 'for the merit of throwing Christian bones on the highway'. Furious, he rushed his servants to the mound, planted the tricolour on top, declaring it the soil of France, and chased the profanators off with sticks, threatening gunfire if they returned.

He gained the day, and complaint to the French Consul at Cairo appears to have confirmed that victory. But in March, 1841, the brother of his servant was bastinadoed and imprisoned for failure to pay land tax. Prisse stormed in to Abdel Karim, the Sub-governor. Nobody rose at his approach. He held out the money and demanded the man's release.

'Out, son of a dog!' cried Abdel Karim, making a grab at him. Prisse snatched a heavy stick from a servant and cracked the Sub-governor on the head. The fight was on. Prisse began with his fists on the attendants, then drew his dagger and wounded three of them. But numbers won. While irons were being fitted, the Comte de Vergennes, who was staying with Prisse, came to see if he could get Prisse out. He too was seized, beaten and dragged by the beard to prison, together with three servants, and all five were chained together. They spent four nights in a filthy prison with twenty-five peasants who had failed to pay land tax. On the fifth day the Governor of Kena sent for them. Nestor l'Hôte happened to be at Kena —he was on his last visit to Egypt—and in his presence the blacksmith came to take off their chains for them to appear before the Governor. They refused his jurisdiction, saying they would make official demands to Mohamed Ali for reparation for abuse of authority. The dread name of the Pasha appears to have been enough for the Governor, for they sauntered off casually to sup with Nestor l'Hôte, not having been fed for twenty-four hours.

Abdel Karim was finally put under arrest for five days, to the utter disgust of Prisse, who wrote in protest to his Consul, 'The Sub-governor must pay with his head for the bloody outrages he has put upon us, to teach the world that a Frenchman is to be respected at least as much as a Turk.' But Abdel Karim retained his head.

Nestor l'Hôte and Prisse d'Avennes had met before, during Nestor's second voyage to Egypt, in 1838. They met at Karnak, in the Chamber of Kings, both digging around for the same things: the blocks missing from sixty-one portraits and cartouches of the chief kings of Egypt up to Thutmose III—a chronological document, in Prisse's opinion, 'quite as important and even more instructive than the Table of Kings of Abydos which ornaments the British Museum'. Though completely disinterested, says his biographer, Prisse had held back from removing this Karnak Table of Kings for the Louvre through fear of censure. It was perfectly true: Prisse was no Saulnier, calculating ahead the cash value of what he was about to purloin. He wanted only the reflected glory of having France possess as good antiquities as England. Now, in 1842, he heard of the arrival of the Prussian expedition led by Karl Richard Lepsius, who, he thought, might be less scrupulous than he. 'So he resolved to save, even at peril of his life, this venerable monument for the benefit of Science and his country.'

Returning from Cairo with a stone-cutter and timber for making cases, he found the quarrying of stone for the saltpetre works creeping nearer to his Chamber of Kings. He must act at once. On 14th May, 1843, with a score of workmen collected secretly, he began to take the roof-stones off. A mud-brick wall had to be built to support the tottering walls of the chamber, and to support the levers, sole machines available. It took fifteen Arabs to move one stone. Despite care, two workers were injured and had to be carried to his tent and cared for. Eventually he was obliged to return them to their homes and pay them double for doing nothing but keeping quiet.

When the roof-stones were off they worked by moonlight or torch, removing the carved stones and sawing the backs off. Lelorrain had worked in secret haste to saw his Zodiac out through fear of detection by Salt, although he had his *firman* from the Pasha. Prisse d'Avennes feared detection by the authorities, for he had no *firman*. To have asked for one would have been to lose the Table of Kings, since the 1835 Ordinance prohibited its export.

Work was well advanced when Selim Pasha, Governor of Upper Egypt, came to Luxor on business. Work was speeded up and pay tripled. Work had to go on in daylight too. Prisse spent part of each day with Selim Pasha and the Governor of Esna to head off a possible visit by the dignitaries, returning at night to direct the work.

At length, after eighteen nights and days, all the blocks were in his tents, packed in cases. He awaited only the departure of the Governor to have them carried to the boat and away to Cairo. To use the delay profitably he packed up some stelae and an Akhnaton block that he found, together with other works 'to enrich our collections' when he was denounced to the Governor of Esna, who was still at Luxor.

The Governor wrote to him on 27th July, 1843, with some restraint, one would say:

> I am very surprised, because you are not ignorant of the orders of His Highness which forbid that anything be taken away from the antiquities or monuments. I demand that you bring here all the antiquities and carvings that you have put into boxes. I forbid you to commit such an offence, and I invite you to quit the temple and go and live in a house somewhere else. I warn you that if you do not come with the boxes as I demand, you will have to take the consequences.

Prisse was, of course, totally in the wrong: he was definitely thieving. While he was busy concocting a reply a posse of Turkish soldiers arrived and tried to enter his tent. He faced them, carbine in hand, and reminded them that his person and dwelling were inviolable under the law. The leader posted his men around and went back to report to the Governor. So did Prisse. He told the Governor that he had no right to search his tent, under the terms of the capitulation with the Porte; and he did not recognize the Governor's authority to order him not to dwell among the ruins of Karnak.

The Governor realized that he ran some risk in forcing entry to a Frenchman's dwelling, be it only a tent. But he effectively blocked Prisse's operation by placing guards ready to oppose any movement of the cases, and by putting an embargo on the boat that was engaged to transport them.

After waiting for a month in hopes of some unexpected opportunity, Prisse decided to take the only way out. It comes as quite a surprise that it was not one of his direct actions accompanied by a breaking of the Governor's head with a thick stick. Prisse merely took the conventional way of making the Governor a sufficiently large present. For appearance's sake, the cases had to be taken aboard by night and sail set immediately for Cairo, where Prisse arrived about mid-September.

By a mischievous quirk of fate, Prisse's boat met that of Lepsius, leader of the Prussian expedition, on its way up. Entertaining his distinguished colleague on the deck of his boat, Prisse offered him a seat. I would like to believe that Prisse was capable of impish malice in doing so; for the seat was one of the cases containing the stones of the Karnak Table of Kings. And as Lepsius sat on it sipping his coffee, he revealed to Prisse in confidence the intention of his present journey: to stop off at Karnak and remove just that very monument.

At Cairo and Alexandria the French Consuls refused to have anything to do with Prisse's 'hot' cargo, to his usual indignation, and he was obliged to put it in the Government store, labelled 'Natural History Specimens', to its peril. By persistence, will-power and audacity he got it to France in May, 1844.

News of the lifting of the Karnak Table spread, and Prisse's home in Paris became the meeting-place of leading men of the day, writes his biographer proudly, adding rather naïvely, 'There the justness and breadth of his outlook, his taste and his knowledge, captivated his listeners, by whom he was not only appreciated, but often admired.'

It is difficult to reconcile the idea of wandering, stormy Prisse d'Avennes with a home at all. He must have been impossible to live with.

In 1845 he was nominated *Chevalier* of the *Légion d'Honneur*, but he never rose higher in the order because, at the investiture, when he was required by his sponsor Letronne to recite the oath of allegiance to King Louis Philippe, Prisse replied, 'I hold to my liberty. I swear allegiance to no man. If I deserve this distinction, give it to me. If not, keep it.'

Prisse gave the Table of Kings to the *Bibleothèque Nationale*, and it is now in the Louvre. But he got little more than a 'thank you' for his free gift to the nation. It was left out in the yard for the winter of 1844 and was damaged by frost and rain. Recollecting that Louis XVIII had paid a king's ransom to Saulnier for the Dendera Zodiac that Lelorrain had spirited out twenty-two years before, one must admit that Prisse had reason to be indignant this time.

For the next thirteen years he did actually remain at home with the family, busy on a dozen projects, editing learned reviews and quarrelling with his confrères. In 1858 he was back in Egypt, sponsored by his Government in spite of his indocility. But there was to be no moonlight removal this time: the Ordinance was strictly in force, and Prisse had a reputation. He had to be satisfied with drawing. Maybe it was as well; for he returned to France in 1860 with 300 folio drawings, 400 metres of paper casts, and many records by the new process of photography, from which he compiled his *Histoire de l'Art égyptien*, the first of its kind to be made from on-the-spot observation of original material, and a most able work.

Five years before his death the French Government recognized his contribution to art and literature with two annual grants of 600 francs; and when he died in 1879 the Government gave him military honours and a subscription of 400 francs towards funeral expenses.

Prisse d'Avennes left two sons and two daughters, 'whose future he had not been in any way able to secure', wails Emile, biographer and younger son. The elder, Eudol Prisse, had volunteered in the 1870 campaign. Captured, he escaped from Germany and died of 'a malady contracted on the field of battle, leaving two children of tender age'. Emile had taken charge of them, and ends the story of his father's life with a more than broad hint that something should be done about it 'to honour the memory of the celebrated Egyptologist to whom intellectual and artistic France has contracted a heavy debt of recognition'.

18 Archaeology and Gunpowder

RICHARD Lepsius had met Prisse d'Avennes before their boats crossed on the Nile, and the gods laughed as Lepsius sat on the stolen goods he was on his way to steal himself. Lepsius had been a distinguished guest at meetings of the Literary Society that had been started by Prisse and Dr Henry Abbott in 1841, when Prisse was living in Cairo. It was really an Egyptological Society and of course Prisse had grand ideas of making it a world centre of Egyptological publishing, with a learned review and large volumes of plates. The printers of Cairo were quite unequipped to cope with this kind of thing, and the Society foundered on the ebullient ambition, as did so many of Prisse's schemes. It endured for exactly the same period as William Stukeley's Egyptian Society in London, and exactly one century afterwards: 1841 to 1844.

Yet while it lasted it is said to have had a hundred members, including eminent men on the spot such as Sir Gardner Wilkinson, whom we visited in his tomb-dwelling above the necropolis of Thebes. It is not likely that Lepsius attended another meeting after he reached Karnak and found only a hole where the Table of Kings should have been. In any case he and his large team were busy up river as far as Abu Simbel during the remainder of the Society's short span. By 1845 the Prussian expedition had culled enough material to publish the twelve elephant-size volumes of *Denkmäler* containing copies of inscriptions and wall-scenes from every important site in Egypt.

This was the last of the great multi-volume surveys of Egypt, of which the first had been the *Description* of

Bonaparte's Expedition. The next were the twin publications of Champollion and Rosellini, practically replicas one of the other. Each survey had been an advance on the last, better informed, more accurate. But there will be no more of them. The day of those heavy, unwieldy sets is over. Specialization has come to Egyptology, and now it is single monuments or even parts of them that are published in detail, and the pity is that there is not more of it. The great tomes, however, were immensely valuable in their day, enabling scholars to study the texts and the historical and religious scenes. They are still valuable, because some of the material has never been published since, and some of it records scenes and inscriptions—even entire monuments—that have disappeared since.

Dr Henry Abbott, co-founder of the Cairo Literary Society, was not really a qualified doctor at all. But he was no quack. He had been orderly to a ship's surgeon in the Royal Navy, and had left his ship at Alexandria to enter the service of Mohamed Ali as surgeon to his fleet. In 1830 he settled in private practice in Cairo, where his Egyptian collection and his hospitality became famous. In 1851 he sent his family to the United States, and followed with his collection; but its exhibition in New York brought poor response. Abbott returned to Egypt in 1854 and bought from A. C. Harris the papyrus by which his name is remembered. The Abbott Papyrus is a vivid account of the investigation of tomb robberies at the time of Ramses IX, and a very important document historically and linguistically. Abbott re-sold it at a profit to the British Museum: and his collection was bought by the New York Historical Society, whence, many years afterwards, it was transferred to the Brooklyn Museum.

Anthony Charles Harris, from whom Abbott bought his papyrus, was a British merchant of Alexandria who collected and dealt in antiquities, and who was something of an Egyptologist. His adopted daughter Selima, a Negress, some forty years his junior, had been educated in England. Intelligent and cultured, she was her father's constant companion, and inheritor of the collection. When she went to England to arrange its sale to the British Museum in 1872 she was made a Lady Member of the Society of Biblical Archaeology. Harris's name lives through the papyri bought by the British Museum. The

Papyrus Harris A is another of several dealing, like the Abbott Papyrus, with the tomb robberies. Papyrus Harris No. 500 is a fanciful tale of how Tahuti took the town of Joppa for Thutmose III by introducing men concealed in jars—probably the origin of Ali Baba and the Forty Thieves. Papyrus Harris No. 1, known as the Great Harris Papyrus, is 133 feet long and nearly 17 inches wide, almost perfectly preserved. It is a funerary recital of all the good deeds of Ramses III, followed by some important historical data.

Some of the Harris papyri were not intact, and a story has been repeated by several writers of good repute that they were damaged when a powder-mill blew up and wrecked part of the Harris home at Alexandria. The incongruous notion of a papyrus being blown up by gunpowder may tickle the humour of the more irreverent of us; but Warren R. Dawson, in the *Journal of Egyptian Archaeology, 35*, explodes the story itself by examining the peculiar behaviour of the alleged upheaval. It left the Great Papyrus unblemished, yet it made off with the last half of the Magical Papyrus without a trace, leaving the first half absolutely intact. On Harris 500, he says, 'the effect was quite different, for instead of half of it being blown to limbo, the whole of it remains' in the state familiar in most papyri subject to ordinary wear and tear. Still more curious was what the blast did to Papyrus B.M. 10054, 'the upper layer of papyrus from part of the recto having been stripped completely off and gummed over the corresponding page of the verso'. Dawson does not suggest that this phenomenal explosion did the gumming as well as the stripping, but he does submit that no explosion would separate fragile layers of papyrus without blowing them into tiny bits. Reliable information leads him to believe, in fact, that half of the Harris Magical Papyrus vanished 'in a much less violent manner', and that the explosion story was a smoke-screen put out by the borrower who had no intention of returning it.

The Abbott and Harris papyri were among the comparatively few to have survived the thousands that perished in flames under the frantic search for more obvious valuables. Study of these documents enlarged the clearing picture of ancient Egypt. The laudatory boasts of 'historical' papyri were checked against inscriptions on temple walls and in private tombs to confirm the framework of history, whose details are still being fitted together. The magical papyri, the judicial and the literary gave life to the bones of history, so that ancient Egypt, the beginning of civilization, has become more familiar to us than the way of life at the beginning of Western civilization in Europe.

The bulk of this knowledge was revealed in the flood of light that flowed in the thirty years following the decipherment of hieroglyphs. By the middle of the last century the story of Egypt that had been lost for fourteen centuries had been revealed with fair accuracy. Thus the reading of documents in stone and papyrus became a science; but the reading of history from purely archaeological sources did not. Excavation still went on in the same haphazard way, with the aim only to unearth museum objects or inscriptions that could be read. Few thought of the information that might be revealed by careful scrutiny of the position of objects and portions of buildings as digging proceeded.

Among those few who used scientific method to examine mute monuments were the two British men, aristocratic Major-General Richard William Howard-Vyse (then a major), and engineer John Shae Perring, who chose pyramids for their special investigation between 1835 and 1837. They have been reproached by critics for 'gunpowder archaeology'. No doubt, had they thought the matter out more carefully, they should have been able to open the Third Pyramid of Giza without blasting their way in. But this was the only clumsy part of their able exploration of many pyramids; and their published plans and descriptions have been the basis for all investigation since.

The first American Egyptologist is likely to have been a foundation member of Prisse d'Avennes's Literary Society. He was George Robins Gliddon, whose father, United States Consul at Alexandria, had taken him there as a boy. George eventually became U.S. Vice-consul himself. He wrote *An Appeal to the Antiquaries of Europe* pleading for the preservation of Egypt's monuments; and in 1842 he went on a lecture tour in the United States that extended as far West as St Louis. He aroused great interest, and sometimes spoke to audiences of 2,000. His book, *Ancient Egypt*, sold thousands of copies, and George R. Gliddon sowed the seeds in America of that interest which has sent forth so many scholars and expeditions to contribute to the science of Egyptology.

Gliddon did not forget his colleagues of Egyptian days. In 1849 he sent a book on the antiquities of the Mississippi valley to his old friend Prisse d'Avennes, who was then in Paris. Prisse, true to form, full of enthusiasm, translated it. But like so many Prisse projects this one too came to naught. The publishers were not interested in that kind of antiquities from over there.

A young Scottish lawyer came to Egypt in 1855 for his health: Henry Alexander Rhind. During two years he organized excavation among the tombs of Thebes, and acquired thence and by purchase fine antiquities that he bequeathed to the Museum at Edinburgh. But Rhind was no ordinary collector. Serious and precise, he wrote:

> There is much room for regret that even after Egyptian antiquities began to be comprehensively studied and sought after by systematic research, attention was almost exclusively directed to obtaining possession of the relics, without sufficiently careful reference to the circumstances under which they were discovered. With Egyptian museums in at least eight capital cities I am not aware that there can be found the contents of a single sepulchre duly authenticated with satisfactory precision as to what objects were present, and as to the relative position these occupied when deposited by contemporary hands. Indeed, for many of the Egyptian antiquities scattered over Europe, there exists no record to determine even the part of the country where they were exhumed.

Rhind goes on to say that there was little prospect of an undisturbed tomb being found for study after the systematic pillage of Salt and Drovetti.

He was only twenty-three when he conducted his search for intact tombs in the hope 'that even by an individual attempt, details of the nature that seemed so highly desirable' might be recorded. He found only one 'in which the repose of the last occupants had remained entirely unbroken', and he gives a step-by-step account of its excavation and the conclusions he reached about the tomb, its spoliation in ancient times, its reoccupation, and the identity of the final occupants. He reached these conclusions by taking note of the position and nature of each object as he came upon it, and from papyri found actually on the mummies of the deceased. This was something quite new. It was not known where any of the great museum papyri came from. Although he had not the background, skill and accuracy of today's excavators, Rhind was absolutely on the right track.

Unhappily he did not live to be the great excavator he surely would have become. His health gave way during another visit to Egypt, and he died at the age of thirty. His name is associated with the Lectureship in Archaeology that he endowed in Edinburgh, and with several papyri, including the Bremner-Rhind Magical in the British Museum.

Generously, Rhind gives credit for the first description of an undisturbed tomb, back in 1823, to Giuseppe Passalacqua, Conservator of the Egyptian Collections in the Berlin Museum. But Passalacqua had come to Egypt as a horse-dealer, and only took up antiquities as a business. Rhind was the first to think out and deliberately put into practice the principles that converted excavation from a treasure-hunt into a science.

19 Mariette

ON that night when Lelorrain was loading his boat at Cairo, on the eve of his departure to take the Dendera Zodiac, 11th February, 1821, a baby was born in Boulogne-sur-mer, you will recollect, and given the name of Auguste Ferdinand Mariette.

He grew up a child full of life, turbulent, and generally good humoured, with no marked enthusiasm for study at the *collège communal* of the town, except for drawing, in which he had real talent. Aimless at home at the age of eighteen, he went to England to teach French and drawing at Shakespeare House Academy at Stratford-upon-Avon. One year of that sufficed, and he tried without success to earn a living as designer for ribbon manufacturers in Coventry. Within months he was back in his home, a teacher in the college where he had been a pupil, on a salary of 166.66 francs a month—about £7—and glad to get it.

Now he discovered in himself an ability and consuming desire to write, and his spare-time articles and novelettes were accepted by editors. He appeared to have found his vocation, and in 1843 he took on editorship of the local paper, *l'Annotateur Boulonnaise*, in addition to his teaching.

This was the very year when the Customs officer, Nestor l'Hôte's father, was transferred to Boulogne after the death of his son the year before. Now it happened that he was related to the Mariette family, and he picked on young Auguste Mariette as the most suitable person to go through his son's papers, seeing that he was a literary type.

To Mariette this was a boring family chore; yet soon he began to be charmed by the notes and descriptions of Egypt, and fascinated by the hieroglyphs. He learned the alphabet and the rudiments of decipherment from the papers before him. By then, unwitting, he was lured. 'The Egyptian decoy-duck,' he told Maspero years later, 'welcomes you blithely, but if you let yourself be duped by his innocent air you are lost! One peck, and he injects his venom, and there you are, an Egyptologist for the rest of your life.'

At first Egyptology was a hobby to be enjoyed between his teaching and his journalism. For seven years he worked alone, testing his new science on the few monuments in Boulogne Museum. Vervoitte the musician, seeing him lying flat before the magnificent coffin acquired by the Municipality six years before, asked him what he thought he was going to get out of that. Mariette replied, 'I'm not sure, but I fancy it is going to take me a long way.' How far, even he could not have guessed.

Another thing he could not have guessed was that Vivant Denon had restored some of the inscriptions on the magnificent coffin in accordance with his fancy. And some of the inscriptions in the *Description* were nonsense-hieroglyphs filled in by some of the draughtsmen of the Expedition who took the lazy way out in the belief that the reading of hieroglyphs would never be solved. Mariette wasted months poring over the puzzling interpretations they yielded. Yet despite his handicaps and isolation he wrote an article on the Egyptian objects in the Boulogne Museum that convinced leading Egyptologists Charles Lenormant and Emmanuel de Rougé that the minor school-teacher of the seventh class at Boulogne-sur-mer had promise.

In 1845 Mariette married Eléonore Millon and promptly became *père de famille*. Turning to his new skill to aid his resources, he got the Mayor and local Deputy to back his offer to go on a scientific expedition to Egypt. The Government turned it down, and this was serious, for Mariette, with optimistic abandon, had burned his boats by resigning his editorship. He had only his teacher's salary to live on. And in 1848 the headmaster told him that teaching was a full-time job, and invited him to give up his learned investigations. Mariette gave up the teaching and headed for Paris. There he studied the Karnak Table of Kings that Prisse d'Avennes had brought at such pains four years before. The seventy-page treatise that Mariette wrote on it gained the praise of Charles Lenormant, Professor of Egyptology at the *Collège de France,* who found him a humble position in the Louvre, cataloguing and mounting papyrus on card.

Mariette brought Eléonore and their three little girls to Paris, where they lived poorly but happily. A Boulogne comrade, Pierre Capet, found him seated at an enormous table overloaded with books in the middle of an almost bare room. He was busy writing, a child on his lap and the other two playing at his feet. 'I never work better than like this,' he told the surprised Capet. 'I like to feel my little world around me.'

In Paris, Mariette made up for the dearth of books in Boulogne. In two years he had read everything published since Champollion's death, and was master of the language as good as any. Then, with Lenormant's help, he realized his ambition to be sent to Egypt. He was to collect rare Coptic manuscript books there.

Bidding wife and children *au revoir,* he embarked at Marseilles on 4th September, 1850. But at Cairo he found the Coptic Patriarch hostile on account of two Englishmen who had made off with an entire library some ten years before, after making the monks drunk on *raki* spirit. Mariette liked to tell that the Patriarch had gathered all the books remaining in other monasteries, and walled them up in his library.

Foiled, Mariette's thoughts turned to his greater interest, Pharaonic antiquities. Climbing to the Citadel one evening, he saw the city below, drowned in mist:

> From this deep sea emerged three hundred minarets like the masts of some submerged fleet. Far to the north, you could see date forests, their roots in the fallen walls of Memphis. To the west, drowned in the golden dust of the setting sun, rose the Pyramids. The sight was overwhelming; it seized me with a violence almost painful. Beneath my eyes I had Giza, Abusir, Saqqara, Mitrahina. My lifelong dream took shape. There, almost within reach, was a world of tombs, stelae, inscriptions, statues. The moment was decisive. The next morning I hired mules and donkeys, bought a tent and foostuffs, all the impedimenta for a journey into the desert, and during the day of 20th October, 1850, I camped at the foot of the Great Pyramid.

Within a week he was combing the necropolis of Memphis at Saqqara. He noticed the head of a sphinx sticking up out of the sand, similar to fifteen others he had seen in private gardens of Cairo and Alexandria, brought from Saqqara by the merchant Fernandez. The sight recalled to him a passage from Strabo: 'There is also a Serapeum at Memphis, in a place so sandy that the winds pile up the sands beneath which we saw the sphinxes buried up to their heads.'

This then, thought Mariette, with a thrill of excitement, must be the avenue of sphinxes that led to the very tomb of the divine Apis bull-gods, one of which Strabo had seen led out of its sanctuary in Memphis for visitors to admire. 'In that instant,' wrote Mariette, 'I forgot my mission, I forgot the Patriarch, the monasteries, the Coptic manuscripts . . . and it is thus that on 1st November, 1850, at one of the most beautiful sunrises I ever saw in Egypt, some thirty workmen were grouped under my orders close to this sphinx that was to bring about such a total change in the purpose of my visit to Egypt.'

It was a gamble. If fortune smiled, it meant sudden glory and an assured future for his family. If he failed, it would be difficult to explain why all his funds went in excavation.

It is often assumed that Mariette had no business to use his funds for digging: that they were for manuscript search only. Certainly manuscripts were the prime objective, yet Lenormant had said in his Report to the *Académie* on 21st June, 1850, 'M. Mariette proposes also to make excavations on sites hitherto imperfectly explored, in order to enrich our museums.' But Mariette would have to find something good to justify his decision.

Mariette had no *firman*, and there were plenty of rivals, native and foreign, to denounce him if he were too successful. For the time being all went well. Sphinx after sphinx came up. To right and left he uncovered tombs of the Memphite empire, in one of which was the famous coloured sandstone statue of the Sitting Scribe, one of the treasures of the Louvre. Many days were wasted when the avenue changed direction and they lost it; and then on Christmas Eve they came upon the statue of a person seated in an armchair. It was the great lyric poet Pindar, and he was not alone. Ten other statues sat on a semi-circular bench where the avenue ended, representing Greek poets and philosophers including Plato, Pythagoras and perhaps Homer. All were in poor style and broken in ancient times, mended with rough stone.

Finding a conventicle of famous Greeks at the end of an avenue of Egyptian sphinxes was enough to upset anybody; but after his first surprise, Mariette pushed on with courage. He found two larger and better sphinxes, bearing the name of Nectanebo I. Between them, on his thirtieth birthday, 11th February, 1851, Mariette found the doorway of a chapel built by Nectanebo in honour of the bull-god Apis. Beyond, two magnificent sandstone lions, now in the Louvre, kept watch. He was clearly on the way to fresh discoveries. But they would be long and costly. Now was the moment to advise the French Government where the 7,000 francs that they gave him to buy Coptic manuscripts had gone. He drew plans and wrote a report which he sent to Lenormant; then he went on digging with money advanced him by the French Consul Le Moyne, who was charmed by his courage and enthusiasm.

He unearthed a statue of the phallic god Bez. 'It is lunch-time,' he wrote. 'Women have come to join the labourers. A sort of procession forms. Evidently Bez is taken for the devil. Women abuse it with lunatic gestures. The men spit at it. Two or three Negroes face the imperturbable god, then suddenly rush off bursting with laughter.' A little later they found two chapels, one Greek and the other Egyptian. In the latter was the magnificent sandstone Apis now in the Louvre. Of this he wrote:

> Towards noon I emerged from my tent without warning. About fifteen women were grouped around the statue of Apis. I saw one of them mount on the back of the bull and stay there some moments as though on horseback, then dismount to make room for another. I was told that this performance, repeated a few times, was a cure for sterility.

Four months under canvas with the dust and glaring sunlight had inflamed Mariette's eyes with the ophthalmia that troubled him from then on. He was forced to go to Cairo for treatment. His return was marked by a brilliant find. Mixed with the sand beneath a pavement his workers found hundreds of bronze statues representing such gods as Osiris, Apis, Ptah, Isis and

Horus, many of them intact, sufficient to have made the fortune of an antiquities dealer. The news spread fast and put the whole city in a ferment. Leading Egyptians, foreign consuls, government employees and especially the dealers in antiquities were filled with jealous envy.

Meanwhile Mariette, convinced that his campaign was going to be a long one, had an expedition house built to shelter himself and his finds. Over this he hoisted the French flag to ensure its immunity from search. His foreman assistant was Bonnefoy, whose first (or second?) name is not known, or his previous history, except that he was, like Mariette, from Boulogne. His devotion to Mariette was returned by affection and trust. Mariette had a way of attracting people, who would give him willing service when he had need of them. The simple secret of his charm was the genuine affection that flowed from him to those in whom he had confidence. It was thus with his Maltese carpenter Fransesco and his *reis,* the foreman of labourers Hamzoui, whom he esteemed much more as valued friends than as servants.

His rivals did not leave him long in peace. On 4th June, 1851, four officials came to seize, in the name of the State of Egypt, the antiquities illegally discovered. Mariette had been denounced to Abbas Pasha, son and successor of Mohamed Ali. Mariette drove them away 'with blows of the *courbash*', or so he claimed. In later years he did admit that although his anecdotes all possessed a basis of truth he did not guarantee the details: 'Every time I tell them I recall that I started out by writing historical novels for the Boulogne papers.'

At all events the matter was patched up by the adroitness of Consul Le Moyne. There was a token stoppage of work and a token handing over of some of the antiquities; five inspectors were appointed, who seldom turned up, and honour was satisfied. Meanwhile the French Government had voted a credit of 30,000 francs for clearing the Serapeum, but had unfortunately assumed that the objects therefrom would go to France. Abbas Pasha was not the man to let this disregard of his rights pass without protest. On 19th November he ordered that antiquities already found could go to France, but digging must stop forthwith and not be resumed until France renounced claim to any future objects found.

This was a blow for Mariette. On 12th November he had at last penetrated to the Tomb of the Apis:

> The upper part of a magnificent door of white sandstone appeared. We set to work with enthusiasm, working through the night. Soon a corner of the entrance was exposed. I slipped through . . .

All was chaos in the vast underground galleries of the Tombs of the Bulls. The immense granite coffins of the bulls stood each in its recess off the galleries, but their lids had been displaced, and the stelae torn from the walls and scattered. But what remained was treasure for the archaeologist. It would have been hard to renounce all this wealth in favour of a ruler who would give it away to important visitors. 'The two supervising officers are absent,' wrote Mariette. 'Thus I need not inform them of the important discovery we have just made.'

Deciding to give up the least possible to the Pasha, Mariette and Bonnefoy installed their packing shop at the bottom of a 40 foot pit reached by a rope ladder. There, Fransesco packed the 513 items ceded to France—and with them he put all the new finds from the Apis tomb. The tomb was searched in secret by *Reis* Hamzoui and six picked men, who entered and left by a trapdoor that was closed in daytime and covered with sand. Beneath it Fransesco had built a wood-lined shaft down into the tomb. The secret work went on for several months until Le Moyne negotiated the resumption of digging. When the tomb was officially opened a great column of blue vapour poured from the north entrance over four hours, as the air of centuries, imprisoned in the vast galleries, escaped.

More ancient galleries yet were found, in which was an unplundered tomb of an Apis from the time of Ramses II. There, with bated breath and deep emotion, Mariette saw in the thin layer of sand on the floor 'the footprints of workmen who, 3,700 years before, had laid the god in his tomb.' Then, on 19th March, 1852, a wooden sarcophagus appeared, little damaged. Within, a golden mask covered the face of the mummy; an amulet of red jasper hung from a golden chain around the neck; a golden hawk, wings outspread, lay on the chest—all in the name of Prince Khaemwase, son of Ramses II, hero of the story of the search for the magic book of Thoth among the tombs of Saqqara thirty-seven centuries ago.

These jewels and much besides reached France through the generosity of the Pasha, whose officials were told to look the other way once Egypt's rights were acknowledged. Mariette was now world-famous; and to crown his happiness Eléonore and the children arrived unannounced to share his triumph. Cairo was sharply divided: his enemies were the jealous dealers and foreign consuls. His supporters were those who admired his courage, his wit, and the good nature that pierced his cloak of roughness.

Travellers were honoured to be shown through the Serapeum by Mariette; and thus one morning in February, 1853, a big jovial man introduced himself as Dr Heinrich Brugsch of Berlin. Mariette knew his writings, and warmly welcomed him to his house. Their instant friendship, born of an affinity of mind and disposition, was lifelong. Brugsch's visit of a few days stretched to eight months. Mariette directed excavation while his friend deciphered, gathering material for his demotic grammar. Big men both, big eaters, big drinkers, big talkers, equally noisy in mirth, they sometimes spent till dawn chatting and laughing in front of a bottle of *raki*: but morning would find each one at his job just as though they had slept all night. Brugsch saw Mariette as 'tall and broad of shoulder; his face, framed by a reddish beard, was as bronzed as that of an Egyptian peasant; its expression was melancholy, yet it could change instantly to one of good humour. His eyes, ravaged by ophthalmia, were red, swollen, weeping, and he was obliged to hide them behind enormous tinted lenses. His hands were rough to the touch and calloused like a mason's. He had a rich native wit, and the making of puns was a natural gift. He planned with great skill in all except his personal affairs. He was indifferent to money and could be generous as a king one moment, yet the next he might not know how to meet the smallest account.'

Around Mariette revolved a world of women, children, servants, native diggers and pets. Thirty monkeys frolicked around the house. There was no comfort inside: a guest's room was furnished with a table, stool and bed all made of planks. Serpents crawled, scorpions lodged in crevices, spider-webs hung like banners from the ceilings. 'Bats flew into my cell,' wrote Brugsch. 'I tucked my mosquito net under the

mattress and commended myself to the grace of God and all
the saints whilst the jackals, hyenas and wolves howled around
the house.' Mariette laughed at these discomforts, and if he
became depressed it was because he realized that one day he
would have to quit his hovel and return to France.

Thus he readily accepted 6,000 francs from the Duc de
Luynes to prove that the Sphinx was not a tomb, for the work
prolonged his stay. He found no tomb, and excavated the
temple of the Sphinx until the money ran out. A few feet more,
and he would have found for France the beautiful head of
Kephren that is now in Cairo Museum. The Serapeum was
cleared, and there was nothing for him but to return to France,
where he was promoted Assistant Keeper of Egyptian Antiquities at the Louvre.

He began to put his notes in order so as to publish his
excavations. But his publications were conceived on too vast
a scale, finance was always insufficient, and his attention
frequently diverted. He never succeeded in doing it. More
than a hundred years later Professor Jean Vercoutter of Lille
wrote, 'It would have surprised the learned world of his day,
enthusiastic over the first great find in modern Egyptology,
to be told that all those objects and inscriptions coming out
of the sand of Mariette's discovery would not yet be fully
published more than a century later. Even now, after the finding
of the royal mummies, Tutankhamon, and the royal tombs of
Tanis, the clearing of the Serapeum remains one of the great
moments of Egyptian exploration.'

Among the 7,000 objects brought out of the tombs of the
sacred bulls were the stelae that Mariette had seen scattered
on the ground when he first crawled inside. He never found
time to publish more than a few of them; and this was not
accomplished until Georges Posner and Jean Vercoutter
honoured the centenary of Mariette's great find with their
Textes biographiques du Sérapeum.

These 'biographical' stelae are peculiarly interesting because
they reveal for the first time the actual ceremony of the funeral
of the bull-gods. They were not put up by later pilgrims, as was
long supposed, but by persons privileged to take active part in
the interment, no matter how humble they might be. The
texts show that the Apis funeral rites were exactly like those

Abu Simbel after sand had been cleared. Engraving by Gau, 1822

John Lewis Burckhardt

The Nefertari temple, Abu Simbel, the first to be seen by Burckhardt. Drawn by Gau, 1822

Ramses II offers prisoners to Amon. Copy by Rossellini from Abu Simbel

Ramses II in his chariot, with a hunting lion. Copied for Rossellini from Abu Simbel

Edward de Montule sets off for the Red Sea by camel

The portico at Hermopolis, later burnt for lime, as Denon saw it in 1799

Right: Giovanni Batista Belzoni. From the portrait in his book

Below: Belzoni moves the colossal head of Ramses II. From a drawing in his book

Henry Salt. After the painting by J. L. Halls,
National Portrait Gallery

Drovetti and his team

The Dendera Zodiac, as drawn by Jollois and his colleagues for *Description de l'Egypte*

Left: Jean-François Champollion

Below: Dr. Thomas Young. *National Portrait Gallery*

The Valley of Kings, Thebes. The walled tomb in the center is Tutankh-amon's. Adjacent on the left is the entrance to the tomb of Ramses VI, in which Champollion, Rossellini and l'Hôte lived. Author's photograph

The Luxor temple, as Denon saw it in 1799. The French took the obelisk on the right to Paris in 1832

Lowering the Luxor obelisk

Emile Prisse d'Avennes in 1843

Sculptors carving colossi, from an 18th-dynasty tomb at Thebes. From Prisse d'Avennes

Drawing by Prisse d'Avennes from temple of Queen Hatshepsut at Deir al Bahri, Thebes

Deceased and his wife from 5th-dynasty tomb of Tiy at Saqqara. Copy by Prisse d'Avennes

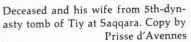

Auguste Mariette in 1861

Statue of seated scribe found by Mariette while excavating the Serapeum. From his *Choix de Monuments*

Mariette at Saqqara

Mariette's house at Saqqara

The temple of Queen Hatshepsut during Mariette's excavation. Below the ruined tower of the monastery is the temple wall from which Mariette claimed Lord Dufferin removed his carvings by night

A modern view of Hatshepsut's temple. Author's photograph

of a human god-king. The ceremonies were directed by the clergy of Ptah, and not by priests of the living Apis, which indicates the importance and popularity of the Apis cult. And it is significant to see very high persons, among them a prince royal and a future king, boast of having taken part personally in the funeral of an Apis, mixing with lesser people whose grief they shared, so that, as one text says, 'there was nothing to distinguish the elevation of their rank'. This humility and active participation in popular cults, says Vercoutter, is something one does not find expressed elsewhere in Egyptian literature. The religious life of individuals is an aspect of Egyptian religion that it is rarely possible to discern.

Mariette could see beyond the external trappings of the Apis cult: 'It was not merely a common animal that the Egyptian came to adore in the temple of Ptah. Through this commonplace symbol he was adoring the sacrifice of Osiris who consented to live within the confines of the flesh, and then to die a death by violence.' The fundamental principle of the Apis cult was the ancient belief in a divine incarnation to mediate between God Supreme and mankind, giving man a sense of intimate contact with the infinite, the secret of which man was for ever seeking.

In Mariette's opinion the Egyptians believed in one Supreme Being whose various attributes were deified. Thus Osiris was the good being *par excellence*, who perished victim of Typhon, descended into hell, rose again, and became man's guide to eternal life. Apis was the incarnation of Osiris, by tradition born of a virgin cow fertilized by the holy spirit from above. When he published these ideas in a paper on the Mother of Apis, devout Catholics were appalled by the suggestion that Christianity might have borrowed from pagan Egypt, and he was advised to express himself on less controversial subjects in future. He did that, yet his resentment smouldered. After a silence of twenty years he stoutly reasserted his view, which had not changed.

Mariette was always a little contemptuous of previous efforts to find the Serapeum. In a letter to Egger, a member of the Institute of France, dated 21st May, 1856, he says he was not the first to see the sphinxes described by Strabo. Dr Marucci had found a couple in 1832, and a few years later the trader

Fernandez had dug up and sold about thirty of them. But nobody had thought of their origin. 'If the Serapeum was not discovered earlier, the blame must be laid on Lepsius,' he wrote. 'He made several bores in the very enclosure of the Serapeum but recognized nothing.'

Mariette surely enjoyed a measure of malicious triumph in knowing that Lepsius, established at leisure on the site with a team of architects and other experts, had not been able to perceive what he, alone and with no resources, had spotted at first glance. He said as much in his publication the same year of *Choix de Monuments,* that gave a foretaste in ten plates of the lavish volumes on the Serapeum that Mariette planned but never carried beyond the first.

When the novelty of being famous had worn off, Mariette began to sigh for Egypt again. His job at the Louvre, so coveted ten years before, was now a cage with little chance of promotion. De Rougé, his superior, was ten years his junior; and his family responsibilities were increasing. 'What can I do?' he said with a shrug. 'I have only to look Eléonore in the eye, and there I am a father again!' His poorly-paid routine job led only to a dull future. In his office, studying some stela, his thoughts would wander:

> I was no longer at the Louvre; I was at the Serapeum, at the spot where I had picked up the stela; I could feel the stuffy air of the galleries; I could hear the voices of Bonnefoy and Hamzoui come to tell me of a fresh discovery. Then I would consign everything to hell; translation, de Rougé—even the Louvre itself. I would start ruminating on some scheme to explore Thebes and Abydos; or I would draft a memo in my head on the importance of setting up a service to protect the monuments—a service of which I, naturally, would be the head.

The opportunity to turn these daydreams into fact came through the retired diplomat, Ferdinand de Lesseps, who took time off from his struggle against opposition to his Suez Canal scheme to meet Mariette. The two practical dreamers found an affinity at once. Mariette put on paper his memo on the protection of monuments, and de Lesseps agreed to place this before Said Pasha, the ruler of Egypt who had succeeded Abbas, assassinated in 1854. Said had esteem and affection for his childhood friend de Lesseps, whose father had helped his own father, Mohamed Ali, to rise to power in Egypt.

But de Lesseps, diplomat, did not baldly present Mariette's paper to Said and startle him with the idea of setting up a brand new administrative service to protect useless monuments. Adroitly, he linked Mariette with the proposed visit to Egypt of Prince Napoleon of France. Thus Mariette, leaving with his family in October, 1857, was somewhat disconcerted to find that he was not going as head of the service he had proposed, but to search for antiquities as gifts to the distinguished visitor when he came.

Well, at least he was back in Egypt, and the Pasha received him affably, gave him money, and put the viceregal river-steamer *Samannoud* at his disposal. Mariette started excavations at Saqqara and Giza. His friend Brugsch came to join him, and together they went up river to dig at Thebes and Abydos, just as he had dreamed at his desk. Results were good, and he returned from the journey with his hands full of booty.

But his enemies were quick to spot the true reason for his return to Egypt. Consuls, middlemen and sly-diggers united to prevent a State monopoly on the ruins. Evil rumours were spread: protection of monuments was only a façade behind which France concealed its intention to seize the country, it was whispered to the Viceroy. Said paid little attention to such guile, however; so that, when a crushing blow to Mariette's hopes was delivered by Prince Napoleon—who cancelled his visit—Said Pasha restored them by appointing Mariette director of all ancient works in Egypt, on de Lesseps's recommendation.

Odious though the appointment was to traffickers in antiquities, it was hailed with joy abroad. Heinrich Brugsch was delighted: 'Said Pasha never had a finer idea than when he conferred upon you the high dignity of director of historic monuments.' The opinion of Brugsch is certainly that of posterity.

20 Consolidation

MARIETTE had realized his dream. Now he could devote all his life to the preservation and publication of the monuments. His situation was nevertheless insecure. He was responsible directly to the Viceroy, relying on his good graces for money. For the proposed museum the best he could obtain were the dilapidated Nile-side stores and offices of a defunct steamship company at Bulac. But he was happy, with Bonnefoy as assistant, and old Hamzoui and his son Roubi supervising in the field.

He had sufficient field staff to make a start, and the Pasha provided labour for the excavations. But there was nothing in the budget for scientific staff to copy and interpret inscriptions. Fortunately the Assistant Keeper at the Louvre Théodore Devéria was willing to come for nothing, for the sake of being in Egypt with his old chief. He arrived early in 1859, just in time to see Mariette find the Table of Kings of Saqqara, listing fifty-eight kings up to Ramses II. Mariette showed him the Serapeum,

> illuminated by candles held in the hands of about 200 children sitting Egyptian fashion, motionless as statues. The effect was truly magical. We examined one of the gigantic sarcophagi of the sacred bulls, beautifully cut from a single block of granite. Eight of us got inside, and we estimated that forty could have stood upright in it. Madame Mariette and her young son were with us; Mariette, who wants to make an archaeologist out of the child, never misses an opportunity to take him visiting the Egyptian monuments. He really is taking him in hand early; the boy is only two years old.

Mariette took Devéria to Upper Egypt on *Samannoud*. At Thebes they saw the temple of Queen Hatshepsut being cleared. There they uncovered the now famous Punt Expedition scenes, and accused the young Marquis of Dufferin and Ava, who was excavating nearby, of breaking their wall by night and stealing their prize pieces. Whether the allegation was true or false, the future Viceroy of India, in his short career as an Egyptologist, acquired a collection of 138 relief carvings which still excites the interest of scholars. Many of the sculptures from the Deir el Bahri temple are still cemented in the walls of Clandeboye, his home in Ireland.

At Karnak, Mariette and Devéria studied the conquests of Thutmose III, just uncovered; at Edfu they watched the native village being removed from the roof of this almost perfect temple. At Abydos, wrote Devéria, Mariette pointed out to his workmen the place where they should dig to disclose a boundary wall. They were astonished when it quickly came to light, bearing inscriptions of the highest interest.

> An old Arab came up and said to him: 'I have never left this village, yet I never even heard say there was a wall there. How old are you that you should remember it?' 'Three thousand years,' replied Mariette imperturbably. 'Well,' said the old man, 'to have attained so great an age, yet to appear so young, you must be a great saint. Let me look at you.' So for three days he came to contemplate the great saint, three thousand years old, who, with unrivalled prodigality, distributed whacks of his stick among the workmen who did not work to his liking.

At Thebes they inspected the clearance of the Medinet Habu temple. It was here that the good Bonnefoy had spent his energies too hard. Early in 1859 he died of heat and exhaustion, to the great grief of Mariette, whose happiest memories of Egypt went with him. Good fortune brought as replacement to this faithful friend an Italian named Luigi Vassalli, no less devoted.

Back in Cairo they received word that Mariette's diggers at Thebes had discovered a coffin richly decorated with gold, bearing the name of a Queen Aa-hotep. Unfortunately the provincial Governor heard of it too, ordered the coffin to be opened, tore the mummy to bits and extracted the Queen's jewels, which he despatched by special steamer direct to the

Pasha, thinking to get in his good graces. Knowing that to let them reach this exalted destination would be to risk losing them for his museum, Mariette set off on *Samannoud* armed with a ministerial warrant to stop all ships carrying antiquities and confiscate them. Devéria wrote home about it:

> We perceived the ship carrying the treasure coming towards us. In half an hour the two steamers were alongside. There ensued a very heated discussion; seeing that he was getting nowhere, and pushed to the limit of patience by their obstinate resistance, M. Mariette employed the only means recognized by all here as being really efficacious: he distributed a few hard punches, proposed to throw one man into the river, to blow the brains out of another, to send a third to the galleys, to hang a fourth, and to treat the rest in a like manner. Thanks to this they agreed to transfer the antiquities to our ship, if a receipt was given. Ten minutes after this scene we were on the way back to Bulac, carrying as prisoner the miscreant supervisor who had handed the mummy over to the Governor. He was very cowed, yet he sat smoking his hubble-bubble pipe philosophically enough. We arrived at Bulac a little before dinner, and only there did we open the famous box, despite its seals. To our great surprise the jewels all bore the name of Aahmes, a king of the 18th dynasty, while that of Queen Aa-hotep was not once mentioned. The workmanship is finer than any of the same kind known, and there are about two kilograms of gold, marvellously worked, incrusted with stones and coloured enamel.

This is the treasure of Queen Aa-hotep, mother of King Aahmes, that Mariette was to rescue later on, in yet another narrow escape, that it might remain one of the marvels of Cairo Museum today. At that time, Mariette was planning to replace his makeshift museum at Bulac with a proper building, for which he had the funds and authority from the Pasha.

But it was now, when everything smiled upon him, that the disease showed itself that was to leave him no rest or peace to the end of his days. Back in France, his family doctor diagnosed sugar diabetes, little understood at the time.

Apparently recovered, he returned to Egypt and started excavations at many fresh points. But within two years, in 1861, he was hastening back to Boulogne for further treatment. This he was not permitted to complete. The Emperor himself disturbed his rest, picking him as a man useful to science and to

French diplomacy simultaneously. He landed back in Egypt on 16th September, calling himself 'a veritable diplomatic mission'. His task was to talk Said into a State visit to France to be dazzled by the Emperor's grandeur while a noose was slipped around his neck in the shape of a financial loan. The mission was extremely distateful to Mariette, yet he dared not refuse: Britain would surely acquire this influence in Egypt if France did not, and then where would his precious museum be?

Mariette had little trouble in bringing the Pasha to the proper state of mind; and while negotiations on the diplomatic level went on, his friend Théodore Devéria joined him on his second voyage to Egypt. Son of a fashionable painter, young Théodore had passed from admiration of Egyptian art to a study of its writing by a strange chance. When the barricades were up in Paris, in 1848, and the National Guard was called out, he was seventeen years old, impulsive and romantic. He intercepted his father's call-up papers, put on his father's uniform, shouldered the long rifle and sallied forth to war. After a fierce fight his battalion took a barricade at the corner of rue Saint-Jacques and rue de la Harpe, where he fired his enormous rifle and was knocked over by the recoil. Then he carried his gravely wounded captain to hospital, where he got a wigging from du Sommerard, a friend of his father, and Director of the Museum. A companion-in-arms was Jules Feuquières, who had printed Champollion's Egyptian grammar in 1836. Through these two he met Mariette, Lenormant and de Rougé, who encouraged him to study Latin, Coptic and Arabic. This in turn led to employment at the Louvre.

Now, in 1862, he went up river with Rondeau and Roquigny, whom he had met aboard *Indus* on his voyage out. That the young men enjoyed their trip is evident from Devéria's diary between January and April. He speaks of the state of the monuments, and the drawings he made; of the villages and the slave-markets; of swimming in the Nile—until they saw seven crocodiles 'and Rondeau did not want to swim any more'. The professional dancing-girls interested the young Frenchmen, although Devéria pronounced them 'rarely beautiful, in fact even ugly for the most part, but their expression often has a lot of character. Their dance consists entirely of a sort of convulsive shivering that has something obscene about it but nothing seductive. These then are the incomparable beauties sung by all the oriental poets.'

At Esna he drew three of the dancing-girls in watercolour. Afterwards 'these ladies so admired my talent that after my declining to enter their dwelling they decided to carry me in. It was only by offering a vigorous resistance that I avoided this honour. Those were strong women!' And at Aswan:

> We discovered the most accomplished Negress it would be possible to see. Young and pretty, she was not varnished at all with castor oil, and she did not stink in any way. Her name was Zaphira and her dwelling most primitive. When we came upon her she was cooking supper outside her door, but that did not stop her doing us the honours of her home.

One must suppose that Zaphira's accomplishments were terpsichorean, for there is no further description of the honours.

In Luxor they met the American Edwin Smith, from Connecticut. Three years before he had 'turned hermit, not to become a saint or to study the ruins, but to give himself entirely to the translation of a treatise on medicine written in fine hieratic on papyrus'. This was the now well-known Edwin Smith Papyrus which his daughter presented, on his death, to the New York Historical Society.

> He showed me too an unique collection of false scarabs, a complete collection of all the cartouches of all the kings of Egypt, product of a too-intelligent Arab to whom the Obelisk Expedition gave this unhappy idea. They would trick the cleverest. Smith, half mummified by the fatigue of several days' excursion with the visiting Prince of Wales, came to lunch on board. The poor fellow had forgotten his French, and we could scarcely get a word out of him. We left him to sleep and went to admire Karnak.

Edwin Smith in fact spent eighteen years at Luxor as money-lender and antiquities dealer, and it is said that he faked many of the trade goods himself, or was accessory to their faking; for he had a scholar's knowledge of the writings.

In April of that year, 1862, Mariette and Devéria embarked together for France, where Mariette was to escort the Viceroy during his impressive visit. When Said passed through Boulogne

Mariette had arranged such a tumultuous welcome that the sovereign could do no less than create him a *bey* on the spot, give him a pension revertable upon his wife, and pay for the education of his children from his privy purse.

Within six months Said Pasha was dead. Mariette was sincerely grieved. He had lost a dear friend. And he was also alarmed about the future. But Ismail, the new Khedive, confirmed all Said's promises and even became so carried away by his own enthusiasm for progress that he promised Mariette a lot more than he was ever able to perform.

Mariette spent this year refurnishing his museum and escorting very important visitors, including Prince Napoleon, who had at last decided to come. But His Royal Highness scarcely stirred from his lounge chair on the Nile steamer *Menchieh*. He found the weather too hot.

Mariette's renown was such that from far corners of the Egyptian Empire came accounts of antiquities sighted by patrolling officers. Thus from Gebel Barkal in Sudan came the tracing of an inscription on a 6 foot stela, in which Mariette read the name of Pianki Meiamun, a king of Cush, and a list of his campaigns against various Egyptian chiefs. He sent for the stela, and meanwhile despatched a copy of the inscription to de Rougé. It interested the veteran Egyptologist so much that he decided to spend the winter of 1863-4 in Egypt, bringing his son Jacques, twenty-one years old, and a promising Egyptologist himself. Jacques lived long enough to attend the Champollion Centenary in 1922. Father and son spent a happy winter copying inscriptions which Jacques published in four volumes the following year. De Rougé's last task in Egypt was to take a copy of the Pianki stela, now safely in the courtyard at Bulac, in a roaring sandstorm. It turned out to be of great historical interest, telling how this king of Cush conquered Egypt, and thus became the first king of the 25th dynasty.

At Abydos Mariette brought to light another Table of Kings, this time in the beautiful Seti I temple, and the best preserved of all. Before Mariette had time to study it, a young German scholar on his first visit to Egypt, Johannes Dümichen, copied it and sent the copy to Lepsius, who did not lose a moment in publishing this interesting addition to knowledge. Unfortunately in the hurry nobody remembered to mention that it was found by Mariette. He never doubted that it was an oversight; yet, as he wrote to Devéria, 'I poured out the wine; it is only right that I should drink it.' There he would have let the matter rest, but the political press turned it into a question of national pride, with brutal attacks on Dümichen and Lepsius. The French Egyptologist Chabas rose in their defence, in all fairness. But he was carried away by his fighting spirit, and attacked Mariette for his slowness in publishing. The result was a coldness between Mariette and these three that never thawed in the case of the Germans.

François Joseph Chabas was an instance of an armchair Egyptologist who never saw Egypt yet was highly respected as a scholar. He seldom stirred from Chalon-sur-Saône, where he was a wine merchant, and where he studied inscriptions supplied by his colleagues. He edited the Harris Magical and other papyri.

In 1865 Devéria accepted a trip to Egypt with a wealthy friend Henri Péreire, and Mariette profited by this to beg once more for his help, this time at Dendera. It was Devéria's third voyage. On New Year's Day he wrote to his mother, 'It is 10 o'clock at night and my companions have not yet returned from the fair at Tanta, where they went this morning by rail to see the dancing-girls and slave markets. Much good may it do them! As for me, Mariette's beautiful museum keeps me too busy to follow them on that kind of expedition.' This is a change of tune from the dancing-girls of his last trip. But of course he was writing to his mother.

Two days later, on 3rd January, they are taken to visit Memphis by Mariette. Arthur Rhoné, one of the party, describes their early morning arrival at Bulac on donkeys. Mariette awaits them, fidgeting impatiently under the trees. 'He shakes our hands impetuously and hustles on to the deck of his steamer which is covered with divans that make it like an open-air drawing-room.' The ship passes through the beautiful morning, past Cairo of those days, until the rose and violet mass of the pyramids of Giza appears. 'The Bey sparkles with lively originality, backed up by M. Sciama, engineer of the Suez Isthmus, whose charming wit will make the journey unforgettable. An excellent picnic lunch was provided from great family baskets that one did not suspect were there . . .'

and Mariette convulses the company with atrocious puns like,
'*Donne ta Memphis, car je Thèbes et tu m'es Caire.*'*

Those were the last of the happy days. A terrible epidemic
of cholera swept over Egypt, and thousands were dying. Life
was tense, terrifying, and there was no mood for merry picnics.
Towards the end of summer, at last, the disease abated, and
they were able to relax. Heinrich Brugsch tells how he joined
Mariette and Eléonore sitting one evening in their garden in
front of the museum. 'The conversation was becoming quite
lively, when suddenly an owl hooted. Madame Mariette
appeared to be frightened, and it was almost with anguish that
she said to me, "Is it calling one of us?" Three hours later she
felt the first attacks of the malady. She died on the 14th. of
August, at dawn.'

Things were never the same again for Mariette. Eléonore had
been wonderful for him. To forget, he took to his infallible
remedy: work, and more work. The faithful Devéria joined him
at forty-eight hours' notice, and they went to Upper Egypt
together to copy everything already found at Abydos and 400
reliefs and inscriptions at Dendera. It was Devéria's fourth and
last voyage. Back in France, he set to work on the plates for a
volume on Abydos.

Mariette joined him soon in Paris, where he stayed for a year
to prepare the Egyptian exhibit in the International Exhibition
of 1867. 'One Thursday evening of that year,' wrote twenty-
one-year-old student Gaston Maspero, 'I heard strange news.'
Two of his classmates had been invited by Desjardins, a friend
of Mariette, to dine with the great man; and they had spoken
of Maspero's inordinate love of hieroglyphs; of how he studied
unaided; and of how he had constructed his own grammar.
Sceptical, Mariette sent him a text. 'A week later the translation
was done, and Mariette, somewhat astonished to find
Egyptology in a college student, wrote on a scrap of paper that
I have guarded preciously, "This young man promises to be an
Egyptologist of the first order." It was the first time I saw
this twisted, hasty writing that was to become so familiar
to me.'

When Sir Gaston Maspero died suddenly while addressing

* Probably directed at his infant son. Unscrambled, the pun presumably
read, *Donne ta main, fils, car je t'aime et tu m'es cher.*

the *Académie* on 30th June, 1916, he had been Mariette's successor in Egypt for thirty-five years.

Mariette's part of the Exhibition was an impressive replica of ancient Egypt, for which many original pieces from Bulac were brought to Paris. He was showered with congratulations and honoured publicly by the Khedive.

But sight of the jewels of Aa-hotep aroused the cupidity of the Empress, who asked the Khedive Ismail to make them his gift to her. The poor man, taken unawares, dared not refuse outright. 'There is,' he said, 'one more powerful than I at Bulac. You should apply to him.'

Approached by the Empress's lady-in-waiting and others, who offered him, most adroitly, high positions as a bribe, Mariette refused them all. In refusing, he lost the support of the Emperor, and weakened his position with the Khedive, on whom the Emperor's displeasure fell too. But he never regretted his firmness. France had given him to Egypt to look after its antiquities, and it was his duty to defend them faithfully. Had he weakened this once, he would have created a precedent that soon would have drained his museum of all its finest pieces.

He returned to Egypt to find his labour force drastically reduced. The Suez Canal was nearing completion; and to wreck this French enterprise the British Parliament appealed to the world to seek an end to the forced labour used to dig it. They had not been so solicitous about the poor workers when the British built railways in Egypt. The fact was that forced labour was not total slavery. The men were paid wages, but were forced out of their farms to work where the Khedive directed. Nobody denied its injustice; but when world opinion forced the Khedive to change to free labour, the Canal was nearly abandoned; and Mariette's excavations suffered too. Only de Lesseps's doggedness and ingenuity saved the Canal, which was opened in a blaze of glory on 17th November, 1869, by the Empress Eugénie herself, aboard the French royal yacht *Aigle*, leading the Khedivial yacht *Maroussa* and ships of the nations bearing crowned heads and royal dukes. The Khedive deputed de Lesseps and Mariette to conduct the royal guests, the one through the Canal, the other up the Nile; and to mark the occasion Ismail asked Mariette to swing back to his old profession of letters, and write the libretto for *Aida*, the opera with an ancient Egyptian theme, for which Verdi composed the music.

To make sure that the stage settings for his opera would look authentic, Mariette went to Paris the next year, travelling with Brugsch. There the friends had to part hurriedly, Brugsch rushing back to Germany: the Franco-Prussian war had started. Mariette remained, enduring shell-fire in Paris with his two children, depressed, with his malady gnawing at him. Devéria was in poor health too, but would not quit his post because of the treasures in his care. Then on 10th January, 1871, a shell struck Devéria's apartment, forcing him out in the intense cold. He was taken really sick and died on the 25th. Utterly miserable, Mariette hurried back to Egypt as soon as the siege lifted, with his two older daughters.

With the Emperor in exile and France no longer strong, Mariette's enemies in Egypt tried to persuade Ismail to replace him with Brugsch, eminent scholar of the victor nation. But Ismail revolted at the base suggestion, and arranged a warm welcome for Mariette. Brugsch wrote to Mariette that he had no part in the intrigues, to which Mariette replied: 'For me you are not a German; you are Brugsch. I love you as a true friend, greatly, with a spontaneous sympathy which nothing has destroyed or ever will destroy.' And nothing ever did destroy it.

Mariette had started on a tour of Upper Egypt when suddenly came news of his youngest daughter Marie, desperately ill in Boulogne. He returned at once to her side. Chabas, with whom there had been a reconciliation, invited him to Chalon. But he could not even pay this desirable visit. The Khedive ordered him back to Egypt to quell further intrigues against him. He had to leave Marie on her sick-bed, and the little girl died when he was two days at sea. She was only sixteen.

During Mariette's absence, a vast tomb near the pyramid of Meidum was excavated by one of Mariette's assistants, Daninos. He was a Greek employed at the Louvre, who came to join Mariette in 1869, and who was later raised to the rank of pasha. The mason who entered the tomb first with a candle came scrambling out in terror, saying that two beings in there had stared at him with living eyes. Daninos then went in to see what terrified the man. 'How great was my stupefaction,' he wrote, 'to find two beautifully modelled heads, the eyes of which, reflecting the light I held, looked so alive as to be really scaring.' The eyes were cleverly made of quartz and rock crystal, giving a lifelike appearance. Daninos had found the statues of Prince Rahotep and Princess Nofret of the 4th dynasty, showing the perfection of portrait art at this remote period. The pair of statues is another of the Cairo Museum's great treasures at the present day.

For a portrait of Mariette himself at the time of this great find we turn to the Vicomte de Vogué who made his acquaintance about then:

> A man of great stature broadly built, aged rather than old, an Athlete roughed out of the mass like the colossi over which he watches. His deep-toned face has a dreamy and morose look, yet how many times, sitting on the bank of the Nile, did he speak with feeling of this strange Egypt, its river, its nocturnal skies. It caused no surprise to see a tear in those eyes reddened by overwork and lack of sleep. This childish tear welled at a symphony of Beethoven, or the farewell of a friend.

De Vogué was in Egypt in 1872 when the death of Charles de Rougé left the chair of Egyptology vacant at the *Collège de France*. Mariette was proposed for it, to give him a secure future. He was tempted, and even said he would go. 'At this,' says de Vogué, 'we would tell him, "No, Chief, you would never desert your children of Bulac." Mariette would get angry, swear we wished him harm—and never quit.' Mariette nominated Maspero, who had been helping him with proofs and plates since Devéria's death.

Winter and spring of 1873 passed in studious calm. The Viceroy unexpectedly authorized the building of a new museum at Giza, and the *Académie des Inscriptions* considered Mariette favourably as a candidate for the 20,000 franc prize for contribution to scholarship. In an atmosphere of peace and almost of elation he prepared for a trip to Europe, when, on the eve of departure, his eldest daughter Joséphine-Cornélie was found dead in her bed.

This brutal blow that struck him at full prosperity left him without hope and with little will to live. Friends forced him to leave as soon as the funeral was over, but he took to his bed in Paris. He dragged himself to Vienna to supervise the Exhibition there, and finished the winter at Boulogne. He did at last pay the long-promised visit to Chabas, cementing a friendship that lasted to the end. He returned to Egypt with his sister Sophie, who had kept house for him since the death of Joséphine; and his spirits rose a little at the terms of praise accompanying the award of the 20,000 franc prize.

The next four years passed without notable incident beyond the mounting financial difficulties of Khedive Ismail that are a part of modern history. Work on the new museum was halted, and digging much restricted. In 1876 Mariette made a careful tour of all his favourite sites along the Nile. Had he, asks Maspero, fond chronicler of Mariette's life, a presentiment that he would not see them often again? Though the journey was leisurely and untroubled, he landed back at Bulac ill and depressed.

Yet he had his encouragements in this period. In 1874 the *Société géographique* awarded him their Gold Medal for the discovery at Karnak of some 600 place-names of Thutmose III, which he published. He decided to publish, too, a detailed account of the Serapeum. 'It is a debt to French science,' he wrote, 'that I am going to try to pay off.' But none of his grand plans for publication ever ran its course. They might have done so, had he not changed his plans incessantly and destroyed the profits of his backers and publishers.

In 1877 he went to France to prepare exhibits for the Universal Exhibition of 1878. But diabetes struck him during the journey, and he had to rest at Boulogne. This malady causes mental depression, and he worried about his publications, his personal finance, and the Khedive's finances. He could not pay the contractors at the Exhibition when they presented their accounts. He received nothing himself, and had to borrow to pay his hotel bills.

Things were worse when he returned to Egypt. The Nile had the most disastrous flood of the century in October, 1878, and Bulac museum was washed out. The antiquities had been put out of reach, but the showcases and fittings were wrecked, and the walls cracked. In his home books and papers, gathered over years, had been soaked to pulp. There was no money in the country to put things right. 'I assure you that during the last three months I have not lived,' he wrote to a friend. 'From day to day I expect to be obliged to offer my resignation to the Khedive. No more excavations, no museum, extreme economy . . . Never did I realize how much I loved Egypt until the day when I knew that from one moment to the next she might perish.'

The Khedive Ismail could do no more for him than confer upon him the rank of pasha. Three weeks later, on 29th June, 1879, Ismail was deposed by the joint action of England and France, and Tewfik reigned in his place.

Power was in the hands of two European ministers on whose goodwill Mariette could count. But he had no time to profit by it. He was called to France urgently by the news that his son Tady had a mortal illness. He spent sad days at Boulogne watching the life fade from the son who, in the happy days, had been carried around the monuments to make an archaeologist of him. When Tady passed away there was little left for him to live for. It is Mariette's noble tragedy that those he loved greatly were taken from him one by one, mostly at moments of his triumph. Sadly he turned once more to his last love, his science, for his last comfort. He continued to speak of his Serapeum publication, but without much conviction that he would ever see it finished. He returned to Egypt to the now unaccustomed experience of receiving his salary at the end of each month without fail. He worked hard repairing his museum, and some of the pyramids at the west of Saqqara were opened up.

This was done at Maspero's request, who believed that some of them might conceal inscriptions, against Mariette's stubborn opinion that all pyramids were mute. But before any conclusions could be reached he had to go to France once more for a cure.

It did no good. 'The leaves are fallen and will never grow again,' he wrote to Desjardins from Boulogne, 18th October, 1880. 'I tried to work a little on the Serapeum, but I had to give it up. This is the biggest of my debts. It is dreadfully stupid, that the Serapeum has been there for thirty years and has still not been shown to the public. Later on I will be blamed for this and rightly. I commenced my career with the Serapeum; I would esteem myself happy if I could finish it with the Serapeum. Unfortunately, I fear, I have wished somewhat too long.'

Yes, somewhat too long. His doctors said that they would not be responsible for his life if he were to try to travel. As soon as he heard this, Mariette's sole desire was to return to Cairo and die there. After a fearful journey during which he suffered two haemorrhages, he reached Bulac somehow. At once he had a lounge chair placed on the porch and began to ask Vassalli for news of the museum and the excavations. Climbing plants were beginning to grow over the trellis. 'Next summer you'll be able to sit here in the shade,' they told him. Suddenly Mariette burst into sobs: 'I shall never be better,' he said. 'And I shall never again make my way through the verandah either to my office or to the museum.'

Indeed he never did. Heinrich Brugsch, who called every day, told him that Maspero was right about pyramids having inscriptions and brought evidence to prove it. 'There are then inscribed pyramids!' exclaimed Mariette with emotion. It was the last scientific delight of his life.

Maspero himself arrived in Cairo on 5th January, 1881, sent by the French Government, anxious that the succession might not pass out of French hands. He found Mariette looking little worse than when he had seen him in Paris in November. Mariette received him cheerfully, making fun of his mission.

But when Maspero came again to Bulac a day or two later, the end was approaching, though the death pangs lasted a whole week, so sturdy was the man. Even his enemies followed with anguish the long phases of Mariette's struggle with death. The Khedive Tewfik sent messages of sympathy. Sailors from Mariette's steamer wandered ceaselessly around the house, crying and disputing as to who could perform last services for their beloved master. Maspero wrote:

I will always remember those distressing hours we passed in the next room exchanging sadly a few words in a low tone. At intervals one of us would go to the door and glance towards the deathbed. The great body moved unceasingly, pulling and pushing at the covers, taking off the *tarbush* and replacing it on the head, some-times silent, but mostly lost in a flow of disconnected words. Twice or thrice a day Mariette's senses cleared, he recognized those around, spoke a few breathless words; but soon intelligence faded and delirium more violent than before set in. At moments it seemed he relived the excavations of his early days. Once the ideal museum of which he had dreamed so many years appeared before him. He saw it finished from threshold to gable, just as he had planned it. On the morning of 18th January he imagined he was going out. He tossed off the covers and stood up. It needed two men to get him back into bed. This was his final effort, and from then he sank fast. He died at seven thirty-five that evening, surrounded by his children and friends.

No matter what has been said in criticism of Mariette's methods, nobody can deny that he accomplished a great work for which he alone had the stature. Without Mariette, Egypt would have gone on destroying her antiquities. He forced Egypt to preserve them; and thus he made possible the great scientific excavations in the years that followed, up to the present day. Without Mariette, the treasures of history and art discovered in recent times would have been scattered to the dealers and the winds, meaningless. And if today Egypt owns the finest museum of ancient art and history in the world, it is certainly owing to him.

Mariette wished to be buried in Old Cairo beside Eléonore and Joséphine. But Egypt, sadly moved by his loss, rendered him almost royal honours. It was decreed that he should have a State funeral and be buried at the very door of his museum at Bulac. And if the museum should be moved elsewhere, he was to be moved with it. So, in front of the new building at Kasr-el-Nil, when it came, Egypt erected a tomb of granite and white marble, and a bronze statue. To mark the feeling that inspired this homage, these words were engraved on the pedestal:

A MARIETTE PACHA
L'EGYPTE RECONNAISSANTE

Bibliography

Ampère, J. J., *Voyage en Egypte et Nubie*. Paris, 1868.

Baikie, James, *Egyptian Papyri & Papyrus-hunters*. London, 1925.

Bataille, A., *Les Memnonia*. Cairo, 1952.

Bell, H. Idris, *Egypt from Alexander to the Arab Conquest*. Oxford, 1948.

Belzoni, Giovanni, *Narrative of the Operations in Egypt and Nubia*. London, 1820.

Bernand, A. & E., *Les inscriptions grecques et latines du Colosse de Memnon*. Cairo, 1960.

Boullaye-le-Gouz, *Voyages et Observations*. Paris, 1657.

Budge, E. A. Wallis, *The Rosetta Stone* . . . London, 1929.
Cleopatra's Needles . . . London, 1926.

Carnarvon, Earl of, & Carter, Howard, *Five Years' Exploration in Egypt*. London, 1912.

Capart, Jean, *Le centenaire de Champollion*. Brussels, 1922.

Carré, Jean-Marie, *Voyageurs et écrivains français en Egypte*. Cairo, 1932.
'Première description du temple de Karnak dans la littérature française.' Article in *Chronique d'Egypte* 13.

Champollion-Figeac, M., *L'obélisque de Louqsor transporté à Paris*. Paris, 1833.

Champollion, Jean-François, *Lettre à M. Dacier* . . . Paris, 1822.
Lettres écrites de l'Egypte. Paris, 1833.
Monuments de l'Egypte et de la Nubie. Paris, 1845.

Clément, R., *Les Français d'Egypte aux XVII & XVIII siècles*. Cairo, 1960.

Combes, Edmond, *Voyage en Egypte, en Nubie*. Paris, 1846.

D'Athanasi, Giovanni, *Researches and discoveries in Upper Egypt under the direction of Henry Salt Esq*. London, 1836.

Davies, Bryn, 'Henry Salt.' Article in *Bulletin*, Faculty of Arts, University of Egypt, Cairo, 1934.

Dawson, Warren R., *The Griffith Studies*. Article on William Stukeley. London, 1932.

De Montule, Edward, *Travels in Egypt in 1818 and 1819*. London, 1821.

Denon, Vivant, *Travels in Upper & Lower Egypt*. London, 1803.

De Verninac Saint-Maur, E., *Voyage du LUXOR*. Paris, 1835.

Erman, Adolf, *Literature of the Ancient Egyptians*. London, 1927.

Forbin, Count de, *Travels in Egypt 1817-1818*. London, 1819.

Forster, E. M., *Alexandria, a History and a Guide*. Alexandria, 1922.

Gau, F. C., *Monuments de la Nubie*. Paris, 1824.

Gauthier, Henri, 'Un précurseur de Champollion.' Article in *Bulletin de l'Institut français*, Cairo, 1906.

Gilbert, Pierre, 'Homer et l'Egypte.' Article in *Chronique d'Egypte* 27, 1939.

Goyon, Georges, *Inscriptions et graffiti des voyageurs sur la grande pyramide*. Cairo, 1944.

Greaves, John, *Pyramidographia*. London, 1641.

Hamilton, William, *Aegyptiaca*. London, 1809.

Henniker, Sir Frederick, *Travels*. London, 1823.

Hogg, Edward, *Visit to Alexandria, Damascus & Jerusalem*. London, 1835.

Hohlwein, N., 'Déplacements et tourisme dans l'Egypte romaine.' Article in *Chronique d'Egypte* 30, 1940.

Jollois, Prosper, *Journal d'un ingénieur 1798-1802* (edited by Gaston Maspero). Paris, 1904.

Kamal, Ahmed Bey (trans.), *Livre des Perles enfouies . . .* Cairo, 1907.

Khater, A., *Le régime juridique des fouilles . . .* Cairo, 1960.

Kircher, Athanasius, *Interpretatio Hieroglyphica*. Rome, 1660.

Lebas, J. B. Apollinaire, *L'obélisque de Luxor*. Paris, 1839.

Legh, Thomas, *Narrative of a Journey in Egypt and the country beyond the Cataracts*. London, 1816.

Lenoir, Alexandre, *Explication d'un manuscrit égyptien*. Paris, 1812.

Lepsius, Richard, *Lettre à M. le Professeur H. Rosellini*. Rome, 1837. *Discoveries*. London, 1852.

L'Hôte, Nestor, *L'obélisque de Louqsor*. Paris, 1836. *Lettres d'Egypte*. Paris, 1840.

Lucas, Paul, *Voyage du Sieur Paul Lucas*. Rouen, 1719.

Mallet, Dominique, *Les premiers établissements des Grecs en Egypte*. Paris, 1893. *Les rapports des Grecs avec l'Egypte*. Cairo, 1922.

Mariette, Auguste, his published works in general, especially *Choix de monuments*. Paris, 1856.
Memoir sur la mère d'Apis. Paris, 1856.
Lettre inédite à M. Egger. Paris, 1856.
Le Sérapéum de Memphis. Paris, 1857.
Voyage dans la Haute Egypte. Paris, 1893.
Monuments divers. Paris, 1889.
Maspero, Gaston, *Contes populaires de l'Egypte ancienne*. Paris, 1882.
Etudes de Mythologie I. Paris, 1893.
Auguste Mariette, notice biographique et oeuvres diverses. Paris, 1904.
Mayes, Stanley, *The Great Belzoni*. London, 1959.
Melly, André, *Lettres d'Egypte & de Nubie*. London, 1852.
Minutoli, Heinrich von, *Reise zum Tempel des Jupiter Ammon*. Berlin, 1824.
Minutoli, Baroness, *Recollections of Egypt*. London, 1827.
Mond, Robert, *The Bucheum*. London, 1934.
Montet, Pierre, *Isis*. Paris, 1956.
Moret, A., *Rois et dieux d'Egypte VII, Homère et l'Egypte*. Paris, 1911.
Petrie, W. A. Flinders, *A Season in Egypt*. London, 1888.
Ten Years' Digging in Egypt. London, 1891.
Pettigrew, Thomas Joseph, *History of Egyptian Mummies*. London, 1834.
Pillet, Maurice, *Thèbes, palais et nécropoles*. Paris, 1930.
Prisse d'Avennes, Emile, *Histoire de l'art égyptien*. Paris, 1879.
Prisse d'Avennes, Emile (fils), *Notice biographique sur Emile Prisse d'Avennes*. Paris, 1894.
Renouf, Peter le Page, *Egyptological and Philological Essays I*. Paris, 1902.
Reybaud, Louis, *Histoire de l'expédition française en Egypte*. Paris, 1828.
Rhind, Alexander Henry, *Thebes, Its Tombs & Their Tenants*. London, 1862.
Rhoné, Arthur, *Egypte à petites journées*. Paris, 1877.
Mariette, sa vie et ses oeuvres. Private issue, Paris, 1884.
Rifaud, J. J., *Voyages 1805-27*. Paris, 1830.
Rosellini, Ippolito, *I Monumenti dell'Egitto e della Nubia*. Pisa, 1832.
Salt, Henry, *Essay on Dr. Young's & M. Champollion's Phonetic System of Hieroglyphs*. London, 1825.
Sandys, George, *Travels*. 7th. edition, London, 1673.
Savary, Claude Etienne, *Lettres sur l'Egypte*. Paris, 1785.
Shaw, Thomas, *Travels relating to several parts of Barbary and the Levant*. Oxford, 1738.
Sottas, Henri, *Préservation de la propriété funéraire dans l'ancienne Egypte*. Paris, 1913.

St John, J. A., *Egypt and Nubia*. London, 1845.

Tagher, J., 'Fouilleurs et antiquaires en Egypte au XIXe siècle.' Article in *Cahiers d'histoire égyptienne*, Cairo, 1950

Vercoutter, Jean, *Textes biographiques du Sérapéum de Memphis*. Paris, 1962.

Wood, Alexander, & Oldham, Frank, *Thomas Young*. Cambridge, 1954.

Index